READINGS IN INDUSTRIAL ECONOMICS

edited by

CHARLES K. ROWLEY

David Dale Professor of Economics
University of Newcastle upon Tyne

VOLUME TWO

PRIVATE ENTERPRISE AND STATE INTERVENTION

Macmillan

First published 1972 by
THE MACMILLAN PRESS LTD
London and Basingstoke
Associated companies in New York Toronto
Dublin Melbourne Johannesburg and Madras

SBN 333 10964 3 (hard cover)
333 10973 2 (paper cover)

Printed in Great Britain by
RICHARD CLAY (THE CHAUCER PRESS) LTD
Bungay, Suffolk

(℮

READINGS IN INDUSTRIAL ECONOMICS

VOLUME TWO

Contents

PART THREE: INVENTION AND THE STATE: A STUDY IN CONTROVERSY

Preface

Industrial economics only too frequently is treated as a descriptive, institutional, even anti-theoretical discipline to which the lesser able and the under-motivated students of economics are directed as a substitute for a vocational course in business studies. It is the principal objective of these *Readings in Industrial Economics* to counteract this impression and to present the discipline as intellectually stimulating and theoretically based, designed to make use of advanced micro-economic theory in the analysis of important problems of public policy. The introductions to both volumes emphasise the need both for a clearly formulated methodology as a basis for positive and for normative analysis, and for reaching out to the testing of hypotheses from a really sound theoretical foundation – an approach which has suffered much in recent years owing to the widespread misuse of standard econometric techniques.

It is usual to justify collections of articles as a means of supplementing standard textbooks in the discipline and of avoiding log-jams in the undergraduate and postgraduate libraries. In this case, there is a more fundamental justification, namely that there is no textbook in industrial economics currently available suitable for advanced undergraduate and postgraduate students. Such a textbook has been commissioned by Macmillan and is presently under preparation by Michael A. Crew of the University of Southampton, and myself. Publication is scheduled for 1973. In the meantime, these volumes provide a foretaste of my thinking in the field and should serve for many years to come as a useful, if not an essential, supplement to our textbook.

I am deeply indebted to all the authors and publishers who so willingly co-operated in giving their permission for their material to be reprinted. Specific acknowledgements and identifications of the original sources are to be found at the beginning of each contribution, whilst a short biography of authors is to be found at the end of each volume. In addition, I should like to thank all my students, undergraduate and postgraduate, who attended my courses in industrial economics during 1967–70 at the University of Kent at Canterbury and who contributed so much to my understanding of the subject. I am deeply grateful also to those of my colleagues and friends who directed my attention to the more fruitful aspects of industrial economics, and most especially to R. A. Cooper, M. A. Crew, H. G. Johnson, Michael Jones-Lee, A. T. Peacock, E. G. West, and Jack Wiseman. Most of all, however, I should like to thank my wife Marjorie, without whose help and encouragement these volumes would never have seen the light of day.

CHARLES K. ROWLEY

Department of Economics and Related Studies,
University of York

Introduction

The organization of economic activity through voluntary exchange – the hallmark of the private enterprise system with which this volume is principally concerned – in no way precludes an important role for government. Even the foremost proponents of free-enterprise capitalism readily concede this point. For there is a general consensus that government intervention is necessary not only for the defence of the realm, but also for the maintenance of law and order, and for the definition, interpretation and enforcement of property rights, as well as for the provision of a stable monetary framework, without which voluntary exchange must be severely impeded. Of course, not everyone would agree upon the precise way in which these functions should be carried out; but there are few demands for private armies, private police forces, courts and judges, whilst the natural monopoly characteristics of central banking present a convincing if not an absolutely overwhelming case for state intervention within the monetary system.

This volume is concerned, however, with wider issues of government intervention within the industrial system, about which there is no consensus at the present time, but, rather, notable disagreement and controversy. No attempt is made in this Introduction to formulate clear-cut conclusions on the issues under debate, for so much depends in this area of economic analysis upon the precise value assumptions imposed, even where the practical consequences of state intervention are exactly identifiable. This Introduction attempts, more modestly, to outline in summary form the principal issues at stake and to catch the flavour of the ongoing debates as they are reflected in the articles and papers reprinted in this volume.

Social Welfare and Value Judgements

There are no rules concerning the proper role of government that can be established by *a priori* reasoning. This, if this alone, is the unambiguous message to be derived from welfare economics. For any discussion of the proper role of government involves value judgements and falls, therefore, outside the scope of positive economics. Indeed, it is a major responsibility of economists engaged in public policy analysis to lay their value judgements squarely on the table so that the reader can judge for himself (or herself) whether or not the premises upon which the discussion is based are acceptable. Unfortunately, far too much of current public policy discussion (perhaps especially in the area of industrial economics) is conducted on a less careful and/or a less scrupulous basis.

Rigorous attempts to discuss state intervention within the industrial system from the viewpoint of social welfare tend to be founded, more or less explicitly, upon the analytical approach established by Vilfredo Pareto. For this reason, a review of the value assumptions and of the welfare maximization implications of the Pareto approach seems necessary in this Introduction.

Although Paretian welfare economics is used automatically by the vast majority of Western economists in approaching formally problems of public policy, it is important to recognize that non-trivial value judgements are deeply embedded in the Pareto principle and that these value judgements may not in fact be universally acceptable [12, 13].

The Pareto principle is based upon four such value judgements. The first establishes the individualistic nature of the approach and directs attention to the welfare of all individuals within a society rather than to the welfare of some organic concept of society. The second – which is frequently modified – directs attention to the economic components of social welfare on the (disputable) assumption that social welfare itself is divisible and that the economic component is separable and distinct. The third endorses the view that the individual is the best judge of his own economic welfare and rejects paternalism save in the cases of lunatics, incompetents and minors. The fourth – which is referred to not infrequently as *the* Pareto value judgement – defines an increase in economic welfare as arising whenever a change in resource allocation increases the welfare of at least one individual without reducing the welfare of any other individual. With this assumption, nothing can usefully be said about the net welfare effects of changes in which there are welfare losers as well as welfare gainers. For this reason, it is impossible to assess whether a social welfare maximum in the sense of Pareto is a local maximum only or whether it is a global maximum. It is impossible, in the absence of a specific social welfare function, to determine which of the infinite number of efficiency possibilities compatible with Pareto optimality should be selected as the most favoured policy objective (i.e. which is the position of constrained bliss).

There are, of course, many alternative social welfare functions, each of which might be employed to resolve the distribution dilemma of the Pareto principle. Indeed, in certain instances the chosen social welfare function might even over-rule, in the interests of equity, the efficiency requirements established by reference to the Pareto principle. In any event, it is important to recognize that economists have no special voice in the selection of a social welfare function, though they are free to make their own choice, always provided that they are explicit about it and do not attempt to obscure value judgements by jargon and mathematical facility. The reader who accepts the individualistic thrust of the Pareto principle but who rejects the constraint upon policy discussion imposed by the fourth value judgement will adopt his own distributional objective as a basis for the search for a social welfare maximum. Those who view industrial economics as being concerned primarily with issues of efficiency in resource allocation and who view equity as being the proper concern of the fiscal authorities may approve of a social welfare function which relies upon the first three value judgements of the Pareto principle whilst introducing strict neutrality as to the equity implications of resource reallocation, viz:

$$\text{Maximize} \quad W = TR + S - (TC - R)$$

where $W =$ net economic welfare, $TR =$ total revenue, $S =$ consumers' surplus, $TC =$ total cost and $R =$ infra-marginal rent.

This particular social welfare function is used explicitly in the articles by O. E. Williamson and by M. A. Crew and C. K. Rowley reprinted in this volume [see also 6, 13, 15, 16]. It is used implicitly in several others, including the articles by L. G. Telser and by K. J. Arrow also reprinted in this volume. It is rejected explicitly by Jack Wiseman, with emasculatory consequences for the public policy debate, in his perceptive contribution to the theory of public utility pricing, also reprinted in this volume. In general, it is the social welfare function which underpins contemporary cost–benefit analysis and which, for better or worse, is increasingly influential in the economics of industrial organization. It is useful, therefore, to outline briefly the necessary conditions for efficiency in exchange and production which are implied by this social welfare function [1].

Exchange efficiency (in Paretian terms) is centrally concerned with the ability of individual consumers to dictate the allocation of resources from the basis provided by the existing distribution of incomes. In the absence of externalities (later to be discussed), a process of unfettered exchange between individuals would ensure that a point would be reached at which further exchange would increase the welfare of one individual only by reducing the welfare of (an) other individual(s). Such a point represents an exchange optimum in the sense of Pareto and would be characterized by the satisfaction of certain necessary marginal conditions. The first marginal condition – which is necessary for efficiency in the distribution of commodities among consumers – is the condition that the marginal rate of substitution between any pair of consumer commodities must be the same for all individuals who consume both commodities. If this condition were not to obtain, one or more consumer(s) might gain from further exchange without harming any other consumer. The second marginal condition – which is necessary if the quantity of each good produced is to conform with consumer preferences – is the condition that the marginal rate of transformation in production must equal the marginal rate of substitution in consumption for every pair of commodities and for every individual who consumes both. If this condition were not to obtain, a shift in the production pattern of commodities would be feasible which would benefit some consumers without harming others. These two conditions, if simultaneously satisfied, ensure efficiency in exchange.

Efficiency in production is concerned with the provision of

the required range of commodities in the most efficient manner, i.e. with economizing in the use of scarce resources. The necessary marginal condition – which ensures optimal conditions of factor substitution in production and distribution – is the condition that the marginal rate of technical substitution between any pair of factor inputs must be the same for all producers who use both factor inputs. If this condition were not to obtain, a reallocation of factor inputs among producers might increase aggregate output without any reduction in the outputs of existing commodities. For the most part, welfare economics has centred disproportionate attention upon exchange efficiency to the comparative neglect of productive efficiency. Very recently, however, this situation has changed since Harvey Leibenstein's seminal contributions on X-inefficiency. In this volume, articles by W. Comanor and Harvey Leibenstein and by M. A. Crew and C. K. Rowley develop the X-inefficiency concept and explore its implications for public policy.

The simultaneous attainment of the marginal conditions necessary for efficiency in exchange and production will provide a social welfare maximum in the sense of Pareto and will maximize the W function outlined in this section. This situation will occur when price is equated with marginal cost in every commodity market and in every factor market, and in this sense universal perfect competition is a sufficient (though not a necessary) condition for a social welfare maximum. Since there are an infinite number of solutions which satisfy these conditions (varying with the initial allocation of property rights), it is theoretically possible to trace out a grand utility-possibility frontier of Pareto-efficient input–output combinations. In order to designate a single 'best position' on this frontier it would be necessary to supply a social welfare function which determined the property-right allocations. Social welfare would then be maximized where the utility-possibility frontier touched the highest contour of the social welfare function. The specific W function here outlined is maximized at *any point* on the grand utility-possibility frontier.

Economists long accepted that any movement within the economy towards satisfying the marginal conditions must lead to an improvement in net welfare, even though the conditions remained unsatisfied in certain sectors of the economy. This belief enabled policy pronouncements to be made with confidence concerning specific sectors of the economy, even though insurmountable obstacles existed to the attainment of the marginal conditions elsewhere. In 1956, however, this belief was rudely shattered by R. G. Lipsey and K. Lancaster [11] in their important article entitled 'The General Theory of Second Best'. As they put it:

> The general theorem for the second best optimum states that if there is introduced into a general equilibrium system a constraint which prevents the attainment of one of the Paretian conditions, the other Paretian conditions, although still attainable, are, in general, no longer desirable. In other words, given that one of the Paretian optimum conditions cannot be fulfilled, then an optimum situation can be achieved only by departing from all the other Paretian conditions.

Lipsey and Lancaster qualified their conclusion by the term 'in general', but the main thrust of the article was in opposition to the piecemeal approach towards public policy grounded upon the Pareto principle. Indeed, their contribution raised serious doubts as to the usefulness of welfare economics propositions in piecemeal public policy analysis. For Lipsey and Lancaster felt unable to lay down any general guidelines as to when the Pareto conditions should or should not be satisfied. Seldom has so destructive an attack been successfully mounted upon a well-established approach to public policy analysis. Almost inevitably, the general response among economists was that of paying lip-service to second-best problems, but proceeding (albeit shamefacedly) to an analysis which assumed more or less explicitly that first-best conditions obtained (or at least were obtainable) elsewhere within the economy.

In 1965, however, fresh support for the piecemeal approach was presented by O. A. Davis and A. B. Whinston [7] in a paper which developed a method of analysis designed to determine whether a specified violation of one or more of the Paretian conditions really did imply that the remaining Paretian conditions should also be violated. Davis and Whinston centred attention upon situations in which at least one actor had a preference ordering, a criterion function, or a technology which deviated from that required for the attainment of the Pareto conditions within the existing decision-making framework. Then, granted the behaviour of the deviant, they examined the behavioural rules for the other actors which would best compensate for the deviant's behaviour. They concluded, following a rigorous analysis, that whenever there was deviant behaviour in a situation where only prices and the variables under the deviant's control entered into his decision rule, the market would take that behaviour into account, since the price mechanism takes into account interconnectedness caused by scarcity. In such circumstances, piecemeal policy was all that was required. But wherever interdependence existed (perhaps as a result of externalities) which caused non-price variables not directly under the actor's control to be in his behavioural rule, the policy-maker must consider the entire system of interconnected actors in order to avoid undesirable consequences. This conclusion must provide comfort for those (like the present author) who are inclined to ignore the problems posed by second-best possibilities and to pursue policy solutions on the assumption that the remainder of the system is perfectly adjusted.

Welfare Economics and Theories of the State

Until recently, the economic theory of public policy centred attention upon situations of likely market failure and upon alternative remedies available via the intervention of the state, treating government for the most part as the omniscient and impartial servant of the public good and paying scant heed to the real-world pressures of the political market-place. Only during the past decade have serious attempts been made to provide a more realistic and relevant approach to political behaviour. In the main, such attempts have been forthcoming from economists concerned with public choice who were increasingly frustrated by the 'nirvana' view of government inherent in conventional economic analysis and by the ascientific approach to their subject which is characteristic of students of politics.

From a normative viewpoint, much attention has been placed in recent years upon the compatibility or otherwise of the Pareto principle with majority-vote systems of political decision-making. In an important contribution, Harvey Leibenstein [10] emphasized that Pareto-superior and Pareto-optimal points are universal consent points. As such, they are inconsistent with democratic choice in all cases where a majority preference point is not also a universal consent point. Thus, if the Pareto principle were to be applied within the political system, a veto power would be available to anyone who favoured the *status quo*. This indeed would provide immense protection for those minorities who opposed change, but almost inevitably at the cost of emasculating the political process. Between majority rule and the complete protection of minority interests a wide range of compromises exist and there is no reason to suppose that the Pareto extreme must necessarily be adopted.

At first sight, the majority-vote system seems to endorse a 'one man one vote' value judgement for public-sector decision-making and to make no allowance for differences in the intensity of preferences among the voting public. But this is not in fact the case, as several commentators (including A. Downs [9] and J. M. Buchanan [2]) have emphasized. There are many situations in which a vote-maximizing government would do well to support minority interests which are known to be strongly held, most especially where the composition of the minority varies with the differing policy issues under consideration. Furthermore, where log-rolling (the free exchange of votes between voters) is at all widespread, majority support for strongly-held minority views may be forthcoming even where a minority-biased decision of the kind outlined above would not occur. This does not imply, of course, that the majority-vote system will always produce public-sector decisions which correspond with the optimality conditions required by the Pareto principle (or indeed by any modification of this principle).

Moreover, as K. J. Arrow has rigorously established, the majority-vote system does not in general give rise to transitive choices, even where each individual voter has perfectly transitive preferences. It is perfectly possible for a voting majority to prefer policy A to policy B, policy B to policy C, and yet policy C to policy A, given that there are a wide variety of individual preferences concerning these policies. Whether or not the presence of such intransitivity in collective decision-making is really such a compelling criticism of the majority-vote system is a matter of opinion. Certainly, there are those who consider it to be of trivial practical importance.

In an ingenious, if somewhat unconvincing, attempt to integrate the collective decision-making processes into the framework provided by the Pareto principle, J. M. Buchanan [2] has distinguished the method by which the rules of the game are determined from the procedures by which particular decision-outcomes are decided. Buchanan suggests that there is some sense in which a majority-vote system may be viewed as a universally acceptable rule and that in this sense particular majority-based decisions may be viewed as being Pareto-preferred to any decisions that might have been forthcoming had a different rule been applied. Buchanan further argues that the role of the political economist should be restricted to that of diagnosing social situations and presenting to the voting public a set of possible policy changes, from which he would select one policy as (in his view) Pareto-preferred and present it as a hypothesis to be subjected to the voting test. Buchanan recognizes that the existence of majority-vote systems must face the political economist with a great temptation to select social alternatives which command majority support rather than consensus. Presumably this would not matter (from a Pareto viewpoint) if Buchanan's view that there is a 'social contract' consensus in favour of the majority-vote system is accepted.

From a positive viewpoint, a great deal of important work has been completed during the past few years, following the seminal contribution by A. Downs [9] in 1957, in connection with predicting the behaviour of political parties from models based upon the vote-maximizing postulate within the context of two-party, majority-vote systems. Since the behaviour of the political parties is clearly of central importance in any analysis of private enterprise and state intervention, a brief outline of the Downs approach may prove illuminating.

Downs developed his model on the basic assumption that politicians are motivated by self-interest and pursue vote-maximizing policies and that the elected government in a two-party, majority-vote system must adopt a vote-maximizing policy platform if it is not to lose control over the governing apparatus to its rival. The election process itself, therefore, is viewed as a political market in which votes are exchanged for policies. A number of testable hypotheses flow from this theoretical framework.

It is a key prediction of the Downs model that both political parties will be pressed into adopting policies favoured by the median preference voters, at least where the voter preference distribution is single-peaked, where voter preferences are clearly registered and are known to be firmly held. Only rarely, in such circumstances, would future-oriented parties diverge from this prescription, sacrificing present votes for future votes in the expectation that voter tastes would shift within the politically relevant time-period. In the main, the policy preferences of minority groups are not expected to exert much influence in formulation of public policy, and the policy platforms of the two competing parties are not expected to diverge significantly. The relevance of ideology is reduced to that of the brand-image of the widely marketed soapless detergent, namely to reduce the transaction costs of acquiring information for those who are incapable of or unwilling to inform themselves about the political market.

The Downs model is easily adjusted to take account of situations in which the policy preferences of the voting public are not clearly registered and/or are suspected to be only loosely adhered to. In such circumstances, it is predictable that the policy utterances of both parties will be ambiguous and that the policy actions of the governing party will be inconsistent. For to formulate policies clearly and consistently would be to run the risk of major net vote-losses which political parties can rarely envisage, especially when elections occur only at widely spaced intervals.

The Downs model also takes account of imperfections of knowledge in the political process and of the transaction costs of communicating information on voter preferences to the politicians, predicting that public policy formation will be disproportionately influenced by producer groups (widely defined), to the detriment generally of consumers. For the interests of producer groups in any single issue of public policy inevitably are more specific than those of consumers, with the implication that producers' pressure-group activities will prove more rewarding for any given outlay than would be the case with consumers. This is a major predictable imperfection in all political markets characterized by uncertainty.

Much work remains to be done in evaluating the predictive properties of the Downs model and in building better models to take account of areas in which its predictions fail. Such testing is still in its infancy and great confidence cannot yet be placed in the model [14, 17]. Preliminary results suggest strongly, however, that the Downs model is a much better predictor of political behaviour than is the traditional 'nirvana' approach to government which is so deeply embedded in the economic theory of public policy.

An Anatomy of Market Failure

Adam Smith, writing in 1776, felt able to conclude that individuals pursuing their own self-interest within the framework of a competitive private enterprise system would be led as if by an invisible hand to actions that in fact promoted the general welfare of all. The technically more advanced modern-day welfare economist would be somewhat more tentative and circumspect in his policy interpretations. At most, he might suggest that on certain restrictive assumptions perfect competition in all goods and in all factor markets would satisfy the necessary marginal conditions for Pareto efficiency in production and exchange, given the initial distribution of income. No economist could seriously claim that perfect competition is universal in the modern industrial economy. Nevertheless, perfect competition provides a useful measuring-rod against which certain aspects of market failure can be evaluated, most notably the welfare implications of monopoly conditions, which feature in such an important role in industrial economics.

The first contribution, by R. A. Berry, makes use of this measuring-rod and centres attention upon the welfare loss arising from monopoly, subjecting the conventional geometrical representation of this welfare loss – the 'Marshallian triangle' – to a highly critical scrutiny. Although Berry correctly emphasizes the interpersonal utility comparisons which are implicit in the Marshallian approach and advances this as a criticism, it is important to emphasize that the criticism is empty once the social welfare function previously outlined in this Introduction is employed, as it is for the most part in discussions of monopoly and competition. Nevertheless, Berry's criticisms of the conventional approach have considerable force, and, always provided they are not allowed to assume disproportionate significance, they stand as a powerful reminder of the simplifications employed in contemporary welfare economics and of the restrictions these impose upon the public policy debate.

The second contribution, by W. S. Comanor and Harvey

Leibenstein, reinforces the welfare economics case against monopoly at least under first-best conditions by demonstrating the additional welfare losses imposed when the existence of monopoly implies higher cost levels, in consequence of X-inefficiency, than would prevail under conditions of competition. Although Comanor and Leibenstein are not explicit in their paper, it is reasonable to infer that X-inefficiency strikes, in part at least, at marginal cost, resulting in shifts in resource allocation additional to those which are observed in the more conventional welfare analysis of monopoly conditions [5]. The significance of X-inefficiency for the conduct of public policy is evaluated in the paper by M. A. Crew and C. K. Rowley reprinted in Part Two of this volume.

The other principal source of market failure relevant for public policy discussion is the existence of Pareto-relevant externalities which are usually taken to imply that even perfect competition cannot achieve a social welfare maximum (in the sense of Pareto) in the absence of some form of state intervention. This view has recently been challenged (most notably by J. M. Buchanan [3]), on the ground that it incorporates an unrealistic presumption that governments are omniscient and impartial and that state intervention will be perfectly designed and meticulously executed to attain the welfare optimum. Buchanan, in particular, has demonstrated, by reference to alternative theories of human behaviour, that as long as individuals are assumed to be similarly motivated in the market-place and in the political process, no direct implications could be derived as to the appropriate organization of an activity beset by Pareto-relevant externalities. The orthodox implications derived by reference to Pigovian welfare economics could be supported only on the assumption that individuals responded to different motives when participating in market and political activities. Otherwise, the only case in which the political process would eliminate externalities which existed under market conditions is that of truly collective goods, with no elements privately divisible and with taxes collected on the basis of marginal benefits. In the real world, commodities with these characteristics are rare indeed.

Fundamentally, the public policy problems posed by externalities, be they of the well-known smoky chimney variety, or the product of indivisibilities in the production function and the inapplicability of the exclusion principle, arise as a consequence of the inadequate specification of property rights. It is appropriate, therefore, that the third contribution, by Paul Burrows, centres attention upon the property-right issues which underpin the externality problem. Burrows evaluates the two principal functions of the law in the treatment of external costs, namely (i) settling disputes over legal rights, and (ii) providing alternative compensation arrangements to those provided by the market and by tax–subsidy schemes. He emphasizes the sharp conflict which exists between the objectives of legal decisions on rights and the existence of institutional constraints on the achievement of optimal outcomes. Burrows makes out a convincing case for adjustments in the existing legal system which would prove instrumental in facilitating private bargains for the redistribution of rights. For example, British legal practice is preoccupied with imposing damages for past events (action which does not influence future behaviour) but with imposing injunctions for continuing activities (thereby preventing such activity even where it would be profitable to continue it if appropriate damages had been payable). Such a preoccupation is not necessarily the most conducive to an optimum solution, though Burrows is careful to distinguish between cases involving large and small numbers and cases involving high and low bargaining costs in formulating his public policy inferences. His contribution is especially important in view of the significance recently attached in the externality literature both to property-right determination and to bargaining solutions [8].

The fourth contribution, by P. A. Samuelson, is the well-known though relatively inaccessible diagrammatic exposition of the public-good problem which clearly demonstrates the inability of a decentralized market or voting mechanism to attain the conditions required for optimality in the provision of public goods. Samuelson noted the polar nature of his public-good theory and did not deny that real-world examples of public goods were difficult to come by. He claimed, nevertheless, a wide public policy relevance for this theory and contended that almost every 'legitimate' function of government was characterized by public-good conditions.

The fifth contribution, by J. G. Head, provides a detailed analysis of public-good theory and of its public policy significance, relating the Samuelsonian concept to the more familiar

Pigovian theory of public policy. Head distinguished clearly between the jointness in supply and the external economies characteristics of public goods, arguing that while jointness was an essential characteristic of a public good, it was the external economies (i.e. the exclusion or appropriability difficulties to an extreme degree) characteristic alone which accounted for the failure of the market mechanism to ensure a revelation of true preferences. Head emphasized that exclusion was never completely impossible even in such obvious cases as national defence, flood control and public health programmes, but that a wide category of commodities was characterized by exclusion difficulties, with the inference that the market would fail to secure optimum production and consumption of the goods in question. On the other hand, goods and services with jointness aspects might well pose no price-exclusion problems, e.g. bus, train and tram fares, although they would pose problems of understatement of preferences by individual members of the collectivity when the government stepped in to promote the more adequate provision of the commodities concerned. In such circumstances, the underprovision of collectively provided public goods was extremely likely. Head's contribution introduces a refreshing element of realism into a field of economic analysis which has frequently attracted highly naïve analyses of the working of the political process.

Implicit in much of the welfare economics literature, and most especially in discussions of market failure, is the assumption that transaction costs are unimportant by comparison with other costs within the economic system. As such, transaction costs are frequently ignored entirely or summarily dismissed as an inconvenient real-world intrusion into what is essentially a theoretical exercise. It is to the lasting credit of Harold Demsetz that he has demonstrated so clearly the theoretical significance of transaction costs for the economic theory of public policy. The sixth contribution to this volume, by Harold Demsetz, is concerned firstly with the fact both that the exchange of goods and the maintenance of control over the use of goods impose economic costs on traders and owners, and secondly to emphasize that there are economic costs attached to collective as well as market activities.

Demsetz demonstrated the relevance of transaction-cost analysis in raising question-marks over the categorical denunciation by economists of situations of market failure based upon externality (and especially public-good) considerations, pointing out that the cost of alternative market and political solutions is seldom introduced explicitly as a relevant variable in the public policy debate. In particular, he emphasized that an insistence that all commodities be priced in the market or that the government should intervene was equivalent to the insistence that there should be no economizing in the cost of producing exchanges or government services. Thus, most welfare propositions concerned with externalities were based on an invalid use of the standard optimality theorems. The relevance of transaction costs for public policy analysis will become especially clear in the concluding debate between K. J. Arrow and Harold Demsetz, concerning the welfare economics of invention.

The Framework of State Intervention

Part Two of the volume centres attention upon two widely utilized techniques of state intervention in the modern industrial economy, namely anti-trust and regulation, though many of the contributions concerning regulation have an obvious relevance also for public enterprise. In a very real sense, these contributions represent the heartland of industrial economics.

The seventh contribution, by O. E. Williamson, presents a case for treating market power not as an unquestionable offence – as by and large is the case in the United States – but as the subject of a complex welfare trade-off between the loss of consumers' surplus on the one hand and the cost savings from scale economies (if any) on the other. Throughout the analysis, Williamson employs the social welfare function previously outlined in this Introduction, thereby suppressing the income distribution considerations of anti-trust intervention. His discussion is restricted to merger activities from which increased market power is anticipated. Williamson indicated that in the usual case the cost savings from scale economies would easily outweigh the loss of consumer benefits from market-power-induced price increases, with the inference that most such mergers could justifiably be allowed to proceed. He took full account of the complicated discounting procedures which would be necessary if the trade-off was to centre attention upon the relevant present values of costs and benefits, and his contribution is a model of careful exposition tied to rigorous economic analysis. Williamson's public policy message is clear. Non-discretionary rules for anti-trust should be replaced by pragmatic investigation – a victory for the United Kingdom over the United States approach to the problem of market power.

The eighth contribution, by M. A. Crew and C. K. Rowley, endorses Williamson's approach to the anti-trust problem whilst challenging the public policy inferences which follow from Williamson's paper, by introducing the possibility that X-inefficiency is an increasing function of market power. In such circumstances, the loss of consumers' surplus would, of course remain as a detriment and the gain from scale economies as a benefit to market power. But the latter benefit would be offset by such X-inefficiency as could be anticipated from the rise in market power. In so far as cost increases from X-inefficiency outweighed the cost savings from scale economies – and to determine this would involve forecasting – the unambiguous neo-classical case in favour of anti-trust would be reinforced rather than weakened. Certainly, Williamson's pro-merger conclusions would be severely weakened. With the introduction of X-inefficiency possibilities, however, the transaction costs of pragmatic 'anti-trust', never low, reach significant proportions, and Crew and Rowley conclude that on an overall assessment non-discretionary anti-trust rules, enforced through the judicial process, probably represent the optimum public policy solution, as evaluated within an all-inclusive framework which takes appropriate account of investigation and policing costs [6, 15, 16].

The ninth contribution, by Jack Wiseman, switches attention away from anti-trust to the problems encountered in regulating the public utilities, and centres critical attention upon the theoretical validity and the practical accountability of the public utility pricing rules which form such a significant part of the conventional regulation literature. Wiseman rejects the social welfare function designed to suppress income distribution considerations and relies instead upon the unqualified value assumptions of the Pareto model. On this basis he clearly demonstrated that welfare criteria gave rise to no unambiguous general rule for the price and output policy of public utilities, since almost every price adjustment implied an income re-distribution effect which could not be evaluated within the context of the Pareto value judgements. Perhaps more import-ant from a public policy viewpoint, however, was Wiseman's emphasis upon the subjectivity of costs – opportunity costs of course – in a world characterized by uncertainty. In such circumstances, a direction to marginal-cost price is little more than an empty order, since the bureaucrat himself would exercise his own subjective judgement on the nature of costs, and public accountability in practice becomes little more than a sham. Wiseman's contribution has ruffled many feathers within the regulation aviary and not without good cause. For it represents a fundamental challenge which no amount of mathematical ingenuity can really answer.

The relationship between cost and choice, which Wiseman emphasized, has been further evaluated very recently by J. M. Buchanan [4], and the issue is sufficiently important both to regulation and to public enterprise to warrant a further comment in this Introduction. Cost in a theory of choice must be reckoned in a utility dimension and must be viewed as that which the decision-maker sacrifices when he makes a choice. In this sense, Buchanan established (i) that cost must be borne exclusively by the decision-maker and could not be shifted, (ii) that cost was subjective, existing only in the mind of the decision-maker, (iii) that cost necessarily was *ex ante*, based on expectations, (iv) that cost could never be realized, (v) that cost was measurable only by the decision-maker himself, and (vi) that cost could be dated at the moment of decision. With these important points established, Buchanan distinguished between choice-influencing and choice-influenced cost. Every choice involves both these costs, but only the former represents a genuine obstacle to choice. Choice-influenced cost is concerned with the consequences of choice, evaluated in terms of the utility losses that are always consequent upon choice, and which may be experienced by parties other than the decision-maker. These costs, the result and not the cause of decision, are the costs with which economists and accountants are apparently primarily concerned, despite the fact that within the context of choice they are not costs at all. Finally, Buchanan demonstrated that only in full competitive equilibrium could the observed money outlays, which in a prostituted sense constitute objective cost, reflect even indirectly the genuine opportunity costs of economic theory. The inapplicability of such conditions to the public utilities is obvious.

The tenth contribution, by Harold Demsetz, raised what is perhaps the most fundamental question of all, namely: why regulate the public utilities at all? Demsetz argued that the theory of natural monopoly was deficient in that it failed to reveal the logical steps from scale economies in production to monopoly price in the market-place, and indeed that there was no inevitable association between the two. For rival sellers could offer to enter into contracts – perhaps annually renewable – with buyers, and in this bidding competition, the rival who offered buyers the most favourable terms would obtain their patronage. There was no reason why competition in bidding should result in an increase in per unit production costs. Always provided that the inputs required to enter production were available to the potential bidders at prices determined in open markets, and that the cost of collusion between bidders was prohibitive, a competitive public utility solution could be obtained without government interference. Strictly, of course, the Demsetz solution is an average-cost pricing solution which would violate the absolute efficiency requirements of the Pareto model, since marginal costs must lie below average cost in a decreasing-cost industry. But Demsetz has never restricted himself to the strait-jacket of Pareto efficiency. To those (like the author) who are deeply concerned by the X-inefficiency consequences of real-world regulation, the Demsetz proposal looks appetizing, judged, as it should be, within a comparative institutions framework [13].

The eleventh contribution, by L. G. Telser, is on the other hand altogether more technical, and is designed to demonstrate, by reference to a specific example, that competition does not yield a welfare optimum in the case of natural monopoly, but rather produces the tangency solution derived by E. Chamberlin in the theory of monopolistic competition, which is generally inefficient. In terms of the welfare criteria applied by Telser, which suppress distribution considerations, some direct price control would be necessary if the industry were privately owned. Telser's contribution is commended on grounds of rigour and clarity of exposition in a field of analysis which is not well known for these qualities. The reader is warned, however, that the important theoretical and practical issues raised by Wiseman and Demsetz are ignored for analytical purposes in Telser's contribution.

The twelfth contribution, by M. Z. Kafoglis, examines the price and output behaviour of the monopoly restrained by 'fair rate of return' regulations, in terms of various non-profit-maximizing theories of the firm, demonstrating the wide range of alternative results which are possible. In particular, Kafoglis demonstrated the likely X-inefficiency consequences of regulation (though he did not explicitly use the X-inefficiency concept), and pointed out that on certain assumptions the output of the restrained firm could be less than, equal to, or might even be pushed beyond the Pareto optimum. The contribution is fundamentally important in that it emphasizes the extreme difficulty of predicting the economic consequences of regulation at least in the present state of knowledge concerning the theory of the firm and of market behaviour.

Invention and the State: A Study in Controversy

The thirteenth and fourteenth contributions, by K. J. Arrow and Harold Demsetz respectively, represent an important debate in which the importance of the assumptions used and the variables introduced for consideration becomes only too clear for the public policy results. Arrow presents a convincing argument to support the view that government finance is necessary for the optimal allocation of resources to invention and that purely private provision will result in a suboptimal allocation. I found the article completely convincing prior to Demsetz's critical response, and I do not class myself as being unduly prejudiced in favour of the interventionist approach. By adjusting certain of Arrow's assumptions – arguably towards a more realistic emphasis – Demsetz turns Arrow's argument upon its head and, at least within the framework of a comparative institutions approach, denies the validity of Arrow's public policy recommendations. If industrial economics, as reflected in these two articles, does not appear to the reader to be the vibrant, exciting discipline that I believe it to be, then he (or she) must indeed be difficult to please.

REFERENCES

[1] F. M. BATOR, 'The Simple Analytics of Welfare Maximisation', *American Economic Review*, XLVII (Mar 1957).

[2] J. M. BUCHANAN, 'Positive Economics, Welfare Economics and Political Economy', *Journal of Law and Economics*, II (Oct 1959).

[3] ——, 'Politics, Policy and the Pigovian Margins', *Economica*, n.s., XXIX (Feb 1962).

[4] ——, *Cost and Choice: An Inquiry in Economic Theory* (Markham, 1969).

[5] M. A. CREW and C. K. ROWLEY, 'On Allocative Efficiency, X-Efficiency and the Measurement of Welfare Loss', *Economica*, n.s., XXXVIII (May 1971).

[6] 'Anti-Trust Policy: The Application of Rules', *Moorgate and Wall Street* (autumn 1971).

[7] O. A. DAVIS and A. B. WHINSTON, 'Welfare Economics and the Theory of Second Best', *Review of Economic Studies*, XXXII (Jan 1965).

[8] ——, 'On Externalities, Information and the Government-Assisted Invisible Hand', *Economica*, n.s., XXXIII (Aug 1966).

[9] A. DOWNS, *An Economic Theory of Democracy* (Harper & Row, 1957).

[10] H. LEIBENSTEIN, 'Notes on Welfare Economics and the Theory of Democracy', *Economic Journal*, LXXII (June 1962).

[11] R. G. LIPSEY and K. LANCASTER, 'The General Theory of Second Best', *Review of Economic Studies*, XXIV (1956).

[12] A. T. PEACOCK and C. K. ROWLEY, 'Pareto Optimality and the Political Economy of Liberalism', *Journal of Political Economy*, LXXX (May/June 1972).

[13] ——, 'Welfare Economics and the Public Regulation of Natural Monopoly,' *Journal of Public Economics*, I (June 1979).

[14] C. K. ROWLEY, 'Monopoly in Britain: Private Vice but Public Virtue?', *Moorgate and Wall Street* (autumn 1968).

[15] ——, *Steel and Public Policy* (McGraw-Hill, 1971).

[16] ——, '*Antitrust and Economic Efficiency*' (Macmillan, forthcoming 1973).

[17] E. G. WEST, *Economics, Education and the Politician*, Hobart Paper 42 (Institute of Economic Affairs, 1968).

PART ONE

An Anatomy of Market Failure

1 A Note on Welfare Comparisons between Monopoly and Pure Competition

R. A. Berry

Welfare economics, in its comparisons between different market structures, has leaned heavily on the concepts of consumers' surplus and producers' surplus. Their acceptance for this purpose has had its ups and downs. Lerner initiated the discussion in his celebrated 1934 article[1] on the welfare implications of monopoly–monopsony, and it has been carried on by a long series of authors since then.

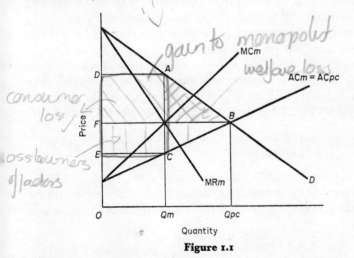

Figure 1.1

In Fig. 1.1 we present the by-now traditional exposition of the welfare loss due to monopoly–monopsony in an industry when all other industries in the economy are purely competitive, and when the alternative in the particular industry is pure competition, economies of scale being absent as soon as a relatively

[1] Abba Lerner, 'The Concept of Monopoly and the Measurement of Monopoly power', *Review of Economic Studies*, 1 3 (June 1934).

Reprinted from *Manchester School*, xxxvii (Mar 1969) 39–57, by kind permission of the author and of the editor.

low level of output is reached. The long-run average cost curve of the monopolistic industry (AC*m*) is assumed to be the same as the long-run average cost (i.e. supply) curve of the purely competitive industry (AC*pc*).[2] Partial demand and cost curves are assumed, i.e. curves based on the assumption that all other prices in the system are fixed. The firm, equating MC*m* and MR*m*, its marginal cost and marginal revenue, produces only OQ*m* units of the good, whereas the purely competitive industry would produce OQ*pc* units. Welfare loss is designated by the area *ABC*. This is the algebraic sum of a loss of *ABFD* to consumers or potential consumers of the good, a loss of *FBCE* to owners of factors used or previously used in producing the good, and a gain of *ACED* by the monopolist.

The reasoning involved is as follows. The marginal utility, in money terms, which the buyer of any particular unit of a good can get from it is given by the demand price of that unit. The marginal social cost of producing that unit is given by the supply price, i.e. by the S*pc* curve. (The conditions under which this is or is not true will be the second main theme of this paper.) Whenever demand price is above supply price, social welfare can be raised by an increase in the quantity produced. The total increase in welfare which would occur in the situation portrayed by Fig. 1.1 if output were raised from OQ*m* to OQ*pc*

would thus be $\int_{OQ_{pc}}^{OQ_m} (Pd - Ps)dQ$ (where *Pd* is demand price

and *Ps* is supply price). This is the area *ABC*.

Criticisms and/or revisions which have been or could be made are based on the following characteristics of the above analysis:

1. The area does not measure the net amount of compensation which would have to be made so that everyone could be as well off without the change to pure competition as he would be with it (analogous to Hicks's 'equivalent variation'), or the amount which would have to be subtracted from people's incomes after the change to pure competition was made to leave each just as well off as

---

[2] We henceforth refer to these two curves as AC*m* and AC*pc*. The corresponding marginal cost curves will likewise be referred to as MC*m* and MC*pc*. We refer to the firm in question as a monopolist, though in fact we will assume it also has monopsony power.

before the change (analogous to Hicks's 'compensating variation') or any other such quantity.

2. It involves interpersonal comparisons of utility and the implicit assumption that the marginal utility of money is the same for everyone.

3. It is based on the assumption that other prices do not change.

4. The pure competition supply curve is assumed to give a correct representation of marginal social costs, and to coincide with the monopolist–monopsonist's average cost curve.

The first two points have been very extensively discussed, with Winch[3] clearing away much of the scattered debris in the area and providing a solid rehabilitation of the Marshallian triangle as a meaningful measure of what he calls 'consumer's gain' (to distinguish the concept from the many other similar ones laying claim to their own terminology). Accepting Winch's conclusions that criticisms based on these first two characteristics are either invalid or not devastating, we consider here the third and fourth respectively.

Partial Curves and Total Curves

When the argument of Fig. 1.1 is expressed using partial curves, there is a fairly obvious error. The true pure competition equilibrium price and quantity in the market for X is not normally the same as it would be if all other prices (i.e. prices of other goods and of all factors) were held constant at what were equilibrium levels when only OQm of X was produced.[4] Yet if we use total curves,[5] it is clear that individuals who are not directly involved in the market for product X, either as buyers or as suppliers of the factors of production used, can be affected

---

[3] D. M. Winch, 'Consumer's Surplus and the Compensation Principle', *American Economic Review* (June 1965). See this article for bibliography on the earlier discussions.

[4] In fact, with constant factor prices and no external diseconomies of scale the ACpc curve in Fig. 1.1 could not slope upward at all. Since we are not concerned with the possibilities of using partial curves we do not worry about this inconsistency.

[5] Total (or general equilibrium) demand and supply curves give, respectively, the demand price and the supply price of X as a function of the amount produced and sold, under the assumption that other prices and quantities in the economy are not fixed but rather are at their equilibrium levels, given each particular output of X.

B

positively or negatively. It is not intuitively clear that these effects are correctly allowed for by the use of the analogous area measure in a diagram like Fig. 1.1 but expressed in terms of total curves. The succeeding paragraphs attempt to show that they are.

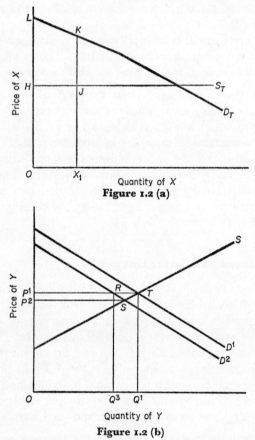

Figure 1.2 (a)

Figure 1.2 (b)

Consider the events in another market, that for product Y, as the output of X rises. Assume Y is a substitute in demand for X and (for simplicity) that the two goods do not use the same or closely linked factors and that the total supply curve of X is horizontal over the relevant range. Thus when output of X rises from zero to OX_1 (Fig. 1.2A) the demand curve (all curves in this diagram are 'total' ones) for Y will shift to the left (Fig. 1.2B), from D^1 to D^2.

If the price of Y had remained at its original level OP^1 the quantity purchased would have fallen to OQ^3. This might suggest that since the consumer's surplus would, under this condition, have decreased in the Y market, the area $HJKL$ in Fig. 1.2A is an overestimate of the increase in total consumer surplus. But this is not the case. The spread between the demand price of another unit of X and its supply price when total curves are being used represents by definition the difference between the marginal utility (measured in money terms) of that amount of money (Px) spent on X and the same amount spent elsewhere, with other prices at their equilibrium levels given the output of X. If prices did not change in any other market as the output of X changed, one would not have to look farther to know whose welfare was being affected and in what direction. The collectivity of consumers would be better off by just the amount $HJKL$ measured in Fig. 1.2A, the gain to consumers of X; non-consumers of X would not be affected. $HJKL$ would be a correct measure even though the apparent consumer's surplus attained in other markets by consumers of X would have fallen. When there are interrelationships between X and other products such as the substitute relationship assumed between X and Y here, the welfare of non-consumers of X can be affected and that of consumers of X may be changed by an amount different from $HJKL$. But these effects net out to zero as we show here. As the amount of X consumed rises, it is only individuals involved in the market for X whose reallocations of expenditure affect, in the first instance, the demand curves elsewhere. Shifts in the demand curve for Y are therefore due to shifts in the demand for Y by people who also consume X. And the decrease in consumer's surplus apparently attained in the market for Y does not mean that in Fig. 1.2B such shifts lead to a fall in the price of Y to OP^2. The people consuming Y after this price fall gain a surplus of P^1RSP^2 and producers or factor suppliers lose an amount equal to P^1TSP^2. If we think of very small increases in output of X leading to very small downward shifts of the demand curve for Y, it is clear that the gain to consumers of Y becomes exactly equal to the loss to factor suppliers. And since the net welfare effect of a shift of finite size is simply the sum of a series of very small shifts it remains true that the gains and losses offset each other perfectly. By a fully analogous argument we can arrive at the same result when the supply curve for good Y shifts as well. And since the result holds in each individual market it is true for all non-X markets as a group.[6]

We thus conclude that a diagram with total demand and supply curves of X is as correct a measure of the welfare change resulting from a change in the level of output of the good where other prices change as the use of a measure based on partial curves is when other prices do not change. So we turn now to the other matter to be discussed, the coincidence of the monopoly–monopsony average cost curve with the pure competition supply curve and the social opportunity cost interpretation to be given to the latter.

Conditions under which AC*pc* Coincides with AC*m*

In the argument that ABC in Fig. 1.1 is a measure of the welfare difference between monopoly–monopsony and pure competition, it is assumed that the monopolized industry would have to pay all the rents paid by the purely competitive one.[7] This, in general, is a necessary but not a sufficient condition to ensure that AC*pc* and AC*m* will coincide. (We will refer to it as Condition 1.) It is necessary since in any situation in which the monopolist does not pay all the rents which the purely competitive industry would have to pay he can, even by using the

---

[6] In Fig. 1.2B the loss to factor suppliers from the discrete price change (P^1TSP^2) *appears* greater than the gain to consumers (P^1RSP^2) because we have not included the area RTS as part of the consumer's surplus. In fact it does represent a surplus which accrued to certain buyers of Y as the price of X fell, with those buyers later moving out of the market for Y as the price of X fell still further. At each moment of time all consumers and producers in other markets such as Y can be grouped as either: (1) consuming the good or supplying factors used in its production both before and after a small change in its price and hence being affected positively or negatively by the price change in exactly offsetting amounts; (2) being marginal buyers of the good or sellers of factors so that moving out of or into the market when price changes does not constitute a gain or loss for them. But the fact that a group of consumers later moves out of the market for Y does not negate the fact that the fall in the price of Y when they were still buying that good constituted an increase in their welfare. When we include this area as part of the increase in consumer's surplus as P_y falls, we conclude that the increase is indeed equal to the decrease in producers' surplus.

[7] One of the reasons for a positively sloping supply curve in a purely competitive industry is normally that as the total output rises and more units of each factor are used, the prices of these factors rise. Since all units of a given homogeneous factor receive the same reward, those units which would have been supplied at a lower level of remuneration are now receiving an 'economic rent'.

same factor combination, achieve a lower average cost. The second necessary condition is that the monopolist must, for any given level of output, combine factors in one of the set of possible proportions (usually only one exists) in which the purely competitive industry could have combined them.[8] If he does this, and also pays the same for each factor unit purchased as the purely competitive industry would have, it is clear that, under the assumptions we are making, the two average cost curves coincide; hence, the pair of conditions is sufficient. That the second condition, like the first, is necessary, can be seen from the following consideration.

We know that at a given output level each firm in the purely competitive industry equates the ratio of value of marginal product to supply price for all factors. This is a necessary condition for equilibrium and its being met implies cost minimization by each firm when the production function is well behaved in the sense of having negative second partial derivatives of output with respect to all inputs. Now for there to be a combination of factor inputs not meeting this condition but costing the monopolist (who by Condition 1 must pay all the rents) the same amount as the combination used in pure competition, the supply curves of the different factors would have to have different degrees of elasticity. But if this is the case the monopolist can always achieve a lower cost by using relatively more of factors with elastic supply curves and relatively less of factors with inelastic supply curves than does the purely competitive industry. (See below, p.13 and note 11.)

A Digression: The Determinants of the Shape of AC*pc*; A Definition of a 'Factor'

A helpful prelude to analysis of these conditions is a consideration of the determinants of the shape of the average cost curve of a purely competitive industry. Given the production function which faces the firms, this shape depends on:

(i) The way in which factor prices ('factor' is defined below) change as an increase in the output of the

[8] Under certain circumstances, more than one combination of factor proportions would give the same average cost; we cannot then say that the monopolist must use the same factor proportions if costs are not to differ. But this is a rather implausible case and will be disregarded.

industry leads to increases in the amounts of the various factors used. In general these prices rise as more of each factor is used; this implies a tendency for the AC*pc* curve to slope upwards.

(ii) The possibility of adding new factors, different from those previously used, as output rises; where the prices of these factors are such that at a certain level of industry output, it becomes profitable to use them, because the prices of the factors used up to that point have risen, the upward slope of AC*pc* is less than it would have been had this alternative not been available.

(iii) The presence or absence of external (dis)economies among the firms in the industry.

The distinction between rising prices of factors of given type or quality as more units of them are used, and rising costs because less productive input units must be used when the supply of the more productive ones is exhausted, is an important one in the analysis which follows. While the distinction may seem somewhat artificial, given the fact that in practical terms a 'factor' must usually be delineated in a rather arbitrary way, it is still worth stressing.

For our purposes we define the term 'factor' as follows:

Definition. Two input units (no. 1 and no. 2) will be said to be homogeneous or to be units of the same factor if the ratio

$$\frac{\text{marginal product of the first unit}}{\text{marginal product of the second unit}}$$

is the same in whatever production process and with whatever combination of other factors the units are likely to be used. In other words, they are perfect substitutes for each other in any production process where they are likely to be employed.

We use the term 'likely' in the above definition since there is no practical value in distinguishing units which are perfect substitutes in all current and foreseeable uses, but might not be in some as yet undeveloped production process or some process for which they are much less suited than other inputs.

From the definition it is clear that two units which are in every way identical are always said to be members of the same factor; such complete sameness is a sufficient but not necessary condition.

Two units may have the same marginal product ratio for all possible uses by a given firm; in such a case they would be perfect substitutes for the firm. But if they are not perfect substitutes for other users, it is still essential to distinguish between them and our definition does imply that they are different factors.

The term 'less productive factor' is defined here as follows:

Definition. a is less productive than b if the ratio

$$\frac{\text{marginal productivity of the first unit of } a \text{ purchased}}{\text{price of first unit of } a}$$

is less than the corresponding ratio for b.

The following situations illustrate the two determinants (rising factor prices and addition of new factors) in a concrete fashion:

(a) Suppose industry X makes a good, in the production of which factors a, b, c are used. The different units of each factor are identical, but the supply curve of each to industry X is not horizontal because, as more units are used by X, less are left to be used elsewhere, with the result that the factor's marginal productivity elsewhere rises, and hence supply price becomes higher. No other factors can be used to produce good X. In this case the ACpc curve for industry X will slope upward because of the positive slope of the supply curve to the industry of each factor. No other consideration need enter the picture.

(b) Suppose industry X can use any of factors a, b, c, d and e, all the units of a given factor being identical. But let us assume that it does not pay to use factors d and e when output is low, since the ratio

$$\frac{\text{marginal productivity of first unit purchased}}{\text{price of first unit purchased}}$$

is lowest for a, b and c. As more of these factors are used and their supply price rises, d and e will be brought into use. This will occur for d (for example) when the ratio of

$$\frac{\text{marginal productivity of the first unit of } d \text{ purchased}}{\text{price of first unit}}$$

is equal to

$$\frac{\text{marginal productivity of another unit of a currently}}{\text{used factor}}$$

marginal cost (equal to price for a firm in a competitive industry) of another unit of a currently used factor.

The above definition of a factor implies that any two units of it are in all respects equivalent to each other regardless of the industry using them. It assumes that owners of these different units will not prefer to supply them to one industry rather than another. If such preferences did exist, it could be cogently argued that two otherwise equivalent units could not in fact be said to be of the same factor.

Relation between AC*pc* and AC*m* (continued)

Let us take each of the three determinants of the shape of AC*pc* listed above and consider how it bears on the two necessary conditions which must be met to have AC*m* coincide with AC*p*.

1. *Rising factor prices*

If there is no possibility of switching to other factors when the prices of those first used rise due to increased demand for them, and there are no external effects, then necessary condition 1 (see p. 8) is met, i.e. if rising factor prices are the sole source of the positive slope of the AC*pc* curve, the condition is met. Since all units of a given factor are by our definition perfect substitutes in their alternative uses, it is impossible for the monopolist to discriminate in any way among different units, and being faced with the same factor supply curve as the purely competitive industry, he must pay the same price per unit to get any given number of units.

Necessary condition 2 (i.e. that the monopolist combines factors in the same proportions as the purely competitive industry), unlike no. 1, will be met only in special cases.[9] The

---

[9] This observation has been made by Joan Robinson in *Economics of Imperfect Competition* (London: Macmillan, 1954) pp. 172–6.

monopolist differs from a single firm in the purely competitive industry in that, since he faces rising factor supply curves, when he equates

$$\frac{\text{marginal productivity of factor } a}{\text{marginal cost of } a}$$

to

$$\frac{\text{marginal productivity of factor } b}{\text{marginal cost of } b}$$

he will in general not be equating

$$\frac{\text{marginal productivity of } a}{\text{price of } a}$$

to

$$\frac{\text{marginal productivity of } b}{\text{price of } b}$$

Only when the ratio of marginal cost to price[10] is the same for all factors (i.e. all have the same supply elasticity) will he combine factors in the same proportions as the purely competitive industry. In all other cases his average cost curve will be below AC_{pc}.[11]

[10] We may assume that the prices of different factors are independent. If we assume dependence, then the marginal cost of another unit of one factor depends not only on how its purchase affects the price which must be paid to previously purchased units of that factor but on how prices of other factors the firm uses are affected.

[11] Total (or average) costs are not minimized by a purely competitive industry since individual firms do not take into account the effects of their purchases of factors on the prices paid by other firms in the industry. When one firm increases its inputs of a factor, assuming the supply of the factor to the industry is not perfectly elastic, its prices rise by a very small amount (so small that we assume the firm disregards it), but when this increase in price is multiplied by all the units of the factor currently used by other firms in the industry, the marginal cost to the industry as a whole is above price. This gap depends on the elasticity of supply of the factor to the industry. Hence, when the purely competitive industry has

$$\frac{\text{value of marginal product of factor } a}{\text{price of } a}$$

equal to

$$\frac{\text{value of marginal product of factor } b}{\text{price of } b}$$

it will nevertheless generally be true that

$$\frac{\text{VMP}_a}{\text{MC}_a} \neq \frac{\text{VMP}_b}{\text{MC}_b}.$$

When this is true, it is trivial to prove that the total cost of any given output could be reduced by substituting some of the factor with the higher ratio for some of the other one. Hence, AC_{pc} is, in general, above AC_m.

In the special case where factor proportions are technologically fixed the monopolist has, of course, no choice in the matter of combining factors and ACm coincides with ACpc. This situation is the same, essentially, as one where there is only a single input.

2. Switching to different inputs

To initiate our discussion of the implications of switching to different inputs as output rises, we consider first an extreme situation (but a particularly easy one to analyse) in which no two units which are perfect substitutes for the industry are likewise perfect substitutes in their alternative uses. We describe this situation by saying that the factor units used by the industry are 'completely non-homogeneous'. Here it is not necessarily true, as in case (1) where we assumed rising factor supply curves, that the marginal cost to the industry of hiring another unit of input is greater than its price. To illustrate this point let us consider the following identity:

$$\mathrm{MC}_a = P_a + \frac{\delta P_a}{\delta Q_a} \cdot Q_a + \sum_{i \neq a} \frac{\delta P_i}{\delta Q_a} \cdot Qi \qquad (1)$$

where a refers to a specific factor used by the firm, and i runs over all other factors it uses. Equation (1) thus tells us that the addition to the total cost of the firm when it hires an additional unit of factor a equals the change in the payments to factor a itself, plus induced changes in payments to other factors resulting from the fact that the various factor prices are inter-related (e.g. if factor b is a substitute for a, a rise in Q_a, which can be taken to raise the price of P_a, would lead to a rise in P_b).

In considering the implications of rising factor prices on the relationship between ACpc and ACm, we implicitly made the simplifying assumption that $\delta P_i/\delta Q_a = 0$ for all i. The equation thus reduced to

$$\mathrm{MC}_a = P_a + \frac{\delta P_a}{\delta Q_a} \cdot Q_a \qquad (2)$$

with MC_a being greater than P_a by an amount depending on $\delta P_a/\delta Q_a$ and on Q_a.

In the present case we have assumed that there is only a single unit of each factor; hence the term $\delta P_a/\delta Q_a \cdot Q_a$ drops out leaving

$$\mathrm{MC}_a = P_a + \sum_{i \neq a} \frac{\delta P_i}{\delta Q_a} \cdot Q_i. \qquad (3)$$

Whether the purchase of an input unit by the monopolist will increase or decrease the price of other units he has purchased all along clearly depends on the degree of substitutability between the two units in their alternative uses.[12] If no two units which he uses are either substitutes or complements in alternative uses we have $\mathrm{MC}_a = P_a$. In this special case we find that the monopolist *pays none of the rent that the purely competitive industry had to pay*, and that, if we make an assumption analogous to that of linear homogeneity, *he combines factors in the same way*. These conclusions require a brief explanation.

That no economic rent is paid by the monopolist is clear since he can hire any given input unit by paying it a price which is greater than it would get elsewhere by an amount arbitrarily close to zero. But why, in the same situation, would the purely competitive industry be paying rent to these factor units? The reason is simple. Consider a factor unit with a value of marginal product of $10, either to the monopolist or to a single firm in the purely competitive industry. If its opportunity cost outside the industry is $5, this is all the monopolist would have to pay it. But in the purely competitive industry, no firm would be able to employ it for less than $10, since the other firms in the same industry would be willing to bid up to that amount for it. The same holds with respect to all input units.

It now remains to consider whether the monopolist uses the same factor combinations as would the purely competitive industry. If we replace the assumption of linear homogeneity (which is meaningless here because only one unit of each factor exists) with the assumption that 'if two bundles of inputs, each of which might be used by an individual firm in the purely competitive industry, are used together, the resulting total output is equal to the sum of the two separate outputs',[13] then this result can be shown to follow. The assumption implies

---

[12] In considering the implications of rising factor prices we made the special assumption that some units were perfect substitutes (those of the same factor) and the rest were neither substitutes nor complements.

[13] This assumption, like that of linear homogeneity in the previous case, is designed to imply that if the monopolist had to pay the same price for each factor unit as did the purely competitive industry, it would be at neither an advantage nor a disadvantage in terms of average cost per unit of output.

first of all that if the monopolist uses the same bundle of inputs as the purely competitive industry, the same output will be forthcoming. Less directly, it implies that he *will* use the same bundle of inputs. For consider the behaviour of the monopolist – one can visualize his having in front of him a shelf of possible input units, each with a price tag attached. To produce any given output he selects first those with the highest VMP/MC ratios, then those with the next highest, until he has enough to produce the desired output. Since there is only one unit of each factor, and no two factors are either substitutes or complements in alternative uses, the marginal cost of each unit equals its price and its price is set by its value of marginal product elsewhere.

Now consider the purely competitive industry producing the same output. The input units would be chosen in exactly the same order as by the monopolist, since, for the last unit hired:

(a) the marginal product is the same for the hiring firm as it would be for the monopolist (this follows from the above assumption);

(b) marginal cost is again equal to price elsewhere.

The only difference is that intra-marginal units have their prices bid up by the competition of the firms in the industry so that their VMP/P ratios are the same as that of the last unit hired.

Given that the monopolist combines factors in the same way as the competitive industry and that he pays no rent, we can show that MCm coincides with ACpc.[14] When a firm in the purely competitive industry increases its output by one unit, the additional factor units which it employs, since they are the last ones added, receive no rent. We know that any firm which is in equilibrium, and is part of a purely competitive industry in equilibrium, has marginal cost equal to average cost.[15] (As we saw earlier, the marginal cost to the industry of the extra unit of output may be greater than that to the firm, but this is not directly relevant here.) Now we just saw that a firm in the purely

[14] Note that this result, and a number of other aspects of the situation as well, is the same as when the monopolist is also a perfectly discriminating monopsonist.

[15] For strict accuracy, we should probably not say that this industry is in purely competitive equilibrium, since the marginal and average cost curves are assumed to be flat for outputs beyond a certain level. But the marginal cost equal to average condition does, of course, hold in this case.

competitive industry uses the same additional factors to increase its output by one unit as the monopolist would, hence its marginal cost equals that of the monopolist. But its marginal cost also equals its average cost, which is given by the height of AC*pc* at that output level. Since this holds for all output levels, MC*m* coincides with AC*pc*.

The case just discussed (where input units are neither substitutes nor complements in alternative uses) serves as a handy benchmark with which to compare other possibilities. Suppose that the input units used by the monopolist tend in general to be substitutes in their alternative uses. Then

$$\text{MC}_a = P_a + \sum_{i \neq a} \frac{\delta P_i}{\delta Q_a} \cdot Q_i$$

and it is no longer true that the monopolist will combine factors in the same way as the purely competitive industry, or that MC*m* coincides with AC*pc*. Instead MC*m* lies above AC*pc*, though AC*m* is still below AC*pc*. The monopolist is paying rent in this case in the sense that when he hires another input unit, he must pay certain other units (which are substitutes in alternative uses for the one just hired) more than before, or they will be bid away by other industries. This payment of rent implies that MC*m* is above AC*pc*.[16]

Finally, we might have the case where the factor units employed by the monopolist are, in general, complementary in their alternative uses. When he hires another unit, the monopolist now finds that the rewards needed to retain previously employed units fall, i.e. $\text{MC}_a < P_a$. When he bids another unit away from some other industry, that industry becomes unwilling to offer as much for the factor units currently used by the monopolist as it was before. By reversing the arguments of the preceding paragraph we now find that MC*m* lies below AC*pc*. Since one would expect that factors which are substitutes in one industry probably would be substitutes elsewhere as well, this case seems less likely than the preceding one.

An extension of the above analysis to cases characterized by some switching, but not by complete non-homogeneity, is fairly straightforward. Perfect non-homogeneity is clearly not necessary for the monopolist–monopsonist to escape paying some

---

[16] The supply curve of a purely competitive industry is the 'marginal cost excluding rent' curve, in John Robinson's terminology. See op. cit., chap. 10.

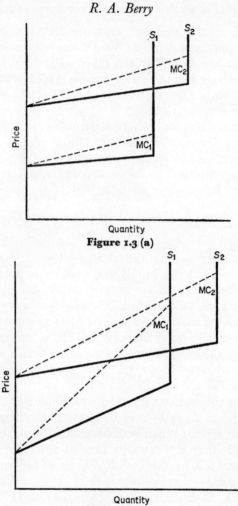

Figure 1.3 (a)

Figure 1.3 (b)

rents paid by the competitive industry. And switching is not a sufficient condition. Switching only creates the possibility of avoiding these rents; they are in fact avoided in those cases where the marginal cost (greater than price) of factors already used is high enough to induce the monopolist to switch to a different factor earlier than the purely competitive industry would.[17]

[17] To illustrate, we might have two factors able to perform about the same services in the industry in question and with supply curves as indicated below. In Fig. 1.3A, the monopolist, like the competitive industry, would employ all the

3. *External effects*

The third determinant of the shape of the supply curve under pure competition is the presence or the absence of external economies or diseconomies, the former making the curve rise less rapidly or fall more rapidly than otherwise, the latter making it rise more rapidly or fall less rapidly. Suppose there are constant factor prices for the industry but external diseconomies leading to a rising supply curve. Then the monopoly marginal cost curve will, if the external economies are symmetrical (by which we mean, roughly, that each firm is the recipient of the same amount of external economies as it contributes to other firms), be marginal to AC*pc*.[18] The same would be true with external economies, where the supply curve was forward falling. Since factor prices are constant, the monopolist's factor proportions cannot differ from those of the purely competitive industry as a result of a divergence between the marginal cost and the price of factors. And the assumption of symmetrical external economies or diseconomies can be shown to imply, subject to certain qualifications, that the purely competitive industry produces any given output in the most efficient manner possible from a social point of view[19] (though it does not

---

units of the first factor before employing any of the second, since the marginal cost of the last unit of the first was less than that of the first unit of the second factor. But with the curves of Fig. 1.3B, the monopolist would start employing the second factor before all units of the first one were employed, and would thereby avoid rents paid by the competitive industry.

[18] If all firms are identical, in the same sense that the production function of any firm can be expressed by the same equation,

$$Q_i = f(a, b, \ldots, m; Q_1, \ldots, Q_i, \ldots, Q_n)$$

where $a, b, \ldots, m$ are factors and i runs over all other firms in the industry, we say that the external effects are symmetrical.

[19] This follows from the fact that with the identical production functions assumed (see note 18), the marginal social cost of production is the same for each firm, so there is no inter-firm reallocation of production which would lower the social cost of a given output level. We assume implicitly that there are not increasing returns to scale, since otherwise pure competition could not be present. This does not follow, however, if a range of different outputs is equally profitable for the individual firm, as in that case there is no mechanism to assure minimization of total social cost. It must also be noted that if there is a determinate maximum profit point at which all firms are producing, so that marginal social cost is equal for all firms, the condition suffices only if marginal external economies fall as the firm's output rises; otherwise the equality of marginal social costs may reflect a local pessimum. (I am indebted to the referee of this paper for making the two points in this paragraph.)

produce the optimal level of output); the internalization of these external effects does not, therefore, lead to increased efficiency. Hence, we find ACm coinciding with ACpc, and MCm marginal to it.

The effects of external economies or diseconomies on the shape of ACpc are additive with the effects of the other two determinants discussed. Those two are, as we saw, rather similar; in a sense they are substitutes for one another. In any case, it is easy to say in qualitative terms how each of the three will affect the relationship between MCm and ACpc even when all are present.

By now it is quite clear that the MCm curve relevant for the analysis of monopoly price and output policy may bear any of a wide variety of relationships to the ACpc curve, depending on the situation. This conclusion implies that monopoly–pure competition comparisons, even in the highly over-simplified static framework with which we are working, are far from a simple, straightforward matter.

Results Concerning Welfare Effects of Monopoly-Monopsony

With the above conclusions in mind, we now make a few brief comments about relative outputs and welfare under monopoly and pure competition.

As we saw, MCm may bear any of a rather wide range of relationships to ACpc. It will lie below ACpc if the factor units are perfectly non-homogeneous, and they are complementary in their alternative uses; at the other extreme it will be marginal to (and therefore above) ACpc when all rents must be paid and either all factors have the same elasticity of supply to the firm or all are perfect complements in the production of the good. It is possible that different factors will have different supply elasticities. This implies

(a) that ACm will be below ACpc (see p. 12);
(b) that the monopolist will not combine factors in the socially most efficient way.

Loss thus occurs both because the wrong amount (from a

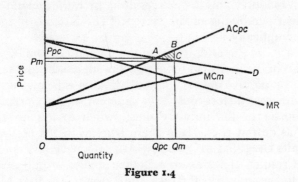

Figure 1.4

social point of view) is produced and because it is produced in a socially inefficient manner.

In most cases monopoly output is below the purely competitive level. Exceptions occur only in certain cases when MC*m* is below AC*pc*. In the absence of external economies, this implies that the inputs of the monopoly tend to be non-homogeneous

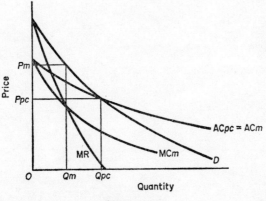

Figure 1.5

and complementary in their alternative uses. A further requirement in this case (illustrated in Fig. 1.4) is that the demand curve be quite elastic.[20] Total income loss here consists of *ABC* (a measure of what loss would be as a result of the overproduction if the output OQ*m* were produced in the socially most

[20] Joan Robinson (op. cit., p. 152) concluded that monopoly output could never exceed purely competitive output unless the average cost curve was downward sloping. This seems to be incorrect.

efficient manner) plus the loss resulting from the fact of socially inefficient combining of the factors. (The latter is not shown diagrammatically.)

When $ACpc$ slopes down (due to external economies among the firms in the industry) monopoly output can be greater than purely competitive output, but only if ACm is below $ACpc$, i.e. either different factors must have different supply elasticities to the industry or the industry must switch to less productive factors as output rises. (It is again true, as in the no external economies case, that MCm below $ACpc$ is a necessary condition for this result.) If we assume factor supplies are all perfectly elastic to the industry, then we know (see p. 18) that MCm is marginal to $ACpc$. Such a case is shown in Fig. 1.5. The monopoly output cannot exceed the purely competitive one since, as a moment's reflection shows, at Qpc MC is greater than MR, since AC = AR and AR is falling faster than AC.

2 Allocative Efficiency, X-Efficiency and the Measurement of Welfare Losses

W. S. Comanor and Harvey Leibenstein

In estimating the loss from monopoly,[1] it has been common to assume that inputs are used as efficiently as in competitive markets. The presumed reason for this assumption is that firms have a clear interest in minimizing costs per unit of output. While the 'carrot' of greater profits may well be a major determinant of firm behaviour, the competitive 'stick' may be equally important, and to this extent, monopoly will affect costs as well as prices. In this context, the welfare loss from monopoly should include the reduction in what one of the authors has called 'X-efficiency'[2] as well as the extent of allocative inefficiency, and therefore the combined welfare loss from monopoly may be very much larger than the usually calculated loss.

Competition may have an important impact on costs because it serves as a major source of disciplinary pressure on firms in the market, which, to a greater or lesser degree, affects all firms in competitive industries. In the first place, the process of competition tends to eliminate high-cost producers, while the existence of substantial market power often allows such firms to remain in business. This is due to the oft-noted fact that the high price–cost margins, which are established by firms with substantial market power, often serve as an umbrella which protects their high-cost rivals. Second, the process of competition, by mounting pressures on firm profits, tends to discipline managements *and employees* to utilize their inputs, and to put

---

[1] In this paper it is recognized that monopoly does not depend entirely on the size distribution of firms but rather rests on the entire set of factors which permits firms to behave differently from what would be enforced in purely competitive markets with similar cost and demand conditions.

[2] Harvey Leibenstein, 'Allocative Efficiency vs. "X-Efficiency"', *American Economic Review*, LV₂ (1966) 392–415.

Reprinted from *Economica*, n.s., xxxvi (Aug 1969) 304–9, by kind permission of the authors and of the Economica Publishing Office.

forth effort, more energetically and more effectively than is the case where this pressure is absent.[3] Thus, a shift from monopoly to competition has two possible effects: (1) the elimination of monopoly rents, and (2) the reduction of unit costs.[4]

Although both of these effects should be included in estimating the welfare losses which result from monopoly, in fact, frequently only the first has been examined. By assuming that actual costs equal minimum costs, Harberger[5] and others have estimated the welfare loss which results from monopoly by calculating approximately the total consumer surplus which is lost. This is illustrated in Fig. 2.1 by the triangle ABC where this area equals $\frac{1}{2}\Delta p\Delta q$, where Δp is the difference between price and actual unit costs and Δq is the corresponding difference in quantities. It is in these computations where actual costs are assumed to represent economic costs, for Δp is also considered to represent the difference in price between monopolistic and competitive equilibrium.

Now let us suppose that a shift from monopoly to competition not only lowers price but also lowers costs (i.e. increases X-efficiency). What are the welfare losses under these circumstances which are due to monopoly? We show below that there is a simple mathematical relation, in the case of linear demand functions, which relates the full reduction in allocative efficiency to that estimated under the limiting assumption noted above. The important implication of our result is that the actual degree of *allocative inefficiency* may be very much larger than the level as heretofore calculated. Furthermore, to this larger sum must be added the volume of *X-inefficiency* for the monopolistically used inputs to obtain the total welfare loss from monopoly.

[3] Cf. R. M. Cyert and J. G. March, *A Behavioral Theory of the Firm* (Englewood Cliffs, N.J., 1963), where the related concept of 'organizational slack' is used to describe the process whereby costs rise above minimum levels.

[4] The hypothesized cost effect of competition is not original to this article but originated as long ago as 1897 in an article in the *Atlantic Monthly* of that year by A. T. Hadley. See Oliver E. Williamson, 'A Dynamic Stochastic Theory of Managerial Behaviour', in A. Phillips and O. Williamson (eds), *Prices: Issues in Theory, Practice and Public Policy*, p. 23. A more recent statement of this hypothesis was made by Tibor Scitovsky in 'Economic Theory and the Measurement of Concentration', in N.B.E.R., *Business Concentration and Price Policy* (Princeton, 1955) pp. 106–8.

[5] Arnold Harberger, 'Monopoly and Resource Allocation', *American Economic Review, Papers and Proceedings*, XLIV (1954) 77–92.

I

In Fig. 2.1, we assume that a shift from monopoly to competition will reduce the monopoly rent per unit of output by a units but that it will reduce unit costs by x units. On this basis, we can distinguish the various components of welfare loss which result from monopoly. W_a is the partial welfare loss which results from allocative inefficiency associated with monopoly, and is illustrated by the triangle ABC in Fig. 2.1. This is the standard

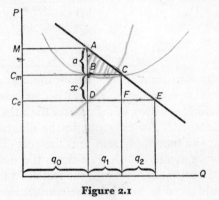

Figure 2.1

measure of the welfare loss which has been calculated in earlier studies. W_{ax}, on the other hand, describes the full measure of allocative inefficiency which results from monopoly under the view that competition affects the level of costs as well as prices. It is measured by the triangle ADE. At the same time, W_x is the welfare loss from X-inefficiency resulting from monopoly, and refers to the higher costs used to produce the restricted level of output. This loss has no allocative component since it is concerned with no change in output levels, and is the rectangle $C_m C_c DB$.

The quantity a is the price–cost margin which exists under monopoly, while the quantity x is the cost difference between monopoly and competition; q_1 is the difference in quantity which results from a shift from monopoly to competition exclusive of the cost effect, while q_2 is the difference in quantity directly associated with the cost reduction. Now let X equal the cost difference in units of a, i.e. X is equal to x/a, which is the ratio of the cost difference to the price–cost margin under monopoly.

As indicated above, $W_a = aq_1/2$, while

$$W_{ax} = (a + Xa)(q_1 + q_2)/2. \tag{1}$$

We can then note that the total welfare loss which results from the allocative inefficiency due to monopoly is some multiple of the welfare loss as measured earlier, and this factor is indicated by

$$\frac{W_{ax}}{W_a} = \frac{aq_1 + aq_2 + Xaq_1 + Xaq_2}{aq_1} \tag{2}$$

and hence[6]

$$W_{ax}/W_a = (1 + X)^2. \tag{3}$$

This relationship implies that where the cost difference due to monopoly is large relative to the price–cost margin, the loss in allocative inefficiency may be far greater than the allocative loss as usually measured. For example, in the diagram above, it is assumed that the monopoly rent and the cost effect are equal, and, as a consequence, W_{ax} is four times the usual measure of welfare loss. If, on the other hand, the ratio of x to a were three, then we would need to multiply the conventional welfare loss by a factor of sixteen.

A numerical example may illustrate the implications of this relationship. Suppose that actual costs are 6 per cent below the monopoly price, and that one-half of the total output of the economy is produced in monopolized sectors. If the price elasticity were equal to two, the welfare loss W_a would be approximately 0·18 per cent of the net national product. Now, suppose that the cost-effect differential is 18 per cent, which does not appear to be an impossible figure. In that case, the full allocative welfare loss W_{ax} is nearly 3 per cent of the net national product – a not insubstantial sum.

The pure X-efficiency effect, apart from the allocative effect, is, of course, likely to be the largest of all. In the numerical illustration above, the welfare loss W_x would be one-half of 18 per cent, i.e. 9 per cent, of the net national product. Furthermore, it should be noted that in fact W_x is likely to be even

[6] We note that $q_2/q_1 = x/a = X$, by similar triangles. Therefore $W_{ax}/W_a = 1 + 2X + X^2$.

larger relatively to W_{ax}, since we have assumed a high price-elasticity of demand.

II

The usual estimates of W_a ignore the problems associated with the theory of the second best, for they indicate only the welfare gain associated with a single change from monopolistic to competitive equilibrium. On this account, they have few policy implications where policy necessarily demands piecemeal and partial measures. A shift, for example, from monopoly to competition in some industries may not improve welfare if the resources allocated to the newly-competitive industry are drawn from uses where they are currently in insufficient supply. In some circumstances, the value of the additional resources used in a newly-competitive industry may conceivably have been higher in the industries where they had been previously allocated. Thus, second-best considerations may make it difficult to determine whether a shift to a greater degree of competition in a particular industry represents a true improvement in allocative efficiency. In the case, however, where there is a reduction in costs as well, and thereby an improvement in X-efficiency, it becomes far easier to conclude that a shift from monopoly to competition in a single industry represents a welfare gain.

Returning to the numerical example of the previous section, we determined that W_x was 9 per cent of net national product. Such gains represent a clear improvement in welfare since they do not depend on a re-allocation of resources. More units of output for particular goods can be produced without reducing the output of other goods in the economy. Furthermore, even if the allocative effect of a single industry shift from monopoly to competition were negative, this gain would represent a positive counter-weight.

Second-best results depend on the structure of inter-relationships among sectors in the economy and focus on the traditional general equilibrium conclusion that 'everything depends on everything else'. While this conclusion is qualitatively correct, it ignores quantitative considerations. The magnitude of the second-best problem for specific sectors depends on the degree of interdependence among industries, the degree of monopoly in sectors related to the one at issue, as well as the structure of input–output relationships. Quantitatively important second-best considerations may depend on a small set of related industries rather than all others, and thereby policy judgements may demand a *specific* rather than a *general* theory of the second best. In such circumstances, it might be possible to estimate the gain or loss in allocative efficiency from a shift from monopoly to competition, and if the latter, to compare it with the clear gain in X-efficiency. In any event, since the X-efficiency improvement may be large and represents a clear gain, we should have confidence that changes which represent both allocative and cost-differential effects are far more likely to represent positive welfare gains as compared to those where only the reallocation of resources is concerned.

One further point should be noted. Because of the higher costs which are assumed to exist under monopoly, the increase in output with competition demands only a partial re-allocation of resources. In Fig. 2.1, xq_0 denotes the volume of redundant inputs under monopoly which could be used to produce xq_0/C_c additional units of output. At the same time, the percentage increase in output, due to a shift from monopoly to competition, is $(q_1 + q_2)/q_0$, which equals

$$(a + x)e/M \tag{4}$$

where e is the absolute value of the elasticity of demand.[7] Then, the increase in output from re-allocated inputs, expressed as a proportion of original output, is

$$\frac{(a + x)e}{M} - \frac{x}{C_c} \tag{5}$$

which equals[8]

$$\frac{ae + x(e - 1)}{M} - \frac{x(a + x)}{MC_c}. \tag{6}$$

The extent to which inputs have to be re-allocated depends

---

[7] This elasticity represents the average value between points A and E such that

$$e \frac{\Delta p}{p} = \frac{\Delta q}{q}.$$

[8] This can be seen by expanding the second term of expression (5):

$$\frac{x}{C_c} = \frac{xM}{MC_c} = \frac{x(C_c + a + x)}{MC_c} = \frac{x}{M} + \frac{x(a + x)}{MC_c}.$$

on the degree to which e is close to unity, and the ratio of x to a (i.e. the value of X). This can be seen by considering the proportion of the total increase in output which must be produced from re-allocated inputs. Dividing both terms in (6) by (4) gives the following expression:

$$1 - \frac{x}{(a + x)e} - \frac{x}{C_c e} \tag{7}$$

In industries where demand is relatively inelastic, no increase in inputs may be required, and it may even be the case that output is increased while the total volume of inputs is reduced. In the latter situation, expression (7) will be negative. And here no second-best problem will arise.

From this analysis it appears that there may be many cases where the clear welfare gain associated with the cost effect of competition is a significant counteracting element to the possible loss on 'second-best' grounds from the re-allocation of inputs. The likelihood of an improved welfare position resulting from a single industry shift from monopoly to competition would seem thereby to be greatly enhanced.

3 On External Costs and the Visible Arm of the Law[1]

Paul Burrows

1. Introduction

In recent years there have been signs that economists are reacting against the earlier, predominantly theoretical, analysis of external costs; the need for research on the practical questions confronting the policy-maker being recognized. This paper considers the two functions of the law in the treatment of external costs: settling disputes over legal rights; and providing alternative compensation arrangements to the market and tax–subsidy schemes. Conflicts between the possible objectives of legal decisions on rights, and the existence of institutional constraints on the achievements of optimal outcomes, are postulated.

The discussion falls into two inter-related parts. Section 2 examines the relevance of economic criteria to the settlement of rights, and section 3 presents an appraisal of judicial solutions, contrasting an idealized form of judicial solution with actual court practice.

2. The Settlement of Legal Rights

The final outcome of a dispute between an external-cost-creating firm or individual, referred to henceforth as the 'offender', and an external-cost-affected firm or individual, the 'offended party',[2] will depend on legal decisions on rights and

[1] I have benefited greatly from discussions with Keith Hartley, Michael Jones-Lee, Alan Peacock, Charles Rowley, Alan Williams, Jack Wiseman, and members of the University of Sussex economics faculty seminar, and am indebted to Dr E. J. Mishan for comments on an early draft and to Mr G. H. L. Fridman for answers to several legal questions. Remaining errors are the property of the author.

[2] The terms 'offender' and 'offended party' are used in a purely descriptive sense of causing or being affected by the interference regardless of the legal decision on liability.

Reprinted from *Oxford Economic Papers*, XXII (Mar 1970) 39–56, by kind permission of the author and of the Clarendon Press.

on redistributions of those rights through bargaining or some other means. An initial settlement of a dispute over rights, which is inevitably a function of the law, will amount to the statement that the 'offender' has or has not the right to continue the imposition of costs (interference) unabated and without compensation to the offended party. The final outcome, defined as the final level of the activity and compensation payment, differs from the initial settlement to the extent that rights are redistributed. The winner of the dispute over rights is assumed to be prepared to forgo (redistribute) his rights if adequately compensated.

The concern of the lawyer in the settlement of rights is to prevent outcomes involving unjust interference; this requires the elimination of 'substantial' and 'unreasonable' interference, unless the offended party is fully compensated.[3] The courts' judgements on the maximum level of interference which is not unreasonable are in practice influenced by circumstances such as the motivation of the litigants and the character of the locality in which the interference occurs. Such decisions could be made independently of the economic effects of the interference, and in what follows it is assumed that 'justice' or 'legal equity' requires the equal availability of protection from interference[4] to all individuals and firms in similar non-economic circumstances.[5] But what would be the economic consequences of the exclusion of economic criteria from decisions on legal rights? And what would the acceptance of economic objectives by the courts imply for the pursuit of justice?

[3] Many cases of external cost involving few litigants lead to (civil) tort actions in nuisance; those involving large numbers of offended parties require an action in public nuisance by the Attorney-General. Nuisance has been defined as interference, in the form of annoyance or physical harm, with the use or enjoyment of one's land. See James [8], Street [16] and *Winfield on Tort* [9].

[4] Defined as equal protection from losses valued in money terms. The major objection to this definition is that, with differences in the marginal utility of income between income groups, the individual's money valuation of a given loss of utility will be a function of his income level. With this problem and the impossibility of checking the honesty of such valuations the courts will be obliged to place their own valuation on the loss of utility. This difficulty does not arise with the external costs imposed on firms.

[5] The possibility of a conflict between justice and economic objectives (p. 40 below) hinges on this definition of the justice objective. To the extent that the courts will accept an economic interpretation of 'similar circumstances' the conflict disappears.

The two economic objectives to be considered are the maximization of community gains from redistributions of rights, and distributive equity. It might be contended that the gain to the community attainable from bargains to redistribute rights is a function of the initial settlement of rights, but it will be shown that this contention depends on the negotiability of legal rights (i.e. whether they can legally be redistributed) and, under certain conditions, on the existence of bargaining costs. A case will be made for adjustments in the law to eliminate obstacles to bargains that redistribute rights; and for caution in accepting the view held by economists,[6] that decisions on legal rights should be related to their allocative (and distributive) consequences.

Initially attention is limited to the dependence of attainable community gains on the initial settlement of rights, the analysis proceeding successively under three sets of assumptions:

(*a*) That bargaining is costless, and that there are no restrictions imposed by the law on redistributions of rights (i.e. there are no institutional obstacles to their redistribution).

(*b*) That bargaining incurs costs but there are no institutional obstacles to the redistribution of rights.

(*c*) That there are institutional obstacles but no bargaining costs.

(*a*) *Costless bargaining, no institutional obstacles*

For simplicity the exposition is limited to the case, illustrated in Fig. 3.1,[7] of the imposition of a cost by one firm (*A*) on another (*B*),[8] though with some qualifications the analysis can be applied to individuals.

In Fig. 3.1A *B*'s marginal loss curve represents the minimum loss he must incur as a result of *A*'s interference. A negotiable settlement of rights in favour of the offended party (*B*) makes point *O* the starting-point. Any privately arranged movement from *O* requires a bargain providing for compensation equal to the value of *B*'s loss to be paid by *A* to *B*. A settlement in the offender's favour states that *OJ* (the maximum level *A* would

---

[6] e.g. Coase [3] section vii; Mishan [13] *passim*.

[7] See Turvey's Fig. 1 ([18] p. 311). We lose little in terms of realism and gain substantially through simplification if we assume *A* to have only one activity.

[8] The non-reciprocal case; see below, pp. 42–3, n. 29.

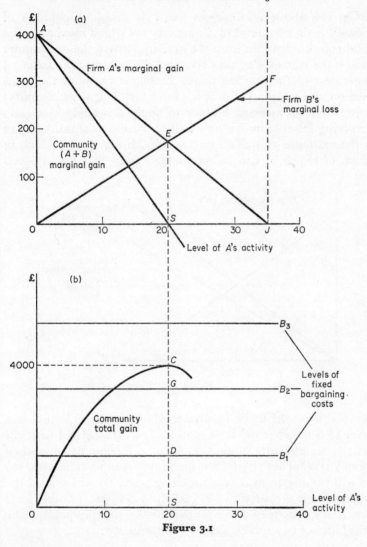

Figure 3.1

choose in the absence of any restrictions) is not unjust, any movement from OJ being a voluntary decision by A presumably in exchange for compensation (paid by B) equal to the forgone gains from the activity.[9]

[9] Note that points O and J are just two of the candidates for the judgement of 'reasonable' interference on non-economic grounds, where O need not represent zero activity. The assumption required by the subsequent analysis is that the activity levels preferred on non-economic and on allocative criteria do not coincide.

34   *Paul Burrows*

On the above assumptions the now classic conclusion of Coase[10] is that the level of A's activity OS which maximizes the total community gain from the activity (where the community gain is the sum of A's gain curve and B's loss curve) is achieved regardless of the starting-point. Problems (such as the comparison and addition of people's monetary valuation of utility) arise when an attempt is made to apply this analysis to cases involving losses of individuals' utility. Perhaps the most serious is the existence of welfare effects (see Mishan [11]), which in terms of Fig. 3.1A can be represented as in Fig. 3.2. A's gain

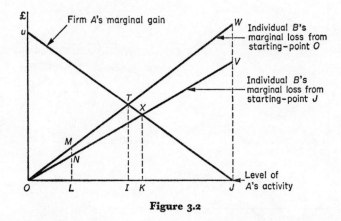

Figure 3.2

curve is assumed to be invariate, which is plausible if A is a firm. If B is better off at O than at J, which he will be if A's activity significantly diminishes his total income position, then for any level of activity OL the amount of compensation (OML) he will require from A (with starting-point O) will exceed the amount he is prepared to pay (ONL) to A to prevent that level of activity occurring at all (with J as the starting-point). The possibility of two loss curves for B depends on:

---

[10] [3] sections 3 and 4. See also Davis and Whinston [5] for a formal demonstration of this result, and Buchanan [1] and Buchanan and Stubblebine [2]. A certain world is assumed – on the implications of stochastic events for Pareto optimality see Williamson, Olson and Ralston [21]. H. Shibata ('Externality, Compensation and Social Policy') argues that, in the case of production-on-production external costs, the same Pareto outcome can be achieved from either starting-point through automatic market adjustments. However, his conclusion requires each party to know the other's production function. We shall refer to private redistributions of rights as if they take place through bargains.

(i) a significant effect of the activity up to OJ on B's total income position; and

(ii) the utility/income curve being non-linear over the relevant range.

The existence of welfare effects influences the maximum community gain attainable from the different starting-points (in the case above, greater for a settlement in the offender's favour) and the associated levels of A's activity, OI and OK. However, the importance of welfare effects can be judged only empirically and it is far from certain that they present a

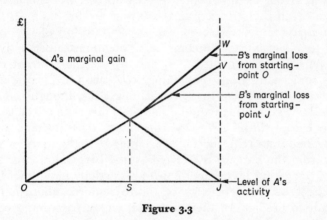

Figure 3.3

problem in more than a small minority of cases. It may be that B's loss curve for each starting-point will differ between starting-points only for the very high activity levels which significantly affect B's over-all position: in which case the chosen activity level and the attainable community gains do not differ.

(b) Bargaining costs, no institutional obstacles

The existence of bargaining costs, i.e. the costs of identifying and reaching agreement with the other parties to the dispute to redistribute rights,[11] will have one effect which is not in dispute: some bargains which would be profitable in the costless situation will no longer yield net gains to the community. Although this will influence the choice of means of redistributing rights it has no direct implication for the settlement of rights. The availability of net community gains to bargains can be dependent

[11] Defined in more detail on p. 37 below.

on the settlement of rights only if bargaining costs are asymmetrical, i.e. differ between the two settlements.[12] Let us accept for a moment the assumption that such an asymmetry exists.

If the costs of bargaining are independent of A's activity level (i.e. are lump-sum), as represented by the lines B_1, B_2 and B_1 in Fig. 3.1B, the costs do not enter the determination of the activity level in the bargain, if they are less than SC, since they do not enter marginal gain and loss curves. A short-run allocative effect results if the bargaining costs from (say) a settlement in favour of the offender exceed SC (i.e. B_3) and from a settlement in the offended party's favour are less than SC (i.e. B_2 or B_1). The former settlement results in a loss of potential gains to a bargain, the outcome being the unrestrained activity at level OJ. If, by contrast, B_1 and B_2 are the relevant cost levels some gains from bargaining (GD) are lost by choosing the settlement leading to B_2 bargaining costs, though the OS activity level is retained and no short-run diversion of resources occurs except through second-order effects on the sectors providing resources required for bargaining.[13] If A's share of the gains from the bargain is affected by the bargaining costs the future (long-run) investment flow to A's activity may differ but the effect on the efficiency of future resource allocation is difficult to predict. In the third case, where bargaining costs exceed SC for both settlements of rights, no bargain yields net community gains from either starting-point. Which polar solution is chosen on allocative grounds is determined by the relative sizes of AEO and EFJ in Fig. 3.1A, i.e. depends on whether the total community gain from OJ is positive or negative.

Clearly even assuming an asymmetry in bargaining costs it is impossible to make *general* statements about the advantages of one settlement of rights over another on allocation grounds.

---

[12] For the theoretical support for an asymmetry in cases involving a large offended group see Mishan ([13] section iv). Coase ([3] section vi) is incorrect in implying that the existence of bargaining costs is a sufficient condition for the settlement of rights to influence 'the efficiency with which the economic system operates'.

[13] If the size of the offended group were functionally related to the level of A's activity the bargaining cost functions in Fig. 3.1B would have positive slopes. An asymmetry in the slopes of the functions affects the chosen activity level but the net attainable community gain may not differ between settlements if there is an asymmetry in the fixed as well as the marginal bargaining costs.

The attainable net gains from bargaining may or may not be affected by the settlement.[14]

The allocative implications of the decision on legal rights become even less certain when the asymmetry assumption is questioned. In the first place, there is no reason to expect any asymmetry in the 'small numbers' cases[15] frequently dealt with by the courts. Second, even where a single offender interferes with a large group (involving small–large bargaining) the presumption of asymmetry is debatable. Consider the argument as it has been presented:[16] bargaining costs will rise exponentially with the size of the group involved and consequently the costs of achieving a solution will be greater if the large group initiates the bargaining than if the offender is forced to do so.[17] This reasoning involves a *non sequitur*. The costs of bargaining will certainly be higher than for disputes involving one offender and

[14] This analysis considers only the effect on attainable gains from bargains. Since this was written, H. Shibata has shown ('Externality, Compensation and Social Policy', to be published) that the decision on rights affects the starting-point for bargaining in the case of external costs on consumption. In Fig. 3.4

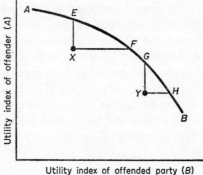

Utility index of offended party (B)
Figure 3.4

(where *AB* is the utility or welfare frontier) *Y* is the starting-point for a settlement in *B*'s favour, *X* the starting-point (with external costs being imposed) for the opposite settlement. Bargaining from *X* and *Y* would lead to moves within the *XEF* and *YGH* quadrants respectively. If no bargains are reached we cannot choose between the outcomes, *X* and *Y*, on Paretian efficiency grounds though their associated income distributions differ. Similarly, different outcomes from bargaining which fall on the welfare frontier differ only with respect to income distribution. Efficiency provides no general case for one settlement over the other whether rights are redistributed or not. (I am grateful to Dr Shibata for permission to reproduce this simplified version of one of his arguments.)

[15] i.e. cases involving few litigants, giving rise to tort actions.

[16] Mishan [13] section iv, esp. pp. 268, 276.

[17] This argument is presented by Mishan, ibid., in support of settlements in favour of offended parties.

C

one offended party, but why does the placement of the incentive to take the initiative itself necessarily affect the costs of small–large bargaining? If the onus is placed upon the offended group the costs include those of identifying other members of the group, of reaching an agreement on a unified policy (of the offer to be made and the share to be paid by each individual), and of contacting and bargaining with the offender. If the offender is liable and must initiate bargaining in order to lift an injunction on his activity, the costs include the identification of the members of the offended group and of contacting and bargaining with the group, together with the costs incurred by the group in reaching agreement on its reaction to offers made by the offender and on the shares to accrue to each member of the group. It is impossible to state categorically which settlement of rights will lead to lower bargaining costs given the complexity of the comparison involved.

Finally, an asymmetry in bargaining costs affects the maximum attainable community gains only where a bargaining solution is more efficient than solutions through other instruments. If some tax–subsidy scheme, court compensation arrangement, merger, provision of separate facilities, or preventive device can be shown to be optimal, a preference for one settlement of rights over another on allocative grounds will rely on a demonstration of an asymmetry between settlements in the availability of the most efficient solution.[18] In fact, the case of large numbers, where an asymmetry in bargaining costs is most probable, may well prove to be one where bargaining does not offer the best prospects of an outcome which maximizes community gains.

(c) *Institutional obstacles, no bargaining costs*

The previous analysis (in common with all the literature on external costs) has assumed that the law permits the settlement of rights to be treated as a starting-point from which the rights can be redistributed. Is this a realistic assumption for Britain? This depends, if a case comes to court, on the ease of out-of-court settlements[19] once the probable settlement of rights is

---

[18] It is suggested in section 3 that asymmetries do arise with respect to some instruments.

[19] An alternative to an out-of-court settlement arises where a temporary ('interlocutory') injunction is applied for to restrain the offender until the case

clear, and on the negotiability of injunctions (which usually accompany settlements in favour of the offended party unless compensation in lieu of injunction is permitted).[20] The legal practice in these respects differs in the small- and large-numbers cases. In cases involving small numbers, dealt with in the civil courts, out-of-court bargains are common; but the negotiability of injunctions, once imposed, is questionable. The court may lift an injunction at the request of the offended party but would be unlikely to reimpose it at a later date in the event of a default in payment of privately agreed compensation. Alternatively, the offended party may refrain, in exchange for compensation, from committing the offender for contempt of court when the conditions of the injunction are not fulfilled; but it may be doubted whether the defendant would be prepared to enter into a bargain enforced by the threat of imprisonment for contempt in the event of his default in payment. If judicial decisions in favour of the offended party are automatically supported by non-negotiable injunctions the economists' analysis of conditions for a market solution is irrelevant in cases where rights cannot be agreed upon without a court decision.

Where interference with a group leads to concerted action through the Attorney-General, a settlement of rights in favour of the offended party is certainly non-negotiable. Public nuisance is treated as a crime and criminal actions offer no opportunity for out-of-court bargains or negotiation *ex post* to redistribute rights. And the civil courts can be used, in cases involving large numbers,[21] only by offended parties who can show losses substantially in excess of those incurred by the rest of the group.[22]

Thus final outcomes can be independent of the decision on rights only if those rights are negotiable. The settlement of

---

can be heard. This requires a preliminary hearing to decide whether there is 'a substantial question to be tried' (*Winfield on Tort* [9] p. 704), and this hearing can be used as an indicator of the likely settlement of the dispute, thus providing a negotiable starting-point, since interlocutory injunctions are dissolvable.

[20] Occasionally an injunction is refused though compensation for past interference is paid. See *Salmond on Torts* ([7] pp. 769–70) and Street ([16] p. 238).

[21] The law is not explicit as to the number which constitutes 'large numbers' (see James [8] p. 138), but public nuisance requires interference with the rights of the 'public at large'. On public nuisance see *Russell on Crime* ([17] vol. 2).

[22] In legal terminology the plaintiff must show 'particular damage'.

non-negotiable rights in favour of the offended party[23] will exclude gains to the community obtainable from 'unreasonable' levels of the interfering activity. The question then arises of the possibility of basing the judgement on 'reasonable' interference (in part) on grounds of the community gains attainable from each settlement. But first we turn to the distributive effects of decisions on rights.

If rights are non-negotiable then a settlement in the offender's favour effectively distributes income to him to the detriment of the offended party; and a settlement in the offended party's favour has the opposite effect. Assuming that compensation exactly equals the value of the external cost, the distributive effect is not altered by negotiability. The effect on the distribution of income of one settlement may be more in accord with the government's income distribution objective than that from the opposite settlement. Whether a conflict occurs depends on the distribution of offenders and offended parties over the income scale. Decisions on rights might be thought to be distributively neutral to the extent that disputants tend to come from the same income group. Where one (or more) of the litigants is a firm the distributive effect of alternative settlements of rights is determined by the income levels of the shareholders of the firm and/or the purchasers of the product depending on the incidence of any cost whose initial impact is on the firm. An estimate of the distributive effect would require income data on these two groups and estimates of the demand and supply elasticities for the product.

If rights were to be settled partly on allocative and distributive criteria a conflict might arise with legal equity (defined on p. 31 above). To take an extreme case, if rights were settled solely on the allocative criterion individuals (or firms) would receive no protection from interferences whose benefits to the community exceed their costs at the margin. Any weighting given to the community gain will imply less protection from loss for those affected by profitable external-cost-creating activities than for those affected by unprofitable activities.

[23] It is worth emphasizing that the same is not true of settlements in favour of the offender: it is settlements in the offended party's favour (Mishan's 'prohibitive law') which limit the outcome to a polar solution. Given the existing institutional constraints one might reach a conclusion diametrically opposed to Mishan's argument that a move towards prohibitive law 'would promote Parento improvements unattainable under the existing system' ([13] p. 281).

With a distributive criterion the implication is that rights will take account of the *ex ante* income positions of the two parties[24] – every dispute over rights involving an investigation of the means of the litigants. But it does not seem improbable that society might make the judgement that legal rights should be independent of position on the income scale.

With negotiable rights and symmetry in bargaining costs the dilemma of a loss of potential community gains does not occur. A settlement of rights on non-economic criteria provides just protection, and redistributions of rights capture the gains to the community. The judgement of reasonableness would be based on the extent of the loss incurred by the offended party independently of the offender's gain curve and consequently would not require information about that curve.

There seems to be a case for making rights negotiable in practice;[25] and in cases where an asymmetry in bargaining costs produces a settlement which prevents potential community gains from an activity (in excess of those obtainable through a non-bargained redistribution of rights), a trade-off is required between the allocative and legal equity objectives.[26] The distributive effects of the settlement of rights are independent of the negotiability of the rights, but it seems doubtful whether the effect on the attainment of the income distribution objective will be sufficient to justify the loss of legal equity caused by a distributive criterion for the settlement. Where the distributive effects are thought to be significant and unfavourable, again a trade-off with legal equity is necessary.

Finally, broadly interpreting the allocative implications of the settlement of rights as the effect on the availability of solutions yielding the highest community gain rather than the effect on the availability of bargaining solutions, an allocative criterion for settling rights requires a comparison of all outcomes available before rights can be decided upon. If one settlement precludes the use of an instrument (e.g. court compensation) that is available under the alternative settlement,

[24] Turvey evidently supports this ([18] p. 311).

[25] To the layman the justification for treating interference with a few people as a civil offence and with a larger group as a criminal offence is obscure though the legal authorities appear to accept it without comment.

[26] The fact that courts do sometimes take the 'social value' of the activities involved to be relevant to the settlement of rights (Street [16] p. 227) perhaps reflects a concession to economic objectives given the non-negotiability of rights.

and this instrument is necessary to maximize gains to the community, the allocative outcomes differ. Given the cost and complexity of such a comparison it does not seem feasible that the courts could adhere rationally to an allocative criterion for all settlements of rights.

In conclusion, the analysis of decisions on legal rights yields two propositions:

(1) That the settlement of rights based on non-economic criteria avoids conflict with the objective of legal equity and only in some cases will it lead to conflicts with economic objectives if rights are negotiable.

(2) That rights are not always negotiable, and that the conflict between the economic and legal equity objectives would be mitigated by reforms in the law to eliminate the institutional obstacles to redistributions of the rights of offended parties.

3. The Redistribution of Rights

Assuming that a just degree of protection is afforded by legal rights and that rights will be redistributed only if the holder of of the rights receives compensation equal to the cost resulting from the consequent interference, the case for a redistribution rests on the capture of community gains.[27]

Economists have analysed the circumstances in which private bargains for polar or intermediate solutions will yield the maximum community gains and those in which government intervention in some form is optimal, when account is taken of bargaining and policy-implementation ('operational') costs.[28] This section suggests some theoretical advantages of court compensation (the judicial solution) and some inadequacies of the existing court compensation methods.

The merits of the judicial solution become clearer in the light of the deficiencies of the bargaining and tax–subsidy solutions. Even if it is assumed that external costs are non-reciprocal[29]

---

[27] In this section institutional obstacles to redistributions of rights are ignored.

[28] Buchanan [1] and Buchanan and Stubblebine [2], Coase [3], Davis and Whinston [4, 5, 6], Mishan [11, 13], Pigou [14], Turvey [18], and Wellisz [19]; Mishan [12] surveys several of these articles.

[29] i.e. a cost imposed by *A* on *B* is not reciprocated. The reciprocity assumption has complicated several recent contributions to the literature (Davis and Whinston [4] and Wellisz [19]). Yet the assumption has not been justified and in fact

the conclusion of Coase (p. 33 above) must be modified, since certain limitations may apply to the operation of private bargaining.[30] One problem lies in the enforcement of private bargains. Can it be assumed that once rights have been redistributed the law will enforce the arrangement? Suppose that a dispute is settled in favour of an injunction and that the offended party accepts compensation in return for the lifting of the injunction. In judging alternative solutions the costs of enforcement (assuming the legal system is flexible enough to provide it) must be added to the costs of bargaining. If the rights are settled in favour of the offender and rights are redistributed (the offender investing in preventive devices or in alternative production techniques in exchange for a promised compensation) and the offended party defaults, the problems of enforcement are more acute. If legally binding contracts for the bargain are permissible, breach of contract could be used to enforce payment. But contracts of this kind would require changes to modify the bargain as tastes and technology change, and the claimed flexibility of the market[31] is lost.

Cases involving large numbers involve heavy bargaining costs, but more interesting are the obstacles peculiar to bargaining involving large numbers.[32] These are generally analogous to the problems of group action in public goods provision, but differ according to the initial settlements of rights. Consider the case of smoke nuisance imposed by a single firm on a large group. If rights are settled in the firm's favour the group must agree on a joint compensation payment; but any individual will be tempted to undervalue the benefit to him of the redistribution of rights in the expectation of reducing his share of the payment without affecting the probability of agreement being reached. If rights are in the group's favour two problems

reciprocal cases seem to be of little more than academic interest, since (except where damage is reciprocated in retaliation) they are difficult to find in practice in or out of court. The distinction between separable (non-marginal) and non-separable (marginal) external costs proposed by Davis and Whinston [4] is not pursued here since in the absence of reciprocity separable external costs raise no problems for bargaining not found in non-separable cases.

[30] Wellisz [19] criticizes the bargaining process because it 'compensates the threat-making party' (p. 361) but this is true only if rights are settled in the offender's favour.

[31] 'A perfectly functioning market . . . automatically adjusts for these changes' (Davis and Whinston [4] p. 252).

[32] Turvey [18] p. 312; Wellisz [19] pp. 353–4.

arise in bargaining. First, any member of the group may exaggerate his losses and expect to raise his share of compensation receipts without affecting the probability of agreement, and second, if some members of the group prefer the activity to cease rather than receive compensation, which formula is to be used for decision-taking? Any decision other than on the basis of unanimity imposes costs on the minority and may not be Pareto optimal.[33]

In the event of market failure or operation at high cost there may be a case for introducing a (Pigovian) tax–subsidy scheme as a substitute. It is theoretically possible (in the non-reciprocal case)[34] to devise a system of tax and subsidy to alter the cost (or utility) functions confronting the two parties in such a way that the levels of the two activities chosen in the absence of the interference are chosen in its presence. Since the value of the external cost is a function of the activity levels of both parties, a tax (= subsidy) which equates its yield to this value cannot be a single-valued function of either activity level. A simple output tax is inappropriate and the computation of the correct transfer (tax and subsidy) must be made by evaluating the external cost for all levels of the interfering activity, and the uniformity and avoidance of casework envisaged in the Pigovian scheme is lost. The procedure required is for the fiscal authority to determine the level of activity which the offended party would choose in the absence of the external cost (or after equivalent compensation) and, given this level, to estimate the offended party's total loss curve (the area under OF in Fig. 3.1A) as a function of the level of the interfering activity; the offender is then confronted with an equivalent tax function and left to select his optimal activity level and tax commitment.[35] As a means of avoiding the information costs involved, Davis and Whinston have proposed an iterative procedure to discover the optimal level of the interfering activity without the relevant functions being revealed to the fiscal authority.[36] Since it is aimed at avoiding the costs of audit (or appropriate investigation for individuals) required by the tax–subsidy scheme as well as by

---

[33] On the external costs created by collective action see Buchanan ([1] p. 21).

[34] The dispute over the theoretical feasibility of a tax–subsidy solution is limited to reciprocal externalities. See Davis and Whinston ([4] p. 257, n. 31).

[35] The option to shift the loss curve by introducing preventive devices is of course open to the offender.

[36] Davis and Whinston [6] section iii.

the judicial solution, the iterative tax proposal should perhaps be judged in terms of its expected operational costs. In the non-reciprocal case the procedure consists of a sequence of choices of the offender's activity level made by the offended party for different subsidy (compensation) levels, and of activity level proposals made by the offender at the corresponding tax levels.[37] When the offended party's choice coincides with the offender's proposal the optimal activity, tax, and subsidy levels have been found.

The over-riding difficulty with this proposal lies in obtaining honest answers from both parties, particularly from individuals in a large offended group. Even assuming the offender has no incentive to bluff unless he is prepared to operate in non-optimal positions,[38] the offended party may not base his choices of the offender's activity level on a true evaluation of the cost imposed. Even though there exists one level of the activity which maximizes joint gains an offended party may attempt to increase his share by exaggerating the cost imposed on him. In these circumstances why should the offender take on faith the valuation of the external cost implicit in the offended party's choice of the level of the interfering activity? In the absence of a penalty on unfounded challenges the offender will challenge the valuation in all cases. If penalties are imposed on discovered exaggerations and on unfounded challenges the decisions on bluffing and challenging amount to a two-person game, with the offended party comparing the returns to overstatement (bluff) and the risk of penalty on a successful challenge, and the offender comparing the predicted returns from a successful challenge with the risk of a penalty on an unsuccessful challenge. A true evaluation even in small-numbers cases can be guaranteed only with challenge, audit, and an imposed tax and subsidy. If the iterative procedure were substituted for small–large bargaining the incentive to individual members of the group to exaggerate their losses would affect the group's choice of the offender's activity level at any subsidy level.

Given deficiencies in the operation of the market and the

---

[37] The full amount of the tax being 'received' as a subsidy by the offended party. Only in the final position does money actually change hands; in earlier stages of the sequence the payments are hypothetical.

[38] Davis and Whinston [6] p. 317.

inevitability of heavy information costs incurred by tax–
subsidy solutions the function of the legal system in providing
judicial solutions is significant. With negotiable rights the
judicial solution becomes an alternative open to parties who
have failed or do not expect to reach redistributions of rights by
agreement.[39] The judicial solution does require a comparison
with the net community gains to solutions through other instruments; but it would be used only if litigants cannot reach a
private bargain. In cases where an available alternative solution (e.g. a cheap preventive device) is clearly more efficient it
will be in the interest of the litigants to avoid the costs of the
judicial solution by adopting that solution.

With rights settled in favour of the offended party the judicial
solution could either take a polar form, total injunction with
zero compensation or the lifting of the injunction in exchange
for compensation equal to the external cost for the duration of
the interference, or yield an intermediate solution with
compensation for interference up to some level with an injunction on higher interference levels. The compensation
would take the form of the above transfer through tax and
subsidy.

Two characteristics of the judicial solution to be considered
are its symmetry and its implementation (including information)
costs.

Ideally the judicial solution would encompass compensation
of the offender by the offended party in cases of interference
judged to be lawful, but it is difficult to imagine the courts
handling such cases and it is realistic to conclude that the
judicial solution is asymmetrical. Although this characteristic
has been ignored, the tax–subsidy scheme also is likely to
redistribute rights only where settlements are made in the
offended party's favour.[40]

The implementation costs of the judicial solution depend on
the extent of disagreement over rights and on the number of
litigants. In small-numbers cases the incremental cost, given the
information on the offended party's loss curve required for a

---

[39] The sequence in the legal treatment might take the form of a settlement of
rights followed by a period for out-of-court bargaining, followed where agreement
is not reached by a judicial solution using the criterion of the maximization of
community gains.

[40] Symmetry requires the possibility of the taxation of the offended party and
the subsidization of the offender.

court settlement of rights,[41] of enforcing the output level chosen by the offender and the associated compensation would not be high. With their participation in the settlement of rights the courts have a comparative advantage over a separate (fiscal) administration in determining outcomes. The small-numbers case, in view of the expected diversity of tort cases and disagreement over rights, will be well suited to the judicial solution as a complement to private bargains. Even if the civil courts were able to accept[42] the repetitive actions arising from the individual treatment of members of large affected groups, the implementation costs would be high in large-numbers cases, though reducible if some form of summary treatment could be adopted to dispense compensation for uniform interference. Frequently the case for government regulation (e.g. zoning) on cost grounds would be irresistible.[43]

Turning to British legal practice we find that the existing principles determining court compensation arrangements diverge from those required for redistributions of rights which maximize community gains. The law and consequently the decisions of the courts reflect a preoccupation with imposing damages for past events and a prejudice in favour of injunction for (potentially) continuing activities. Many external costs are single or spasmodic events (particularly where the cause is accident or momentary negligence) and the courts are concerned with compensating those injured. Once the isolated event has occurred compensation is irrelevant from an allocative viewpoint, except as a deterrent to activities which run the risk of similar events. Compensation in such cases consists of a lump-sum payment equal to the sum of the estimated cost previously borne by the offended party. Unfortunately a similar propensity to compensate is not apparent with continuous interference. Apart from the large-numbers cases involving actions in public nuisance where the criminal interference is inevitably banned, the law is loath to regard compensation as a substitute for an

---

[41] The information required for the settlement of rights is the actual loss incurred by the offended party at the past level of interference. The court compensation arrangements suggested above require an extension of this information to estimates of A's loss levels at other levels of interference; i.e. A's loss function must be estimated.

[42] In the absence of 'particular damage' defined on p. 39 above.

[43] These would be second-best solutions of the kind outlined by Turvey ([18] p. 312).

injunction. An all-or-nothing approach is adopted with the 'solution' being identified with the settlement of rights. The law does provide the courts with the power to impose compensation in lieu of injunction, but with conditions so stringent as to render the solution inapplicable in all but cases of minor interference. The attitude towards the judicial solution seems to be that the courts would not 'allow a wrong to continue simply because the wrongdoer is able and willing to pay for the injury he may inflict',[44] and that to do so is to 'fix judicially the price which an intending tortfeasor could pay for a licence to commit a wrong'.[45] Consequently damages in lieu of injunction are payable only if the case meets four conditions:

1. If the injury to the plaintiff's legal rights is small,
2. and is one which is capable of being estimated in money,
3. and is one which can be adequately compensated by a small money payment,
4. and the case is one in which it would be oppressive to the defendant to grant an injunction.[46]

If the agreement of the offended party is required before a judicial solution is sought it is difficult to see that full compensation in lieu of injunction is an infringement of rights whatever the degree of interference. And does even the refusal of an injunction in favour of compensation in lieu seriously conflict with the requirements of justice? Condition (2) is not difficult to accept, though the problems of utility measurement, where individuals rather than firms are involved, are common to all instruments as well as the market. Condition (3) is the monetary corollary of (1). On efficiency grounds, in view of the costs of arranging and enforcing continuing compensation, it is likely that only for cases requiring large payments will the arrangement of compensation in lieu of an injunction be worth while. Condition (4) is hardly disputable but it is not sufficient. At no point do these conditions recognize the significance of the relative magnitude of the offender's gains and the resultant losses by the other party at different levels of the interfering activity.

[44] Lindley L.J. in *Shelfer* v. *City of London Electric Lighting Co.* (1895) 1 Chapter 287, p. 315, quoted in James ([8] p. 396).
[45] Lord Sumner in the House of Lords debate on *Leeds Industrial Co-operative Society Ltd.* v. *Slack* (1924) A.C. 851, quoted in *Winfield on Tort* ([9] p. 707, n. 51).
[46] A. L. Smith L.J. in *Shelfer* v. *City of London Electric Lighting Co.* See also *Salmond on Torts* ([7] pp. 770–2).

In addition to the reluctance to substitute compensation for injunction, where compensation is permitted the law requires a lump-sum advance payment of compensation for expected future interference. Thus, the award of damages 'may take account of future as well as past damages'.[47] The compensation for future interference is based on a prediction of the sum of the costs to be imposed in the future assuming the existing activity levels continue. If the degree of interference increases, the offended party must take a new action to obtain further compensation. Such a solution does not give the offender an incentive (provided by continuing payments tied to the degree of interference) to reduce future interference, since he has no opportunity to claim back compensation previously paid.

Decisions on compensation levels typically are influenced by objectives other than pure compensation for loss;[48] and where pure compensation is the aim some types of loss are disregarded. In accordance with the view that damages are imposed on the offender as a deterrent, 'exemplary' or 'punitive' damages may be awarded in addition to compensatory damages, with the intention of teaching the offender that 'tort does not pay'.[49] Such damages awards, if extended to cases of continuing interference, would lead to a sub-optimal level of the interfering activity. A number of legal authorities oppose exemplary damages on the grounds that it is unreasonable for the plaintiff to receive them as a windfall gain (and that punishment should be left to the criminal courts) and the economic effects strengthen the case against such damages.[50] In other cases, in setting compensation levels the courts have often been reluctant (due to measurement difficulties) to allow for losses of utility, awards being limited to pecuniary loss from physical injury and damage to property. An instance of this has been the cautious treatment of cases of nervous shock.[51]

[47] Street [16] p. 237.

[48] See G. Williams [20] for a survey of the legal controversy over the objectives of damages awards in tort actions.

[49] *Bell* v. *Midland Rail Co.* (1861) 10 C.B.N.S. 287, quoted in James ([8] p. 373). See James's part iii, chap. 2, on other types of non-compensatory damages.

[50] At least the non-compensatory element could be paid to the Exchequer. James ([8] p. 373, n. 3) suggests that 'possibly the punitive element in tort was better met in the old law of trespass where a fine could be imposed as well as damages . . .'.

[51] See Street ([16] p. 227; [15] pp. 4–13).

The analysis of this section yields two further propositions:

1. The judicial solution is complementary to the market in the determination of outcomes, and is advantageous (in an idealized form) in the small-numbers cases in which disputes over rights necessitate court actions.
2. The courts do not adhere in practice to damages awards which correspond to the judicial solution in its idealized form.

REFERENCES

[1] J. M. BUCHANAN, 'Politics, Policy and the Pigovian Margins', *Economica* (Feb 1962).

[2] —— and W. C. STUBBLEBINE, 'Externality', *Economica* (Nov 1962).

[3] R. H. COASE, 'The Problem of Social Cost', *Journal of Law and Economics* (Oct 1960).

[4] D. A. DAVIS and A. WHINSTON, 'Externalities, Welfare, and the Theory of Games', *Journal of Political Economy* (June 1962).

[5] —— and ——, 'Some Notes on Equating Private and Social Cost', *Southern Economic Journal* (Oct 1965).

[6] —— and ——, 'On Externalities, Information and the Government-Assisted Invisible Hand', *Economica* (Aug 1966).

[7] R. F. V. HEUSTON, *Salmond on the Law of Torts*, 14th ed. (Sweet & Maxwell, 1965).

[8] P. S. JAMES, *General Principles of the Law of Torts*, 2nd ed. (Butterworths, 1964).

[9] JOLOWICZ and LEWIS, *Winfield on Tort*, 8th ed. (Sweet & Maxwell, 1967).

[10] I. M. D. LITTLE, *A Critique of Welfare Economics*, 2nd ed. (Oxford Paperbacks, 1960).

[11] E. J. MISHAN, 'Welfare Criteria for External Effects', *American Economic Review* (Sep 1961).

[12] ——, 'Reflections on Recent Developments in the Concept of External Effects', *Canadian Journal of Economics and Political Science* (Feb 1965).

[13] ——, 'Pareto Optimality and the Law', *Oxford Economic Papers* (Nov 1967).

[14] A. C. PIGOU, *The Economics of Welfare*, 4th ed. (Macmillan, 1932).

[15] H. STREET, *Principles of the Law of Damages* (Sweet & Maxwell, 1962).

[16] ——, *The Law of Torts*, 3rd ed. (Butterworths, 1963).

[17] J. W. CECIL TURNER, *Russell on Crime*, 12th ed. (Stevens, 1964).

[18] R. TURVEY, 'On Divergences between Social Cost and Private Cost', *Economica* (Aug 1963).

[19] S. WELLISZ, 'On External Diseconomies and the Government-Assisted Invisible Hand', *Economica* (Nov 1964).

[20] G. WILLIAMS, 'The Aims of the Law of Tort', *Current Legal Problems*, IV (1951).

[21] O. E. WILLIAMSON, D. G. OLSON and A. RALSTON, 'Externalities, Insurance and Disability Analysis', *Economica* (Aug 1967).

4 Diagrammatic Exposition of a Theory of Public Expenditure

P. A. Samuelson

In the November 1954 issue of the *Review of Economics and Statistics* my paper on 'The Pure Theory of Public Expenditure' presented a mathematical exposition of a public expenditure theory that goes back to Italian, Austrian, and Scandinavian writers of the last 75 years. After providing that theory with its needed logically-complete optimal conditions, I went on to demonstrate the fatal inability of any decentralized market or voting mechanism to attain or compute this optimum. The present note presents in terms of two-dimensional diagrams an essentially equivalent formulation of the theory's optimum conditions and briefly discusses some criticisms.

A Polar-case Model of Government

Doctrinal history shows that theoretical insight often comes from considering strong or extreme cases. The grand Walrasian model of competitive general equilibrium is one such extreme polar case. We can formulate it so stringently as to leave no economic role for government. What strong polar case shall the student of public expenditure set alongside this pure private economy?

One possibility is the model of a group-mind. Such a model, which has been extensively used by nationalists and by Romantic critics of classical economics, can justify any, and every, configuration of government. So there is perhaps little that an economic theorist can usefully say about it.

My alternative is a slightly more sophisticated one, but still – intentionally – an extreme polar case. It is consistent with individualism, yet at the same time it explicitly introduces the vital external interdependencies that no theory of government can do without. Its basic assumption is an oversharp distinction between the following two kinds of goods:

Reprinted from *Review of Economics and Statistics*, xxxvii (Nov 1955) 350–6, by kind permission of the author and of the editor.

(i) A *private* consumption good, like bread, whose total can be parcelled out among two or more persons, with one man having a loaf less if another gets a loaf more. Thus if X_1 is total bread, and X_1^1 and X_1^2 are the respective private consumptions of Man 1 and Man 2, we can say that the total equals the sum of the separate consumptions – or $X_1 = X_1^1 + X_1^2$.

(ii) A *public* consumption good, like an outdoor circus or national defense, which is provided for each person to enjoy or not, according to his tastes. I assume the public good can be varied in total quantity, and write X_2 for its magnitude. It differs from a private consumption good in that each man's consumption of it, X_2^1 and X_2^2 respectively, is related to the total X_2 by a condition of *equality* rather than of summation. Thus, by definition, $X_2^1 = X_2$, and $X_2^2 = X_2$.

Obviously, I am introducing a strong polar case. We could easily lighten the stringency of our assumptions. But on reflection, I think most economists will see that this is a natural antipodal case to the admittedly extreme polar case of traditional individualistic general equilibrium. The careful empiricist will recognize that many – though not all – of the realistic cases of government activity can be fruitfully analyzed as some kind of a blend of these two extreme polar cases.

Graphical Depiction of Tastes and Technology

The first three charts summarize our assumptions about tastes and technology. Each diagram has a private good, such as bread, on its vertical axis; each has a public good on its horizontal axis. The heavy indifference curves of Fig. 4.1 summarize Man 1's preferences between public and private goods. Fig. 4.2's indifference curves do the same for Man 2; and the relative flatness of the contour shows that, in a sense, he has less liking for the public good.

The heavy production-possibility or opportunity-cost curve AB in Fig. 4.3 relates the total productions of public and private goods in the usual familiar manner: the curve is convex from above to reflect the usual assumption of increasing relative marginal costs (or generalized diminishing returns).[1]

Because of our special definition of a public good, the three diagrams are not independent. Each must be lined up with *exactly the same horizontal scale*. Because increasing a public good for society simultaneously increases it for each and every man, we must always be simultaneously at exactly the same longitude in all three figures. Moving an inch each in one diagram moves us the same amount east in all.

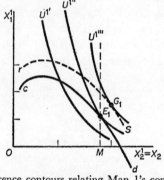

Figure 4.1 Indifference contours relating Man 1's consumption of public and private goods

The private good on the vertical axis is subject to no new and unusual restrictions. Each man can be moved north or south on his indifference diagram independently. But, of course, the third diagram does list the total of bread summed over the private individuals; so it must have a larger vertical axis, and our momentary northward position on it must correspond to the sum of the independent northward positions of the separate individuals.

Tangency Conditions for Pareto Optima

What is the best or ideal state of the world for such a simple system? That is, what three vertically-aligned points corre-

---

[1] Even though a public good is being compared with a private good, the indifference curves are drawn with the usual convexity to the origin. This assumption, as well as the one about diminishing returns, could be relaxed without hurting the theory. Indeed, we could recognize the possible case where one man's circus is another man's poison, by permitting indifference curves to bend forward. This would not affect the analysis but would answer a critic's minor objection. Mathematically, we could without loss of generality set $X_2^1 =$ any function of X_2, relaxing strict equality.

sponding to a determination of a given total of both goods and a determinate parcelling out of them among all separate individuals will be the ethically preferred final configuration?

To answer this ethical, normative question we must be given a set of norms in the form of a *social welfare function* that renders

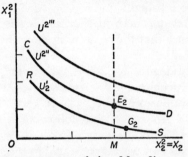

Figure 4.2   Indifference contours relating Man 2's consumption of public and private goods

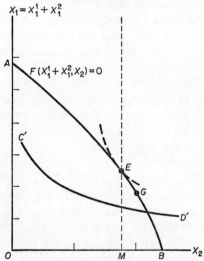

Figure 4.3   Transformation schedule relating totals of public and private goods

interpersonal judgments. For expository convenience, let us suppose that this will be supplied later and that we know in advance it will have the following special individualistic property: leaving each person on his same indifference level will leave social welfare unchanged; at any point, a move of each man to a higher indifference curve can be found that will increase social welfare.

Given this rather weak assurance about the forthcoming social welfare function, we can proceed to determine tangency conditions of an 'efficiency' type that are at least necessary, though definitely not sufficient. We do this by setting up a preliminary maximum problem which will eventually necessarily have to be satisfied.

Holding all but one man at specified levels of indifference, how can we be sure that the remaining man reaches his highest indifference level?

Concretely, this is how we define such a tangency optimum: Set Man 2 on a specified indifference curve, say his middle one CD. Paying attention to Mother Nature's scarcity, as summarized in Fig. 4.3's AB curve, and following Man 1's tastes as given by Fig. 4.1's indifference curves, how high on those indifference curves can we move Man 1?

The answer is given by the tangency point E_1, and the corresponding aligned points E_2 and E.

How is this derived? Copy CD on Fig. 4.3 and call it $C'D'$. The distance between $C'D'$ and AB represents the amounts of the two goods that are physically available to Man 1. So subtract $C'D'$ vertically from AB and plot the algebraic result as cd in Fig. 4.1. Now where on cd would Man 1 be best off? Obviously at the tangency point E_1 where cd touches (but does not cross) his highest attainable indifference contour.[2]

How many such Pareto-optimal points are there? Obviously, for each of the infinite possible initial indifference curves to put Man 2 on, we can derive a new highest attainable tangency level for Man 1. So there are an infinity of such optimal points – as many in number as there are points on the usual contract curve. All of these Pareto-optimal points have the property that from them there exists no physically-feasible movement that will make every man better off. Of course we cannot compare two different Pareto points until we are given a social welfare

---

[2] The reader can easily derive rs and the tangency point G_1 corresponding to an original specification of Man 2's indifference level at the lower level RS rather than at AB. He can also interchange the roles of the two men, thereby deriving the point E_2 by a tangency condition. As a third approach, he can *vertically add* Man 2's specified indifference curve to each and every indifference curve of Man 1; the resulting family of contours can be conveniently plotted on Fig. 4.3, and the final optimum can be read off from the tangency of AB to that family at the point E – as shown by the short broken-line indifference curve at E. It is easy to show that any of these tangencies are, in the two-good case, equivalent to equation (2) of my cited paper; with a single private good my equation (1) becomes redundant.

function. For a move from one Pareto point to another must always hurt one man while it is helping another, and an inter-personal way of comparing these changes must be supplied.

Fig. 4.4 indicates these utility possibilities on an ordinal diagram. Each axis provides an indicator of the two men's respective indifference curve levels. The utility frontier of

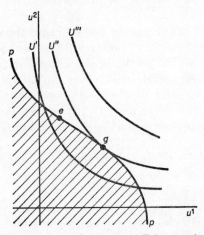

Figure 4.4 Utility frontier of Pareto-optimal efficiency points and its tangency to highest attainable social welfare contour

Pareto-optimal points is given by pp: the double fold infinity of 'inefficient', non-Pareto-optimal points is given by the shaded area; the pp frontier passes from northwest to southeast to reflect the inevitable conflict of interests characterizing any contract locus; the curvature of the pp locus is of no particular type since we have no need to put unique cardinal numbers along the indifference contours and can content ourselves with east–west and north–south relationships in Fig. 4.4 without regard to numerical degree and to uneven stretchings of either utility axis.

The Optimum of All the Pareto Optima

Now we can answer the fundamental question: what is the best configuration for this society?

Use of the word 'best' indicates we are in the ascientific area of 'welfare economics' and must be provided with a set of norms. Economic science cannot deduce a social welfare function; what it can do is neutrally interpret any arbitrarily specified welfare function.

The heavy contours labelled U', U'' and U''' summarize all that is relevant in the provided social welfare function (they provide the needed ordinal scoring of every state of the world, involving different levels of indifference for the separate individuals).[3]

Obviously society cannot be best off inside the utility frontier. Where then on the utility frontier will the 'best obtainable bliss point' be? We will move along the utility frontier pp until we touch the highest social indifference curve: this will be at g where pp tangentially touches, without crossing, the highest obtainable social welfare level U''. In words, we can interpret this final tangency condition[4] in the following terms:

(i) The social welfare significance of a unit of any private good allocated to private individuals must at the margin be the same for each and every person.

(ii) The Pareto-optimal condition, which makes relative marginal social cost equal to the sum of all persons' marginal rates of substitution, is already assured by virtue of the fact that bliss lies on the utility frontier.[5]

[3] These social welfare or social indifference contours are given no particular curvature. Why? Again because we are permitting any arbitrary ordinal indicator of utility to be used on the axes of Fig. 4.4.

An ethical postulate ruling out all 'dog-in-the-manger phenomena' will make all partial derivatives of the social welfare function $U(u^1, u^2, \ldots)$ always positive. This will assure the usual negative slopes to the U contours of Fig. 4.4. However, without hurting the Pareto part of the new welfare economics, we can relax this assumption a little and let the contours bend forward. If, at every point there can be found at least one positive partial derivative, this will be sufficient to rule out satiation points and will imply the necessity of the Pareto-optimal tangency condition of the earlier diagrams.

[4] This tangency condition would have to be expressed mathematically in terms of numerical indicators of utility that are not invariant under a monotonic renumbering. However, it is easy to combine the tangency with the earlier Pareto-type tangency to get the formulation (3) of my cited paper, which is independent of the choice of numerical indicators of U, u^1 or u^2.

[5] A remarkable duality property of private and public goods should be noted. Private goods whose totals add – such as $X_1 = X_1^1 + X_1^2$ – lead ultimately to marginal conditions of simultaneous equality – such as $MC = MRS^1 = MRS^2$. Public goods whose totals satisfy a relation of simultaneous equality – such as $X_2 = X_2^1 = X_2^2$ – lead ultimately to marginal conditions that add – such as $MC = MRS^1 + MRS^2$.

Relations with Earlier Theories

This completes the graphical interpretation of my mathematical model. There remains the pleasant task of relating this graphical treatment to earlier work of Bowen[6] and others.

To do this, look at Fig. 4.5, which gives an alternative depiction of the optimal tangency condition at a point like E. I use

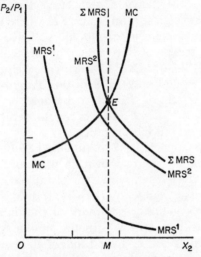

Figure 4.5 Intersection of public good's marginal cost schedule and the vertically-summed individual's marginal rates of substitution, as envisaged by Lindahl and Bowen

the private good X_1 as numeraire, measuring all values in terms of it. The MC curve is derived from the AB curve of Fig. 4.3: it is nothing but the absolute slope of that production-possibility schedule plotted against varying amounts of the public good; it is therefore a marginal cost curve, with MC measured in terms of the numeraire good.

The marginal rate of substitution curves MRS¹ and MRS² are derived in a similar fashion from the respective indifference curves of Man 1 and Man 2: thus, MRS¹ is the absolute slope of the $u^{1\prime\prime}$ indifference curve plotted against varying amounts of the public good; MRS² is the similar slope function derived

[6] Howard R. Bowen, 'The Interpretation of Voting in the Allocation of Economic Resources', *Quarterly Journal of Economics*, LVIII (Nov 1943) 27–49. Much of this is also in Bowen's *Toward Social Economy* (New York, 1948) chap. 18.

from Man 2's indifference curve *CD*. (All three are 'marginal' curves, bearing the usual relationship to their respective 'total' curves.)

These schedules look like demand curves. We are accustomed to adding horizontally or laterally the separate demand curves of individuals to arrive at total market demand. But this is valid only for private goods. As Bowen rightly says, *we must in the case of public goods add different individuals' curves vertically.*

This gives us the heavy ΣMRS curve for the whole community. Where is equilibrium? It is at *E*, where the community MC curve intersects the community ΣMRS curve. Upon reflection the reader will realize that the equality MC $=$ ΣMRS $=$ MRS^1 $+$ MRS^2 is the precise equivalent of my mathematical equation (2) and of our Pareto-type tangency condition at E_1, E_2 or E. Why? Because of the stipulated requirement that Fig. 4.5's curves are to depict the absolute slopes of the curves of Figs. 4.1–3.

Except for minor details of notation and assumption, Fig. 4.5 is identical with the figure shown on p. 31 of the first Bowen reference, and duplicated on p. 177 of the second reference. I am happy to acknowledge this priority. Indeed anyone familiar with Musgrave's valuable summary of the literature bearing on this area[7] will be struck with the similarity between this Bowen type of diagram and the Lindahl 100 per cent diagram reproduced by Musgrave.[8]

Once the economic theorist has related my graphical and mathematical analysis to the Lindahl and Bowen diagrams, he is in a position, I believe, to discern the logical advantage of the present formulation. For there is something circular and unsatisfactory about both the Bowen and Lindahl construc-

---

[7] Richard A. Musgrave, 'The Voluntary Exchange Theory of Public Economy', *Quarterly Journal of Economics*, LIII (Feb 1939) 213–17. This gives citations to the relevant works of Sax, De Viti de Marco, Wicksell, and Lindahl. I have greatly benefited from preliminary study of Professor Musgrave's forthcoming treatise on public finance, which I am sure will constitute a landmark in this area.

[8] Musgrave, op. cit., p. 216, which is an acknowledged adaptation from Erik Lindahl, *Die Gerechtigkeit in der Besteuerung* (Lund, 1919) p. 89. I have not had access to this important work. This diagram plots instead of the functions of Fig. 5.5 the exact same functions after each has been divided by the MC function. The equilibrium intersection corresponding to *E* now shows up as the point at which all persons will together voluntarily provide 100 per cent of the full (unit? marginal?) cost of the public service. (If MC is not constant, some modifications in the Musgrave diagram may be required.)

tions: they show what the final equilibrium looks like, but by themselves they are not generally able to find the desired equilibrium. To see this, note that whereas we might know MC in Fig. 4.5, we would not know the appropriate MRS schedules for *all* men until we already were familiar with the final E intersection point. (We might know MRS^2 from the specification that Man 2 is to be on the AB level; but then we wouldn't know MRS^1 until Fig. 4.1's tangency had given us Man 1's highest attainable level, $u^{1'''}$.) Under conditions of general equilibrium, Figs. 4.1–3 logically contain Fig. 4.5 inside them, but not vice versa. Moreover, Figs. 4.1–3 explicitly call attention to the fact that there is an infinite number of different diagrams of the Lindahl–Bowen type, one for each specified level of relative interpersonal well-being.[9]

Concluding Reflections

I hope that the analytic model outlined here may help make a small and modest step toward understanding the complicated realities of political economy. Much remains to be done. This is not the place to discuss the wider implications and difficulties of the presented economic theory.[10] However, I should like to comment briefly on some of the questions about this theory that have been raised in this *Review*.[11]

(i) On the deductive side, the theory presented here is, I

[9] The earlier writers from Wicksell on were well aware of this. They explicitly introduce the assumption that there is to have been a *prior* optimal interpersonal distribution of income, so what I have labelled E might better be labelled G. But the general equilibrium analyst asks: how can the appropriate distribution of income be decided on a prior basis *before* the significant problems of public consumptions have been determined? A satisfactory general analysis can resist the temptation to assume (i) the level of government expenditure must be so small as not to affect appreciably the marginal social significance of money to the different individuals; (ii) each man's indifference curves run parallel to each other in a vertical direction so that every and all indifference curves in Fig. 4.1 (or in Fig. 4.2) give rise to the same MRS^1 (or MRS^2) curve in Fig. 4.5. The modern theorist is anxious to free his analysis from the incubus of unnecessarily restrictive partial equilibrium assumptions.

[10] At the 1955 Christmas Meetings of the American Economic Association and Econometric Society, I hope to present some further developments and qualifications of this approach.

[11] Stephen Enke, 'More on the Misuse of Mathematics in Economics: A Rejoinder', *Review of Economics and Statistics*, xxxvii (May 1955) 131–3; Julius Margolis, 'On Samuelson on the Pure Theory of Public Expenditure', ibid., xxxvii (Nov 1955) 347.

believe, a logically coherent one. This is true whether expressed
in my original mathematical notation or in the present diagrammatic form. Admittedly, the latter widens the circle of
economists who can understand and follow what is being said.
The present version, with its tangencies of methodologically the
same type as characterize Cournot–Marshall marginal theory
and Bergson–Pigou welfare theory, should from its easily
recognized equivalence with the mathematical version make
clear my refusal to agree with Dr Enke's view that my use of
mathematics was limited 'to notation'.

(ii) In terms of the history of similar theories, I hope the
present paper will make clear relationships to earlier writers.
(In particular, see the above discussion relating my early diagrams and equations to the Bowen–Lindahl formulation.) I
shall not bore the reader with irrelevant details of independent
rediscoveries of doctrine that my ignorance of the available
literature may have made necessary. Yet is it presumptuous to
suggest that there does not exist in the present economic
literature very much in the way of 'conclusions and reasoning'
that are, in Dr Margolis's words, 'familiar'? Except for the
writers I have cited, and the important unpublished thoughts of
Dr Musgrave, there is much opaqueness in the literature. Much
of what goes by the name of the 'voluntary exchange theory of
public finance' seems pure obfuscation.[12]

(iii) Far from my formulation's being, as some correspond-
ents have thought, a revival of the voluntary exchange theory,
it is in fact an attempt to demonstrate how right Wicksell was to
worry about the inherent political difficulty of ever getting men
to reveal their tastes so as to attain the definable optimum.
This intrinsic 'game theory' problem has been sufficiently
stressed in my early paper so that it has not been emphasized
here. I may put the point most clearly in terms of the familiar
tools of modern literary economics as follows:

Government supplies products jointly to many people. In
ordinary market economics as you increase the number of

[12] See Gerhard Colm, 'The Theory of Public Expenditure', *Annals of the
American Academy of Political and Social Sciences*, CLXXXIII (Jan 1936) 1–11, reprinted
in his *Essays in Public Finance and Fiscal Policy* (New York, 1955) pp. 27–43, for
an admirable criticism of the Graziani statement, 'We know that the tax tends
to take away from each and all that quantity of wealth which they would each
have voluntarily yielded to the state for the satisfaction of their purely collective
wants' (p. 32).

sellers of a homogeneous product indefinitely, you pass from monopoly through indeterminate oligopoly and can hope to reach a determinate competitive equilibrium in the limit. It is sometimes thought that increasing the number of citizens who are jointly supplied public goods leads to a similar determinate result. This is reasoning from an incorrect analogy. A truer analogy in private economics would be the case of a bilateral-monopoly supplier of joint products whose number of joint products – meat, horn, hide, and so on – is allowed to increase without number: such a process does not lead to a determinate equilibrium of the harmonistic type praised in the literature. My simple model is able to demonstrate this point – which does have 'policy implications'.

(iv) I regret using 'the' in the title of my earlier paper and have accordingly changed the present title. Admittedly, public expenditure and regulation proceed from considerations other than those emphasized in my models. Here are a few:

(*a*) Taxes and expenditure aim at redistributing incomes. I am anxious to clear myself from Dr Margolis's under-standable suspicion that I am the type of liberal who would insist that all redistributions take place through tax policies and transfer expenditures: much public expenditure on education, hospitals, and so on, can be justified by the feasibility consideration that, even if these are not 100 per cent efficient in avoiding avoidable dead-weight loss, they may be better than the attainable imperfect tax alternatives.[13]

(*b*) Paternalistic policies are voted upon themselves by a democratic people because they do not regard the results from spontaneous market action as optimal. Education and forced paces of economic development are good examples of this.

(*c*) Governments provide or regulate services that are in-capable of being produced under the strict conditions of constant returns that go to characterize optimal self-regulating atomistic competition.

(*d*) Myriad 'generalized external economy and diseconomy' situations, where private pecuniary interest can be

[13] See my 'Evaluation of Real National Income', *Oxford Economic Papers*, n.s., II (Jan 1950) 18 ff., for analytic discussion of this important truth.

expected to deviate from social interests, provide obvious needs for government activity.

I am sure this list of basic considerations underlying government expenditure could be extended farther, including even areas where government probably ought not to operate from almost anyone's viewpoint.

(v) This brief list can end with the most important criticism that the various commentators on my paper have put forth. They all ask: 'Is it factually true that most – or any! – of the functions of government can be properly fitted into your extreme category of a public good? Can education, the courts, public defense, highway programs, police and fire protection be put into this rigid category of a "public good available to all"? In practically every one of these cases isn't there an element of variability in the benefit that can go to one citizen *at the expense* of some other citizens?'

To this criticism, I fully agree. And that is why in the present formulation I have insisted upon the polar nature of my category. However, to say that a thing is not located at the South Pole does not logically place it at the North Pole. To deny that most public functions fit into my extreme definition of a public good is not to grant that they satisfy the logically equally-extreme category of a private good. To say that your absence at a concert may contribute to my enjoyment is not to say that the elements of public services can be put into homogeneous additive packages capable of being optimally handled by the ordinary market calculus.

Indeed, I am rash enough to think that in almost every one of the legitimate functions of government that critics put forward there is to be found a blending of the extreme antipodal models. One might even venture the tentative suspicion that any function of government not possessing any trace of the defined public good (and no one of the related earlier-described characteristics) ought to be carefully scrutinized to see whether it is truly a legitimate function of government.

(vi) Whether or not I have overstated the applicability of this one theoretical model to actual governmental functions, I believe I did not go far enough in claiming for it relevance to the vast area of decreasing costs that constitutes an important part of economic reality and of the welfare economics of monopolistic competition. I must leave to future research discussions of these vital issues.

Economic theory should add what it can to our understanding of governmental activity. I join with critics in hoping that its pretentious claims will not discourage other economic approaches, other contributions from neighboring disciplines, and concrete empirical investigations.

5 Public Goods and Public Policy

J. G. Head

1. Introduction

One of the most interesting developments in the Anglo-American public finance literature of recent years has been the appearance, under the formidable aegis of Professor Samuelson, of a prescriptive theory of public expenditure based on the alien Continental concept of a 'public good'.[1]

1.1. The concept of a 'public good', which first flourished in the Italian, German and Scandinavian literature on public expenditure theory of the late nineteenth century,[2] never really penetrated the English-speaking countries, where prescriptive theories of public expenditure and economic policy generally were founded on such concepts as external economies and diseconomies and consequent divergences between private and social cost–benefit calculations, imperfections of competition including those due to decreasing cost phenomena, and inequities in the distribution of income. The main lines of this largely independent English development can be found very firmly laid down in Pigou's great classic, *The Economics of Welfare*. Although the occasional article did appear in which the 'public good' concept was employed or referred to,[3]

[1] P. A. Samuelson, 'The Pure Theory of Public Expenditure', *Review of Economics and Statistics* (1954); 'Diagrammatic Exposition of a Theory of Public Expenditure', *Review of Economics and Statistics* (1955) (pp. 52–65 above); and 'Aspects of Public Expenditure Theories', *Review of Economics and Statistics* (1958).

[2] Extracts from some of the most important contributions by Mazzola, Wicksell, Sax and others can be found in English translation in R. A. Musgrave and A. T. Peacock (eds), *Classics in the Theory of Public Finance*.

[3] See, for example, F. Benham, 'Notes on the Pure Theory of Public Finance', *Economica* (1934); R. A. Musgrave, 'The Voluntary Exchange Theory of Public Economy', *Quarterly Journal of Economics* (1938–9); H. R. Bowen, 'The Inter-

Reprinted from *Public Finance*, no. 3 (1962) 197–219, by kind permission of the author and of the managing editor.

its precise relationship to its more familiar Pigovian rivals was barely discussed, let alone made clear, and it remained, for most of the English-speaking economic world, yet another mystery in the Pandora's box of Continental esoterica.

1.2. Stimulated by the researches of Professor Musgrave, Samuelson has now opened this still far-from-empty box, and has set loose upon an ill-prepared literature a fully fledged mathematical theory of public expenditure, based upon this concept alone. This theory, it is probably fair to say, is still, eight years and two re-expositions later, something of an enigma to most economists, though it is nevertheless felt to be of considerable importance. In the course of his three articles, Samuelson refers to external economies, along with certain other considerations, as important elements in any completely general theory of public expenditure, but, except perhaps to the specialist, the precise relationship between the various concepts remains unclear.

It is the aim of this article to examine the meaning of the public good concept as it appears in Samuelson's theory, and relate it to the more familiar Pigovian and Keynesian theories of public policy. In this way we hope to be able to show the place and importance of the concept in a general prescriptive theory of public policy.

We shall begin (section 2) with a brief outline of Samuelson's theory. Then (section 3) we shall set out in some detail the main characteristics of the public good concept on which the theory is based. Finally (section 4) we shall try in various ways to relate these characteristics, both to one another and to the more familiar concepts of modern theories of market inefficiency.

2. Samuelson's Theory of Public Expenditure

2.1. In the following quotation from his original mathematical exposition in 1954, Samuelson provides what appears to be a singularly clear definition of the public good concept, which is

---

pretation of Voting in the Allocation of Resources', *Quarterly Journal of Economics* (1943–4), and *Toward Social Economy*, chap. 18; and (in French) A. T. Peacock, 'Sur la Théorie des Dépenses Publiques', *Économie Appliquée* (1952).

to provide the foundation of his normative theory of public expenditure, viz.:

> I explicitly assume two categories of goods: ordinary *private consumption goods* $(X_1, \ldots, X_n)$ which can be parcelled out among different individuals $(1, 2, \ldots, i, \ldots, s)$ according to the relations $X_j = \sum_1^n X_j^i$; and *collective consumption goods* $(X_{n+1}, \ldots, X_{n+m}$ which all enjoy in common in the sense that each individual's consumption of such a good leads to no subtraction from any other individual's consumption of that good, so that $X_{n+j} = X_{n+j}^i$ simultaneously for each and every ith individual and each collective consumption good.[4]

In his geometrical re-exposition in 1955 we find a similar definition of a 'public consumption good', which 'differs from a private consumption good in that each man's consumption of it . . . is related to the total by a condition of *equality* rather than of summation'.[5]

2.2. On the basis of this definition, and making the usual convexity assumptions, Samuelson shows algebraically and geometrically that the familiar Pareto-optimum condition of welfare economics, requiring equality between marginal rates of substitution and marginal rates of transformation, no longer holds. Where, in the case of two private goods and two individuals 1 and 2, the condition was $MRS^1 = MRS^2 = MT$, what is now required, where one of the two goods is 'public', is equality between the marginal rate of transformation and the *sum* of the marginal rates of substitution, i.e. $MRS^1 + MRS^2 = MT$.

Thus, given the same 'New Welfare' value-judgement, that the goal of economic life should be a situation in which it is impossible to make someone better off without making someone else worse off, i.e. a Pareto optimum, the characteristic features of the allocation of resources which will achieve this goal will change with the introduction of public goods.

2.3. Samuelson points out that this change in the Pareto-optimum conditions with the introduction of public goods has

---

[4] Samuelson, op. cit. (1954) p. 387.
[5] Samuelson, p. 52 above. For one of the clearest of many similar definitions in the traditional Continental public good literature, see that of Sax, in Musgrave and Peacock, op. cit., p. 183.

disastrous implications for 'duality', i.e. for the ability of a competitive market to compute these conditions, even under otherwise ideal circumstances. In particular, charging individuals a common price equal to the marginal cost of producing a unit of the good (or even 'average marginal cost' per individual served by that unit) will not be efficient in the case of public goods. Highly idealized multiple pricing will be required if output of these goods is to be optimal, but 'no decentralized pricing system can serve to determine optimally these levels of collective consumption'.[6]

Furthermore, circumstances are otherwise far from ideal. As Samuelson expresses it, 'one could imagine every person in the community being indoctrinated to behave like a "parametric decentralized bureaucrat" who *reveals* his preferences by signalling in response to price parameters or Lagrangean multipliers, to questionnaires, or to other devices. But . . . by departing from his indoctrinated rules, any one person can hope to snatch some selfish benefit in a way not possible under the self-policing competitive pricing of private goods.'[7] 'It is in the selfish interest of each person to give *false* signals, to pretend to have less interest in a given collective consumption activity than he really has'.[8] In short, even with ideal multiple pricing, the market will fail because true preferences will not be revealed.

It is, therefore, in somehow promoting adequate provision of these public goods, that at least some[9] of the proper economic functions of government are to be found.[10] Samuelson warns, however, that these functions are not likely to be easy to perform efficiently, and emphasizes in particular that the benefit theory offers no perfect practical solution.

[6] Samuelson, op. cit. (1954) p. 388.

[7] Ibid., p. 389.

[8] Ibid., pp. 388–9.

[9] The apparent implication of the first article, that *all* legitimate governmental functions must be of this sort, is considerably modified in 'concluding reflection' (iv) of the second (see above, pp. 63–4).

[10] Samuelson speaks of 'public expenditure and regulation' and 'economic functions of government' as well as public expenditure, and it is clear that all expenditure and therefore, by implication, the necessary revenue-raising activities and hence all economic functions of government are, at least potentially, under consideration. Such outlays as those required to support the multifarious activities of a central bank, price control or import-licensing authority, etc., would therefore be included. As we shall see below, the services of such agencies can indeed quite properly be regarded as 'public goods'.

D

3. The Characteristics of a Public Good

Turning now to detailed consideration of the public good concept on which this theory is based, it appears that Samuelson's public good has two main characteristics, 'jointness of supply', 'indivisibility' or 'lumpiness' on the one hand, and external economies on the other.

3.1. *'Jointness'*

3.11. The first and most obvious implication of the equal consumption requirement $(X_{n+j} = X_{n+j}^i$ for each and every individual) is that Samuelson's public good is in joint supply, in the special sense that, once produced, any given unit of the good can be made equally available to all. Extension of the supply to one individual facilitates its extension to all. Supply of a given unit to one individual, and supply of the same unit to other individuals, are clearly joint products.[11] Alternatively we could describe this characteristic as a special type of lumpiness or indivisibility of product.[12] As we shall see,[13] it is this 'jointness' which alone accounts for the change in the Pareto-optimum conditions and the consequent need for a highly idealized system of multiple pricing referred to above, a need which a competitive market cannot meet.

3.12. Are there many goods which would appear to fall into this category? In his first article Samuelson offers no example. In the second, he instances an outdoor circus and national defence. In the third a battleship and a television programme are mentioned. None of these, nor any of a host of other traditional governmental activities, seems, however, to satisfy this very stringent requirement to perfection. 'Capacity limits' are usually met well before the good has become equally available to all, this applying alike to roads, bridges, hospitals, courts,

---

[11] Samuelson uses the term 'joint supply' only once, on p. 355 of his second article (p. 62 above), to describe this property. He also refers to 'jointness of demand', traditionally reserved for 'bacon and eggs' type phenomena. Musgrave uses the term 'joint consumption'. I have preferred 'jointness of supply' which is closest to traditional usage. Lindahl (see Musgrave and Peacock, op. cit., p. 221) uses a joint supply analogy to good effect in his derivation of the 'optimum conditions' for the public good case.

[12] This is common usage in traditional public good discussions. Mazzola, Sax and Bowen, for example, all use the term 'indivisibility' to describe public goods.

[13] See below, section 4.21.

police, and even flood control measures, irrigation, national defence, and public health schemes such as vaccination programmes and draining of malarial swamps. Furthermore, even before capacity limits in any strict sense are encountered, quality variations usually occur. Crowded roads and other facilities are usually regarded as giving inferior service to that provided by the same 'goods' less fully utilized.

Under pressure on this particular point from such critics as Enke and Margolis,[14] Samuelson admits in his second article that his public good concept is properly to be regarded only as an 'extreme polar case', which the student of public expenditure can set against the 'logically equally-extreme category of a private good', in order to bring out the essence of the case for government activity. Accordingly he reformulates the theory with this change of emphasis, to avoid the apparent overstatement of the original article.

It is, however, no more than a change of emphasis. 'To deny that most public functions fit into my extreme definition of a public good is not to grant that they satisfy the logically equally-extreme category of a private good.... Indeed I am rash enough to think that in almost every one of the legitimate economic functions of government that critics put forward there is to be found a blending of the extreme antipodal models.'[15]

3.13. 'Jointness' thus remains an essential characteristic of a public good, though it is now to be understood in the less extreme sense that a given unit of the good, once produced, can be made at least partially available, though possibly in varying degrees, to more than one individual. Only beyond a point does additional consumption by one person imply the need for a corresponding reduction in consumption by others.

The presence of public good elements in this sense is quite sufficient to cause the change in the Pareto-optimum conditions and consequent failure of market catallactics described in section 2.3.[16] Modified in this way, the public good concept, and hence the theory of public policy based on it, thus becomes much more realistic and important. A whole host of activities,

---

[14] S. Enke, 'More on the Misuses of Mathematics in Economics: A Rejoinder', *Review of Economics and Statistics* (1955); and J. Margolis, 'A Comment on the Pure Theory of Public Expenditures', *Review of Economics and Statistics* (1955).

[15] Samuelson, p. 64 above.

[16] See Samuelson, p. 52 above, esp. note 1.

including all those listed earlier and many more, can be found which will satisfy this less demanding requirement.

3.2. *External economies*

3.21. The second important characteristic of Samuelson's public good is that it gives rise to external economies. In his first article he speaks of the 'external economies or jointness of demand intrinsic to the very concept of collective goods' and the 'external effects basic to the very notion of collective consumption goods'. Describing his theory in the second article, he states that 'it explicitly introduces the vital external interdependencies that no theory of government can do without', and in the third that it 'is the natural model to formulate so as to give strongest emphasis to external effects'.

3.22. There are indications at various points in his articles that Samuelson may be using the term 'external effects' in a rather broader sense than is now usual, and possibly even as a generic term to cover all causes of market inefficiency. To make quite sure that we do not get trapped in a semantic snarl, it may therefore be wise to begin with a brief discussion of the meaning of external economies and diseconomies.[17]

In its narrowest modern sense the concept of external economies, applied to a given good, indicates that a change in the production and/or consumption of that good will affect the utility and/or production functions for other goods. The 'reason' usually given by economists for the existence of these external economies or diseconomies is perhaps most succinctly described by Ellis and Fellner[18] as 'the divorce of scarcity from effective ownership', i.e. imperfections in property titles. Following Sidgwick,[19] we might describe the problem as one of 'non-appropriability', it being impossible for private firms and individuals, through ordinary private pricing, to appropriate the full social benefits (or be charged the full social costs) arising directly from their production and/or consumption of certain goods. An identical concept to be found in the important works of Bowen and Musgrave is 'impossibility of exclusion',

[17] For a very useful summary of the subject and references to the extensive literature, see F. M. Bator, 'The Anatomy of Market Failure', *Quarterly Journal of Economics* (1958) section ii.

[18] H. S. Ellis and W. Fellner, 'External Economies and Diseconomies', *American Economic Review* (1943) p. 511.

[19] Henry Sidgwick, *Principles of Political Economy*, 3rd ed., pp. 406–7.

meaning that it is impossible for private firms and individuals, through private pricing, to exclude other firms and individuals from at least some part of the benefits (or be charged the full social costs) arising directly from their production and/or consumption of certain goods. The extra-market benefits in question are here to be interpreted narrowly in terms of use or enjoyment of the product itself.

The effect of these external economies and diseconomies is to create divergences between private and social costs and benefits, and thus to prevent the satisfaction of the optimum conditions. Some economic units can enjoy some of the benefits of certain activities without having to pay for them, and it would of course be grossly unrealistic to expect them to contribute voluntarily. These activities will therefore be under-expanded, and government expansion of them is justified. Similarly, where the full social costs cannot be charged to an economic unit through the pricing process, again voluntary contributions by way of compensation or expenditures to reduce the costs in question cannot reasonably be expected. Overexpansion of these activities is therefore likely, and their restraint is a legitimate economic function of government.

But for these ownership difficulties encountered by the consumer or producer of the good in physically excluding other users, there is no reason inherent in the external economies concept why a competitive market could not ensure optimum output of it. The external economies concept in this sense is clearly not a generic term covering all causes of market inefficiency.

3.23. Do Samuelson's public goods exhibit external economies in this sense? Perhaps the easiest way of seeing that they do, is to notice the resemblance between Samuelson's definition and the Bowen and Musgrave concepts of goods for which price-exclusion is completely impossible,[20] and which therefore exhibit external economies to an extreme degree. These goods are refered to by Bowen as 'social goods' and by Musgrave as goods satisfying 'social wants'. According to Musgrave, 'Social wants are those wants satisfied by services that must be consumed in equal amounts by all. People who do not pay for the

---

[20] H. R. Bowen, *Toward Social Economy*, pp. 172–3; and R. A. Musgrave, *The Theory of Public Finance*, pp. 8–9. Our definition of 'impossibility of exclusion' above is less restrictive than this.

services cannot be excluded from the benefits that result; and since they cannot be excluded from the benefits, they will not engage in voluntary payments. Hence the market cannot satisfy such wants.'[21]

In this definition the equal consumption requirement and the impossibility of exclusion appear side by side. Samuelson on the other hand does not explicitly refer in his definition to the possibility or otherwise of price-exclusion. On reflection, however, it should be clear that impossibility of exclusion is a direct implication of his formulation of the equal consumption condition for public goods. The latter is clearly to hold by definition in all situations, optimal and non-optimal alike; public goods, once produced, not only *can* but *must* be made equally available to all. If exclusion were possible, however, consumption would not be equal for all individuals in innumerable non-optimal situations of private pricing, since those unwilling to pay the inefficient private price would be excluded. The assumption also shows up in his conclusion that true preferences for public goods will be understated in the market.[22]

The second implication of the equal consumption requirement which defines Samuelson's public good is therefore that such a good exhibits external economies, i.e. exclusion or appropriability difficulties, to an extreme degree. As we shall see, it is this characteristic alone which accounts for the failure of the market mechanism to ensure revelation of true preferences.

3.24. Are there many goods which would appear to exhibit this characteristic? The answer would seem to be that there are none. Exclusion is never *completely impossible*, even in such obvious cases as national defence, flood control and public health programmes.

Samuelson does not explicitly consider this question.[23] Both Bowen and Musgrave appear, however, to employ the concept only to emphasize the essential feature of this particular market weakness. A less extreme usage is fairly clearly indicated, if perhaps underemphasized, in both cases.[24]

---

[21] Ibid., p. 8.   [22] See above, section 2.3.

[23] In the passages referred to in section 3.12 above, and in other places, he seems much more concerned to acknowledge that his jointness concept requires modification in the light of such considerations as capacity limits and quality variations.

[24] Bowen, op. cit., pp. 196–7; and Musgrave, op. cit., p. 8.

There are in fact innumerable goods which will pose price-exclusion problems, and thus exhibit external economies (and diseconomies) in the less restrictive sense of section 3.22, without approaching *complete impossibility* of exclusion. A theory of public expenditure based on this less restrictive, and hence more realistic and important concept, is itself correspondingly more realistic and important, with the important conclusion still justified, that, because of exclusion difficulties, true preferences will be understated, and the market will therefore fail to secure optimum production and consumption of the goods in question.

4. The Relationship between Jointness, External Economies and Other Concepts in the Theory of Public Policy

We have distinguished two important properties of Samuelson's public goods, namely jointness and external economies. Are they, however, conceptually quite distinct, or are they related in some way, or perhaps even identical? And what is the relationship between them and the various concepts of the more familiar theories of public policy? We shall consider these two questions in turn.

4.1. *Jointness and external economies*

In the light of Samuelson's own definition and that of Musgrave, quoted earlier, and indeed of the whole traditional public good literature, in all of which the two characteristics appear to be merged, it is clearly important to ask whether they are in fact independent, somehow related, or one and the same.

4.11. We shall begin by considering whether the existence of jointness necessarily implies the existence of external economies and thus of price-exclusion problems. In other words, does it follow from the fact that a good *can* be made equally available to all, that it *must* be made equally available to all? Most public good concepts exhibit both characteristics, but does the one necessarily entail the other in this manner?

It is certainly true that some of the best examples of goods with jointness characteristics also pose the most difficult exclusion problems. National defence, flood control and public health programmes are excellent examples of goods exhibiting both characteristics to a high degree.

The fact remains, however, that goods and services with jointness aspects may, and in fact often will, pose no price-exclusion problems. Bus, train and tram fares are too obvious to need comment, though in each case elements of jointness in the public good sense certainly exist.[25] Tolls are common in the case of roads and bridges. Fees are charged in the case of the courts, postal and telephone services, hospitals, etc., and could easily be extended, if necessary, to a host of similar services. Concerts, football matches and circuses (even outdoor ones!) can usually be fenced off and admission charges levied. Unscrambling devices may be perfectly feasible in the case of television and radio programmes and the services of lighthouses. In short, the existence of jointness in no way necessarily entails the existence of price-exclusion problems. This point is explicitly recognized by both Samuelson and Musgrave.[26]

This is not of course to suggest that the imposition of charges will not occasionally, or even frequently, be extremely costly to the private firm and/or inconvenient to the user. In these cases it is perfectly possible that a socially superior service could be provided 'free' by the government. We would therefore agree that there are often important exclusion problems coexisting with jointness, which may enormously reinforce the case for government intervention, without conceding that exclusion is the only problem involved, or, for that matter, that exclusion is in any literal sense 'impossible'.

4.12. Although joint supply or indivisibility in our present sense in no way necessarily implies the existence of *price*-exclusion difficulties, it is important to recognize that it does create a very similar problem for the effective functioning of political choice or voting mechanisms.

We have seen that there is no necessary problem in principle of ensuring, under a price system, that individuals will reveal their true preferences for goods exhibiting Samuelsonian joint-

[25] The last bus can be made available to sixty people, etc.

[26] Samuelson, op. cit. (1954) p. 389, and (1958) p. 335; and Musgrave, op. cit., p. 10, n. 1. Musgrave, however, fails to see the point stressed by Samuelson, and perhaps the distinguishing feature of his whole theory, that jointness as such (and the consequent need for multiple pricing) gives rise to market inefficiency. Indeed he appears to suggest the contrary. This is in curious contrast to his account in the Introduction (with A. T. Peacock) to *Classics in the Theory of Public Finance*, p. xiv. The point is, however, clearly recognized by Bator, op. cit., p. 371, and p. 376, n. 5.

ness characteristics. Market inefficiency arises here because of the independent phenomenon of jointness.

If, however, the government steps in to promote, by extra-market means, more adequate provision of the service in question, the problem of determining true preferences immediately becomes acute. Whatever the nature of the political system, individuals and small groups will know that, if prices are not to be charged, the supply to them of this service 'equally available to all' will depend overwhelmingly upon what the rest of the community is induced or forced to contribute, and to only the slightest extent on their own contributions. Each therefore has an enormous incentive to try to minimize his own contribution by understating his true preferences in public statements, bargaining, voting or other political activity relevant to the determination of the sharing of the burden. With large numbers behaving in this way, there is clearly a grave danger of underexpansion of the service when provided 'free' by government:

This is precisely Wicksell's overwhelming objection to even the relatively refined benefit theory of Mazzola as a *practical* solution to the problem of securing adequate provision of public goods,[27] and the same point is also to be found in the articles by Benham, Musgrave, Bowen, and Peacock referred to in section 1.1.[28] Samuelson also emphasizes in all three articles 'the inherent *political* difficulty of ever getting men to reveal their tastes' for public goods.[29]

It is important to stress again that this difficulty is a consequence of jointness, and arises whether price-exclusion is

[27] Wicksell, in Musgrave and Peacock, op. cit., pp. 81–2.

[28] See note 3 above. As some of these later writers have pointed out, the objection applies also, though much less forcefully, to the 'Positive Solution' of Lindahl, which represents the final development of the benefit theory. Lindahl's theory is intended to be descriptive as well as prescriptive, and he depicts the political mechanism in a democracy as a bargaining process between major parties with equal power. Since large parties are involved, supply of public goods will now depend significantly on own contributions, and the incentive to understatement of true preferences is correspondingly much weaker. If his theory were valid as description, the problem of switching from private to tax-financed government provision of public goods would, therefore, be a comparatively minor one. Since, however, it is not, it remains merely a rather quixotic prescription for political organization in a democracy.

[29] Like these other writers, and even Musgrave in *The Theory of Public Finance* (p. 10), he fails to make it clear, however, that this difficulty is basically a consequence of jointness, rather than of price-exclusion difficulties.

possible or not, and it applies to almost any conceivable voting mechanism, including that suggested by Wicksell. The problem is, however, considerably exacerbated where price-exclusion is impossible, since this removes the possibility of using previous market choices as some check on true preferences in the political activity following the switch to 'free' government provision of the service.[30]

4.13. If joint supply does not necessarily entail price-exclusion problems, why do writers such as Bowen and Musgrave bring the equal consumption requirement with its implications of jointness into the forefront of definitions of public goods, the essential characteristic of which is apparently intended to be complete impossibility of price-exclusion?

The answer suggested by Musgrave[31] is that, although jointness does not necessarily entail exclusion problems, the existence of exclusion problems does imply the existence of elements of jointness. If no economic unit can be price-excluded from any part of the good, it follows *ipso facto* that each unit of the good is, and hence can be, made equally available to all, i.e. we have Samuelsonian jointness.

In many cases of extreme exclusion difficulties it is true, as we have already noted, that joint supply is also involved. It is far from clear, however, that the exclusion problems in any way necessarily imply the existence of jointness. Oil wells drawing on a common pool would appear to be a case in point. New wells in the neighbourhood of a strike may drastically reduce output from the original well, with the firm which made the original strike possibly quite unable to price-exclude others from peacefully expropriating a significant part of its 'property'. The good in question, oil, is, however, strictly 'private' in Samuelson's sense of being 'like bread whose total can be parcelled out among two or more persons with one man having a loaf less if another gets a loaf more'. If one economic unit gets more oil, there is a corresponding reduction in the quantity which can be made available to others. Other similar examples could be cited. It is of course perfectly true that all can take part in the scramble for the scarce supply, but this is the only

---

[30] Musgrave, ibid., overstates, however, when in making substantially this point he implies that it is the impossibility of price-exclusion which is the fundamental reason for preference-revelation problems in the political process.

[31] Ibid., p. 10, n. 1.

sense in which 'equal potential availability' can be claimed. In a sense, that is, the good is 'indivisible', in so far as secure property titles to the individual units of it are difficult to grant, and this problem of parcelling out of the total for purposes of legal ownership has doubtless contributed to the misunderstanding.[32] Such 'equal availability' of 'indivisibility' is clearly in no way related to Samuelsonian jointness.

From the above analysis we can conclude that jointness and external economies are conceptually quite distinct properties of Samuelson's public good, and are in no way related. A clear differentiation between them is therefore extremely important to preserve.

4.2. *Jointness, external economies and other concepts*

Finally, let us consider possible relationships between these two characteristics of a public good and the more familiar concepts of Pigovian and Keynesian theories of public policy. We have already seen that the external economies which characterize the public good are simply an extreme category of external economies in the narrowest modern sense. The precise nature of jointness, however, requires further examination, as does the relationship between both these characteristics and the other elements which go to make up modern theories of market inefficiency.

4.21. What, first of all, is the precise relationship between jointness, which is the distinguishing characteristic of the Samuelson concept,[33] and these other theories of public policy?

The answer seems to be the obvious one suggested by the occasional use of the term 'indivisibility' in this connection, namely that we are dealing here with a special case of *decreasing costs*.

4.211. This is perhaps most easily seen by recognizing that one of the most traditional examples of decreasing cost problems discussed in the public finance literature dealing with pricing policies for nationalized industries,[34] namely that of a bridge, is

---

[32] It is possible that Bowen (op. cit., p. 173) intended initially to use the term 'indivisibility' in this sense only, though he goes on to speak without qualification of equal availability.

[33] In contrast, as we have seen, to the superficially very similar concepts of Bowen and Musgrave where impossibility of exclusion is the essential feature.

[34] This literature dates back at least to Jules Dupuit's celebrated article of 1844, now reprinted in English translation in *International Economic Papers*, no. 2. The lively

a perfect example of a good exhibiting jointness characteristics.
Up to a point it is possible for some individuals to have more,
without the need for anything like a corresponding reduction in
the service available to others.

With a uniform toll being charged in a given period, as under
private pricing, to (say) cover average cost in that period, it is
quite likely that the bridge would not be used to 'capacity', and
some individuals who would be willing to pay marginal social
cost would be excluded by the average cost price. As has been
pointed out again and again in the literature, this is not Pareto-
efficient pricing and, in a world in which all other optimum
conditions are satisfied, the position could be substantially
improved by lowering the uniform price towards the true
marginal social (opportunity) cost of supplying the service to
the last user. In the case of the bridge this will be zero if we
neglect wear and tear, and lowering price to this level will
therefore necessarily result in substantial losses, since overheads
will be uncovered. Clearly these losses are due to spectacularly
decreasing costs. In the absence of government action in the
form of a subsidy or complete takeover, this financially disastrous but socially ideal pricing policy can clearly not be
expected of a private firm. Whatever the form of the action
taken, the losses should be covered by non- (or not too-)
distorting taxation.

Alternatively, and this is the familiar verbal conclusion which
Samuelson has effectively demonstrated mathematically and
geometrically in his articles, a system of *multiple pricing*[35] or

controversy of the 1940s was sparked off by Hotelling's classic, 'The General
Welfare in Relation to Problems of Taxation and of Railway and Utility Rates',
Econometrica (1938). For an excellent critical summary of this controversy, see
I. M. D. Little, *A Critique of Welfare Economics*, 2nd ed., chap. xi. Also Nancy Ruggles,
'Recent Developments in the Theory of Marginal Cost Pricing', *Review of Economic
Studies* (1949–50). Wicksell's brilliant 1896 discussion (for which see Musgrave
and Peacock, op. cit., pp. 97–105) is another landmark which is well worth
attention.

[35] Or, more strictly, as Samuelson's demonstration clearly shows, an infinite
set of such systems, corresponding to the infinite set of conceivable post-policy
distributions of welfare. See his objection (p. 60 above), on precisely this point,
to the formulations of Wicksell, Lindahl and Bowen. Only if we adopt the
Bergson–Samuelson, 'Social Welfare Function' version of the New Welfare
Economics, is one of these systems likely to be better than the others. This is
also the point which lies at the heart of Musgrave's contention (op. cit., pp. 8,
84) that Samuelson's normative theory is indeterminate 'if we apply the criterion of efficiency as understood in the determination of market price . . . a more
specific welfare function is needed to secure an optimal solution'.

multi-part tariffs could be employed, mulcting the consumer surplus of intra-marginal users to cover overheads. Under this system, each user would be charged a price which would equate his individual demand for the service with the fixed supply equally available to all. This is of course nothing more than a careful application of the general rule, familiar from the pricing debates referred to above, that where all other optimum conditions are satisfied, price, in the particular industry under consideration, should be set at marginal social cost and equate supply with demand.[36] It is also familiar, at least by implication, from this branch of the literature, that no decentralized pricing system can compute this multiple pricing solution, and indeed that only the very roughest approximation to such a solution such as a two- or few-part tariff could, let alone would, be attempted by a central (private or public) pricing authority.[37] It has always been clear, in addition, that this problem is in no way related to exclusion difficulties in the narrow external economies sense.

4.212. The case of a bridge is only one of a number of cases of decreasing costs discussed in the literature, which are basically examples of Samuelsonian jointness. Wicksell[38] lists roads, ports, canals, railways, postal services and public squares as well as bridges. Little,[39] writing more than fifty years later, mentions museums, parks, passenger trains and buses, broadcasting, water supply and roads. In all these cases the decreasing cost problem is due very largely to elements of jointness, in the sense that at least up to a point, once a given unit of the good has been produced, additional consumption by one individual does not imply a corresponding reduction in the quantity which can be made available to others.

The decreasing cost implications of Samuelson's public good concept should indeed be evident on reflection from his definition, which implies very directly, even if it does not state, that the opportunity cost of supplying more of the service, and more specifically of supplying the same unit to more users, is zero. Modified in the direction of realism to take account of capacity limits, quality variations, and minor wear and tear effects due

---

[36] Optimum price and output are thus, of course, mutually determined.
[37] See Little, op. cit., pp. 199–200, on the feasibility of such a solution.
[38] Ibid., pp. 99–100.
[39] Ibid., p. 195.

to additional use, the essential point remains, that opportunity cost is likely to be almost negligible and certainly very low in relation to average cost, i.e. we have sharply decreasing costs. In all these Samuelsonian cases, as long as any individual is excluded who has paid or is willing to pay any necessary 'marginal customer cost' (the cost of installation of the telephone, the price of the television or radio receiver or vehicle, etc.), and who is also willing to pay the relatively small marginal social cost due to wear and tear (zero in the extreme Samuelson case), price to such users should be lowered.[40, 41] It is unlikely that even a private firm in a monopoly position could do this without incurring losses, and in the absence of public policy it would therefore never be done.[42]

These are not of course the only examples of decreasing cost industries. Other cases traditionally quoted, such as steel and other heavy industries, are due to indivisibility of factors with no elements of jointness of product in our sense.[43] There can be little doubt, however, that Samuelsonian cases are amongst the most numerous and important. It is also clear, both from the

[40] Most economic functions of government are necessarily desirable individually, only if all other functions necessary to achieve the optimum are simultaneously performed. Where marginal cost is actually zero, however, as in the extreme Samuelson formulation, the general case for satisfying this condition no longer depends upon the simultaneous satisfaction of all other optimum conditions.

[41] In some instances, and particularly in certain periods, demand will already be pressing up against the capacity limit, and marginal social cost, properly interpreted, may be well above an average price. Consumption is then no longer in the decreasing cost range, and there is no apparent need for either multiple pricing or the financing of deficits by non-distorting taxation under marginal cost pricing. No problem remains – except to expand capacity to an adequate level, ration existing capacity efficiently by charging the marginal cost price which will equate supply and demand, and dispose of the surplus by multiple pricing (lower prices to intra-marginal users) or non-distorting subsidies!

[42] It is interesting to note the similarity between this problem and that posed by an uneven time-pattern of demand, the so-called 'problem of the peak'. Peak and off-peak services, like the services of public goods to different individuals in the same period, are essentially joint. Charging a uniform average cost (or even long-run marginal cost) price is likely to prevent the use of off-peak units for which someone would be perfectly willing to pay marginal social cost (e.g. labour and materials costs), whilst at the same time failing effectively to ration peak use. Public goods usually exhibit both kinds of jointness. On this problem see P. O. Steiner, 'Peak Loads and Efficient Pricing', *Quarterly Journal of Economics* (1957); and J. Hirschleifer, 'Peak Loads and Efficient Pricing – Comment', *Quarterly Journal of Economics* (1958).

[43] Though the often slightly artificial distinction between factor and product tends to obscure a fundamental similarity.

theory and from practical experience, that the resulting economic function of government is likely to be far from easy to perform efficiently even without price-exclusion difficulties.

4.213. It seems then that in terms of the usual theories of public policy, what is perhaps *the* essential characteristic of Samuelson's public good, namely its jointness of supply or indivisibility in the sense of equal potential availability, gives rise to a very important category of decreasing cost problems. It is interesting to observe the growing appreciation of this crucial point in his three articles. In the original mathematical exposition there is no mention whatever of decreasing costs. In the geometrical version we find, in the penultimate paragraph, the completely enigmatic statement that 'whether or not I have overstated the applicability of this one theoretical model to actual governmental functions, I believe I did not go far enough in claiming for it relevance to the vast area of decreasing costs that constitutes an important part of economic reality and of the welfare economics of monopolistic competition'.[44] Finally, in the third article, in the course of developing, with reference to television programmes, the argument that impossibility of exclusion is far from the be-all and end-all of his public good concept, and under the general heading 'Decreasing-cost phenomena', we find a brief but clear and explicit exposition of this basic point.[45]

4.22. We have now seen that the first characteristic of Samuelson's public good, viz. jointness or indivisibility, accounts for an important part of the familiar concept of decreasing costs. The second characteristic, namely complete impossibility of exclusion, is a special and extreme case of the modern external economies concept.

Is there not, however, a sense in which decreasing costs and external economies are related? And is there perhaps

[44] Samuelson, p. 64 above.
[45] Samuelson, op. cit. (1958) p. 335. He notes that broadcasting is, in a way, a perfect example of his public good, in spite of the possibility of exclusion with the help of unscrambling devices. Market inefficiency arises here because 'our well-known optimum principle that goods should be priced at their marginal costs would not be realized in the case of subscription broadcasting. Why not? In the deepest sense because this is, by its nature, not a case of constant returns to scale. It is a case of general decreasing costs.' And again, 'what after all are the true marginal costs of having one extra family tune in on the program? They are literally zero.' See also Bator, op. cit., p. 376.

some general relationship between these and the other major elements which go to make up modern theories of market inefficiency?[46]

4.221. Referring back to our earlier summary of the explanations which have been offered for the existence of external economies and diseconomies, we defined non-appropriability as that property of a good which makes it impossible for private economic units to appropriate, by ordinary private pricing, the full social benefits from their production and/or consumption of that good. So far, following the mainstream of the modern external economies doctrine, we have interpreted these 'full social benefits' in a very narrow sense to refer only to use or enjoyment of the product itself. By price-exclusion problems we have therefore simply meant difficulties in physically excluding, from use or enjoyment of the product itself, other economic units who have not paid for the privilege.

Interpreting these full social benefits in the widest sense, however, it is clear that non-appropriability or impossibility of exclusion accounts for all decreasing cost problems as well as external economies in the narrow modern sense. By lowering price from (say) average cost to marginal cost in a situation in which all other optimum conditions are satisfied, a decreasing cost monopolist could provide *resource-allocation benefits* such that, as a result, it would be possible to make someone better off without making anyone else worse off. The firm could not, however, as a general rule, charge for these social benefits, and the individual beneficiaries could not be expected to contribute voluntarily. The possibly quite substantial losses that would be incurred by the monopolist through the lowering of price would not therefore in general be covered by other means, even though it would be possible for the community, by co-operative action, to compensate him and still enjoy a net benefit, with some members better off and none worse off than before. Since such spontaneous and voluntary co-operation cannot be relied upon, the average cost price and consequent misallocation will persist in the absence of government, and the reason is precisely *the non-appropriability of these potential resource-allocation benefits*. Exactly the same general argument applies to

[46] The analysis of this section is based upon the highly suggestive extensions of the external economies concept contained in W. J. Baumol, *Welfare Economics and the Theory of the State*.

Samuelsonian as to other forms of lumpiness, and indeed to the much more general category of imperfections of competition from whatever cause (including decreasing cost phenomena).

4.222. It is interesting to notice that, in this more general sense, non-appropriability or impossibility of exclusion also accounts to a considerable extent for Keynesian and post-Keynesian vagaries of aggregate demand and supply and their associated inefficiency concepts of unemployment 'equilibrium' and inflation. An economic unit increasing its consumption- or investment-spending, or accepting a substantial money-wage cut in a situation of unemployment equilibrium, can by no means appropriate to itself, through private pricing, the full social benefits in the form of multiplier and real balance effects on the incomes and profits of other economic units. Instead, the individual consumption-spender risks severe later hardship and insolvency; the investment-spending firm risks heavy losses and ultimate bankruptcy; the single trade union or employee accepting a wage cut loses both absolutely and relatively to less socially-minded employee groups; and the small nation risks international insolvency and consequent further employment difficulties. With the signs changed, a similar argument applies to the inflation case, where again the full benefits from reduced inefficiencies of all sorts are not appropriable. The non-appropriability case for government activity in the stability field is therefore clear.

Again, in the case of sub-optimal economic growth, the full benefits in terms of rising real wages from growth-promoting behaviour, such as thrift, risk-bearing, dividend- and wage-restraint, are seldom anything like fully appropriable from the point of view of the economic unit which must bear the full cost of such behaviour. Competitive depreciation and tariff and export-subsidy wars, including beggar-my-neighbour remedies for unemployment, provide further examples of cases in which socially responsible behaviour fails to receive anything like its just reward.

In all these cases it would be possible for the community, by means of voluntary co-operative action, to compensate potential losers from socially desirable changes, and still enjoy a net benefit with some members better off and none worse off. Such co-operative effort will seldom be forthcoming in the absence of coercion and the inefficiency due to non-appropriability will therefore persist.[47]

In a broad but very real and important sense then, domestic and international economic stability, domestic and international allocation of resources in accordance with consumers' wishes and an optimal rate of growth can all quite properly be regarded as public goods, for adequate provision of which public policy must be relied upon.

4.223. Of the most important elements in the usual theories of market inadequacy only such slippery, though undoubtedly vital, concepts as inequitable income distribution (including therefore important aspects of economic stability and growth), imperfect knowledge and irrational motivation remain outside this wider non-appropriability net, and even here some part of the problem can undoubtedly be ascribed to exclusion difficulties.

The most important of these concepts, namely the gross inequalities of income which result from the free functioning of the market, is a concept which is in fact alien to the New Welfare ethical foundations on which the whole of the above theory is based.

In our account we have adopted a goal of economic organization in the Kaldor–Hicks 'hypothetical-compensationist' tradition of a situation in which it is impossible to make someone better off without making someone else worse off, and have regarded any resulting redistributions of income as of negligible importance. Alternatively, in the 'actual-compensationist' tradition we could have postulated the same goal, but insisted at the same time that losers from any policy leading to the goal be compensated in costless lump-sum fashion, thus making the policy implications of the theory 'more generally acceptable'. Following this latter approach still further, we could insist in addition that the government's first policy act be to correct any initial, *pre*-policy, inequities in the distribution of income.[48]

[47] It might be suggested that this extension of the non-appropriability concept to cover so many causes of market inefficiency robs it of all explanatory significance, and reduces it to a synonym for such inefficiencies. There can be little doubt, however, that the approach does yield valuable insights into the persistence of these malfunctions, and the extension therefore seems well justified.

[48] This is the approach followed by Wicksell and Lindahl, and adopted also by Musgrave in *The Theory of Public Finance.* It is this form of the theory which Musgrave (ibid.) and Musgrave and Peacock (op. cit.) have noted as indeterminate, though this also applies *a fortiori* to the two previously mentioned variants. The point here is that, even given the *pre*-policy distribution of welfare, there is

A further extension of this approach would be the Bergson–Samuelson formulation, under which it is the *post*-policy distribution of income in the 'bliss state' which is to be made ideal (or 'swung to the ethical observer's optimum') using costless lump-sum taxes and subsidies. Finally, in the limit, we could demand that the government ensure that the initial distribution of income is ideal, and also that, in implementing the policies necessary for 'efficiency', incomes be simultaneously redistributed to maintain an ideal income distribution throughout the process.

In other words, it is possible in various ways to graft considerations of income distribution on to the formal framework of a basically New Welfare theory of public policy. The operation is, however, rather artificial, and the crucial questions regarding the appropriate distribution of income are either ignored or begged, in accordance with the fundamental tenet of New Welfare that the economist *qua* economist has little to contribute on this important but controversial subject.[49]

---

still an infinite set of *post*-policy distributions, which will satisfy the requirement that someone has been made better off and no one worse off. The suggestion by Musgrave, and Musgrave and Peacock, that this indeterminacy problem is in some way peculiar to the provision of 'public goods', narrowly defined, is, however, unjustified and highly misleading. The ambiguity lies in the welfare criterion itself.

[49] For an excellent critical survey of the New Welfare literature see Little, *A Critique of Welfare Economics*.

6 The Exchange and Enforcement of Property Rights[1]

Harold Demsetz

Our economic system, with its specialization of economic activities into separate ownership and decision units, requires both control over goods and exchange of goods if it is to cope with the diversity of wants of specialist producers. This paper is concerned with the fact that the exchange of goods and the maintenance of control over the use of goods impose costs on traders and owners. It is also concerned with the cost of government alternatives to the market place. We seek to establish both the importance and the wide role of these costs in economic life.

A large part of our argument will be illustrated by two important controversies in welfare economics in which we will show, on the one hand, that zero pricing of scarce goods need not result in inefficiency, and, on the other, that zero pricing of 'public' goods may result in inefficiency. The standard criticisms of resource allocation by the market, which turn on the market's failure to price 'external' effects and on its tendency to price 'public' goods, are shown to be invalid. To do this we extend the well-known axiom that there is no such thing as a free scarce good by including such goods as markets, government bureaus, and policing devices.

Throughout this paper, our attention is confined to the problem of efficiency within the framework of smoothly running markets and governments, in the sense that we assume that persons, whether in their capacity as civil servants or as private citizens, do not make arithmetic errors in calculating, or, at least, that they do not tend to make more errors in one role than in another. We do not concern ourselves with problems of

[1] The author wishes to thank Armen A. Alchian, Gary S. Becker, William H. Meckling, Peter Pashigian, and George J. Stigler for their comments.

Reprinted from *Journal of Law and Economics*, VII (Oct 1964) 11–26, by kind permission of the author and of the editor.

monopoly by either a firm or the government, but the problem of imperfect knowledge is treated.

Instead of 'external effects' or 'neighborhood effects' we will use the phrase 'side effects' to identify those for which no account *seems* to be taken in the market place. This avoids the flavor of location and of being *necessarily* outside of the market place that seem to be associated with the more common names for these effects.

1. Exchange Cost

Recent developments

R. H. Coase,[2] in an important article written recently for this *Journal*, demonstrates that there is, in general, nothing special about side effects that rules out the possibility of their being taken account of by the market. These effects can be taken into account by market transactions between the parties affected once the courts have established who has what right of action. Under competitive conditions and assuming zero exchange costs, these transactions will result in an efficient solution to the scarcity problem. Thus, if ranchers are given the right to allow their cattle to roam and the cattle stray accidentally onto unfenced farm land, it will be in the farmer's interest to bring the damage they cause to the rancher's attention by offering to pay the rancher to reduce the number of cattle foraging nearby. If the rancher disregards this offer, he sacrifices a potential receipt equal to the crop damage. Thus, the crop damage becomes a private cost to the rancher of raising additional cattle and will be taken account of in his calculations. Moreover, Coase points out the efficiency of the solution with respect to the number of cattle and the size of the crops in the absence of exchange costs is independent of whether the farmer or rancher is legally liable for the damage. The party not held liable, of course, acquires the right to act in ways which may have harmful side effects. The assignment of the liability for crop damage to the rancher would lead to a direct accounting for this cost in his operations and he would need to decide whether to reduce his herd or pay the farmer to reduce the crop he plants. Whether the farmer will find it worthwhile to pay enough to the rancher to reduce

[2] Coase, 'The Problem of Social Cost', *Journal of Law and Economics*, III (1960) 1–44.

his herd or whether the rancher can pay enough to the farmer
to reduce the area he cultivates depends on whether the value
lost because of the crop reduction is greater or less than the
value lost because the size of the herd is reduced. Whichever
way the rights are initially assigned, the outcome of the subsequent bargaining will be that which maximizes the value of
output.

Coase has advanced the analysis of the roles that can be
played by the market and the government a step beyond its
previous position. For now Coase has shown that if exchange
costs are positive, it is necessary to ask whether government can
take the harmful effects of an action into account at less cost
than can the market or, indeed, if the resulting resource realignment is worth the cost of taking the side effects into account
at all.

Misapplication of optimality theorems

The question which asks whether or not realignment is worthwhile brings to light an improper usage to which we frequently
have put our optimality theorems. The cost of using the market
relative to the cost of using a political mechanism has seldom
been considered explicitly or in detail in the bulk of the theory
of welfare economics. This has led to an improper usage of those
theorems. As a consequence of the conventional approach to
these problems, it has not been recognized that the very conditions under which side effects are believed to lead to inefficiency are those conditions for which the welfare theorems
used are inapplicable.

The usual analysis of market inefficiency in such cases attributes the difficulty to the absence of markets in which 'appropriate' prices for measuring side effects can be revealed.[3] But

[3] Cf. Arrow, 'Uncertainty and the Welfare Economics of Medical Care',
American Economic Review, LIII (1963) 941, 944–5:

'An individual who fails to be immunized not only risks his own health, a dis-
utility which presumably he has weighed against the utility of avoiding the
procedure, but also that of others. In an ideal price system, there would be a
price which he would have to pay to anyone whose health is endangered, a
price sufficiently high so that the others would feel compensated; or, alternatively,
there would be a price which would be paid to him by others to induce him to
undergo the immunization procedure. . . . It is, of course, not hard to see that
such price systems could not, in fact, be practical; to approximate an optimal
state it would be necessary to have collective intervention in the form of subsidy
or tax or compulsion.'

absence of a market or of a price can be consistent with efficiency when optimality theorems are appropriately interpreted. *For produced goods*, the optimality theorems require equalities among various marginal rates of substitution. These same optimality conditions, however, do not require such equalities for goods and services that are *not produced* in the final efficient equilibrium; for these we have corner solutions involving inequalities. Thus, a basic premise in requiring equalities is that we are talking about goods which we require to be produced in positive quantities.

We then turn to the competitive model and observe that market prices will often bring about the equalities required for produced commodities and services. But, we ask, what if some goods produce side effects which are not exchanged over a market? We answer that the market fails to provide us with incentives which will guide behavior to take account of the side effects and that, therefore, the required equalities will be absent. The allegation is that even perfectly competitive markets fail to achieve efficiency. But, this reasoning generally fails to take account of the fact that the provision of a market (for the side effect) is itself a valuable and costly service. Where a market, or the political action which would be its counterpart, does not exist, this service is not being produced. If this service is not being produced some *in*equalities (instead of the equalities required for produced goods) among our marginal rates of substitution and marginal rates of transformation may be consistent with efficiency, as will be the case if the cost of taking account of side effects through either the market or the government exceeds the value of realigning resources. In such cases zero amounts of market pricing or the government equivalent will be efficient. In asking the implications of the nonexistence of some markets, we seem to have forgotten the cost of providing market services or their government equivalent. The existence of prices to facilitate exchange between affected parties has been

---

and Bator, 'The Anatomy of Market Failure', *Quarterly Journal of Economics*, LXXII (1958) 351, 353–4:

> 'Pareto-efficient . . . points . . . are characterized by a complete set of marginal-rate-of-substitution . . . equalities (or limiting inequalities) which, in turn, yield a set of price-like constants. Where no such constants exist, reference will be to *failure of existence* (of prices, and hence, of efficiency).' (Parenthetic phrase added.)

too much taken for granted. A price for every produced good or service is not a necessary condition for efficiency, so that the absence of a price does not imply that either market transactions or substitute government services are desirable. If we insist either that all actions (services or commodities) be priced in the market or that the government intervene, we are insisting that we do not economize on the cost of producing exchanges or government services. Thus, most welfare propositions concerned with side effects are based on an invalid use of the standard optimality theorems, i.e. they ignore the cost of some of the goods.

Some examples

We shall consider two examples to illustrate our point. In the first rights of action are clearly defined; in the second they are not.

Our first example is zero-priced parking at shopping plazas in which unpaid-for benefits exist insofar as shoppers, in the prices they pay, confer benefits on nonshopping parkers. Most economists, regardless of their philosophical persuasion, would probably argue that the number of spaces is nonoptimal. But, when we say nonoptimal, we must have some idea of what is the optimal number of spaces. Assuming the absence of increasing returns, the less careful of us are apt to reply that the proper number of spaces is the number that would clear the market when a charge is levied to cover construction cost. A more careful reply would include exchange costs in the charge. *Neither* answer is necessarily correct.

It is true that the setting and collecting of appropriate shares of construction and exchange costs from each parker will reduce the number of parking spaces needed to allow ease of entry and exit. But while we have reduced the resources committed to constructing parking spaces, we have increased resources devoted to market exchange. We may end up by allocating more resources to the provision and control of parking than had we allowed free parking because of the resources needed to conduct transactions. By insisting that the commodity be priced, we may become less efficient than had we allowed persons to ration spaces on a first come, first serve basis. Similarly, rationing by government involves its own costs and may be no better. Those who purchase merchandise and indirectly pay for parking spaces may prefer to substitute the smaller total cost of constructing additional spaces to accommodate free-loaders rather than ration out the nonbuying parkers by paying the required exchange costs minus the savings of constructing fewer parking spaces. Since the cost of providing additional parking spaces depends largely on the price of land, it follows that we should expect to observe free parking allowed more frequently in suburbs than in the center of towns because of the differential prices of land. Given this differential, both methods of allocating parking may be efficient.

Is this example consistent with competition? Will not competing stores open nearby and charge lower prices because their customers use a free parking lot supplied by a competitor? Will they, thereby, force their competitor out of business? The desirability of providing parking spaces implies that we are dealing with a world of finite dimension in which all cars cannot be parked at zero cost on a dimensionless point. For this reason, differential land rent will be taken into account. Owners of land surrounding the free parking lot will enjoy windfall profits, a question of wealth redistribution, but potential competitors will have the advantages of the nearby lot capitalized and included in the rent they pay; they will enjoy no competitive advantage. The equilibrium is a stable competitive one although it gives rise to differential land rent. If the windfall is expected to be large enough to warrant the additional transactions required to purchase surrounding land, the (prospective) owners of the shopping plaza could take account of these gains in their calculations by purchasing the surrounding land before free parking is allowed. This option, which Coase refers to as extending the role of the firm, is alternative to both exchange and government action.[4]

In this particular example, the efficiency of producing this costly but zero-priced parking depends on the supplier being

[4] The existence of unique locations does not necessarily imply the inefficiency usually associated with monopolistic competition. Cf. Demsetz, 'The Welfare and Empirical Implications of Monopolistic Competition', *Economic Journal*, LXXIV (1964) 623–41. It should also be noted that if the landowners could know of the differential land rents that would result from the superior technology offered by free parking, they would be inclined to enter into an agreement sharing the differential rent accruing to land adjacent to the shopping plaza. If they did not enter into such an agreement there would be an inclination to let the free parking facility be built on the other man's property.

able to recoup the cost by other means, namely in the prices of his merchandise. This method of financing the parking lot becomes economically superior *only* if demand interrelations are such that a sale in combination arrangement reduces exchange costs sufficiently. Both the loose combination sale (not all parkers need to buy merchandise) as well as tighter tie-ins may, in fact, be methods which reduce the cost of allocating and which lead to optimal quantities of goods. We will have more to say on the relevance of this for the problems posed by public goods.

For contrast, our next example, one that has become a favorite, involves neither tie-in arrangements nor defined rights of action. It is the case in which market transactions do not take place in the use of nectar by bees, so that prices do not arise which reflect the beneficial effects of apple blossoms on the productivity of bees. Clearly, as Coase would probably point out, it is possible for beekeepers and apple growers to strike a bargain over how many trees are to be planted, the bargain taking account of an apple tree's contribution to honey production and a bee's contribution to cross-fertilization of trees. Further, were there significant predictable benefits from the interaction, significant enough to offset any diseconomies of underspecialization, beekeeping and apple growing would be carried on by the same farmer. However, the benefits may be small relative to the costs of forsaking specialization. Merger will not then be the solution. Suppose, also, that estimates of benefits are small relative to estimates of the cost of developing the science of the apple–bee interaction and to either the costs of transacting in the market or providing substitute government services. Then efficiency requires that bees be allowed to 'help themselves' on a first come, first serve basis, which is, after all, an alternative arrangement for settling scarcity problems.

Here no combination sales are directly involved. A valuable and costly good, nectar, is provided free of charge because it would be too costly to take account of the indirect benefits to beekeepers. In contrast to the parking and merchandising example, the separate marketing of the two products, apples and blossoms, is costly. Hence a zero-priced good may be efficient even though no combination sale is used. Since no low cost combination sale seems possible, the good (nectar) will be provided free if apples, *per se*, are worth producing. If apples are not worth producing, or recognition of the existence of a benefit to beekeepers will not make the production of apples desirable, for the cost of inducing the apple grower to take this benefit into account is too high to make it worthwhile.

2. Police Cost

Up to now we have largely limited our attention to situations in which direct bargaining between individuals requires an exchange cost that is larger than the benefits derived from the exchange. To take account of these side effects, the interested parties, therefore, resort to combination sales, to extensions of the firm, or they find it expedient not to modify these effects. All of these alternatives are consistent with efficiency and yet all fail to exhibit a market in the side effect. There are situations, however, which are somewhat different in that the cost of *policing* the effects of actions, rather than the cost of exchange, may be so high as to cause additional complications. The following discussion of these situations is designed to reveal the roles played by police cost and private property and to help clear up some public good problems.

Property rights and the valuation problem

There are two tasks which must be handled well by any acceptable allocative mechanism. These are, firstly, that information must be generated about all the benefits of employing resources in alternative uses, and secondly, that persons be motivated to take account of this information. To the extent that both these tasks are solved by the allocative mechanism, the problem of attaining an efficient allocation of resources reduces to arithmetic. Setting aside the second problem, we turn to the first and, in particular to the necessity for protecting the right to use economically valuable resources if we are to obtain accurate information about benefits.

It is well known that prices can serve as guideposts to where resources are wanted most, and in addition, that exchangeability of goods at these prices can provide incentives for people to follow these guideposts. However, analytical concentration on the price mechanism has kept us from closely examining what it is that is being traded. The value of what is being traded depends crucially on the rights of action over the physical commodity and on how economically these rights are enforced. The enforcement of the accompanying property rights has an important impact on the ability of prices to measure benefits. An emphasis on this aspect or view of the problem, in conjunction with our emphasis on exchange cost, will allow us to unify our treatment of what is now largely a collection of special cases in which our measures of benefits diverge from actual benefits. The petroleum and fishery 'pool' problems are good examples of problems created by treating economic goods as free goods. The general conclusion reached by the analysis of pool problems is that a resource, be it petroleum, fish, or game, is too rapidly worked. This conclusion is correct and if we think in terms of producible inventories, the absence of property right enforcement also can be shown to result in too little production of the good, or in too small an increment to the pool or inventory of the good. This is because the prices, which reflect private benefits, fail to measure the whole of the social benefit derived from the good. As a special case of this general proposition, if we assume that it costs nothing to police property rights, it follows that there exists a direct relationship between the degree to which private benefits approach social benefits and the degree to which the conveyed property rights are enforced. This relationship can be illustrated with two examples.

Given any definition of the rights that accompany ownership in an automobile, the price mechanism will ration the existing stock of automobiles. But the total private value of this stock will depend on the degree to which auto theft is reduced by our laws and police. If we pass a law *prohibiting* the arrest and prosecution of auto thieves, and also prohibiting the use of private protection devices, the bids that persons subsequently offer for the purchase of automobiles will fall below the social value of automobiles. The lower bids will result from the reduction in control that a purchaser can expect to exercise over the use of a purchased auto and, in addition, from his ability to 'borrow' at no charge those autos which are purchased by others. The bids submitted after the passage of such a law will underestimate the social value of autos, for we can assume for our purposes that the usefulness of an auto remains the same whether it is used by the purchaser or by the legal thief. This is true even though the existing stock of autos is efficiently distributed among owners. The total value of autos will fall below social value and the subsequent increase in the stock of autos will be less than it should.

The lowering of bids that results from our law is similar to the lowering of bids that will take place when high police cost reduces the degree of private control that it is economical to guarantee owners. The provision of national defense provides us with a classic example of the impact of high police cost. Voluntarily submitted bids for defense will be lower than the social value of defense because the bidder can count on being able to enjoy (some of) the defense bought and also enjoyed by his fellow citizen. The effect on bidding is similar to that which takes place in our example of legalized auto theft except that the reason for lack of control is not merely the absence of an appropriate law but, rather, it is the high cost of defending a purchaser from a foreign aggressor while at the same time preventing his neighbors from enjoying protection. The cost of excluding those who have not contracted for benefits from the enjoyment of some of these benefits is so high that a general attitude of letting others bear the cost of defense can be expected. Consequently, voluntarily submitted bids will underestimate the social value of defense.

If a low cost method is available and is used to prevent those who do not contract for defense from benefiting from the defense bought by others, the market would reveal accurate information about the social value of defense. Such information would be extremely useful if the market or the planner is to allocate resources efficiently.

The institution of private property, which attempts to exclude nonpurchasers from the use of that which others have purchased, should, therefore, not be looked upon as either accidental or undesirable. On the contrary, its existence is probably due in part to its great practicality in revealing the social values upon which to base solutions to scarcity problems. This is precisely why we do not worry that bids for, say, candy will fail to reveal the social value of candy. The price of candy is accurate in its measure of social value because reflected in it is the ability of each purchaser to control the use of his purchase, whether that use be for resale or for charity, for his children, or for his own consumption. This valuation function is related to but distinct from the incentives to work provided by a property system, for even in a society where work is viewed as a pleasurable activity, and, hence, where incentives to work are not needed, it would still be necessary to properly value the varieties of alternative output that can be produced.

We have already observed that the value of what is being traded depends upon the allowed rights of action over the physical good and upon the degree to which these rights are enforced. This statement at once raises the question of which rights and which degrees of enforcement are efficient. If changing the mix of property rights that accompany ownership increases the value of property, such a change will be desirable from the viewpoint of wealth maximizing. For example, if the problem is whether to allow automobile owners to increase the speed at which they travel on side streets, one could assess whether there would result an increase in the total value of affected property. Would people be willing to pay higher prices for automobiles? It is by no means clear that they would, for some prospective owners may fear high speed more than they value it. And, if there would result an increase in the price of automobiles, would it be large enough to offset any increase in the cost of insuring life, limb, and home (i.e. the resulting decline in the value of other property)? If a net increase in the total value of property follows a change in the mix of rights, the change should be allowed if we seek to maximize wealth. Not to allow the change would be to refuse to generate a surplus of value sufficient to compensate those harmed by the change. The process of calculating the net change in value will, of course, involve the taking into account of side effects and this is a problem that we have already discussed. The enforcement of rights can be viewed in the same way. Indeed, we can insist that a proper definition of a right of action include the degree to which the owner or the community is allowed to enforce the right. Enforcement thus becomes the specification of additional rights and can be included in the above analytical framework. The conclusion we have reached depends, of course, upon the existence of competitive entry in the exercise of particular rights. It is therefore necessary to exclude rights which confer monopoly by restricting entry and to insist that all owners have the same rights of action. There are some difficult problems which we do not take up here. For example, since everyone has the right to take out a patent or a copyright on 'newly created' goods or ideas, does the granting of this right involve the granting of monopoly power?

It is, of course, necessary to economize on police cost, so that we will not always want to guarantee full control to the purchaser; more will be said below about this aspect of the problem. But, this aspect aside, it is essential to note that the valuation power of the institution of property is most effective when it is most *private*. It is ironic, therefore, that one of the strongest intellectual arguments for expanding the role of government has been based on the alleged necessity for eliminating exclusivity and for allowing free access to the use of certain types of resources. These resources have been given the name 'public goods' and they are characterized by their alleged ability to confer benefits on additional persons without thereby reducing the benefits conferred on others. The provision of national defense is a well-known example.

The public goods problem

The relevance of what we have been discussing for public goods is that if the cost of policing the benefits derived from the use of these goods is low, there is an excellent reason for excluding those who do not pay from using these goods. By such exclusion we, or the market, can estimate accurately the value of diverting resources from other uses to the production of the public good. Thus, even though extending the use of an existing bridge to additional persons adds nothing to the direct cost of operating the bridge, there is good reason for charging persons for the right to cross the bridge. Excluding those who do not pay for the use of the bridge allows us to know whether a new bridge is likely to generate more benefit than it is likely to cost.[5] Why should we desire information about a new bridge if the direct marginal cost of using the existing bridge is zero? Firstly, the bridge may depreciate with time rather than with traffic, so that the question of replacement remains relevant even though the marginal cost of use is zero. Secondly, there is a private marginal benefit to users of the bridge, at least in lessening their driving costs, and this benefit can be measured by pricing the use of the bridge. Such information would allow us to ascertain

[5] See Coase, 'The Marginal Cost Controversy', *Economica*, xiii (1946) 169–82, for an early application of this point in reference to the use of multipart pricing in natural monopoly situations. See also Minasian, 'Television Pricing and the Theory of Public Goods', *Journal of Law and Economics*, vii (1964) 71.

whether it is economic to have a new bridge closer to some persons than is the present bridge.

For some goods, air for example, the supply is so plentiful that diversion from some uses is not required to increase the intensity with which they are used elsewhere. Only where scarcity is absent is it *a priori* reasonable to charge a zero price. Superabundance is the only true *a priori* case for a zero-priced public good. All other goods are such that their provision forces us into resource allocation problems. To solve these problems efficiently, we need information which is obtained by excluding nonpurchasers, *provided that the additional information is worth more than the exchange and police costs necessitated*. In cases where the costs are greater, a zero price can be reconciled with efficiency requirements. If we must distinguish among goods, we had best do away with the 'public goods' *vs.* private goods dichotomy and instead classify goods according to whether they are truly free or economic and classify economic goods according to whether marketing costs are too high relative to the benefits of using markets and to the costs of substitute nonmarket allocation devices.

Alternative devices

The use of taxation for the provision of scarce goods must be defended on grounds other than the usual rationale of their being public goods. As we have seen, insofar as efficiency is concerned, the fact that side benefits can be derived by nonpurchasers from the acquisition by others of these goods is inconclusive. If the planner's or the market's calculation of benefits can be improved by a small expenditure to protect or to confer property rights, the use of price rationing to measure these benefits may be justified. The problem can be viewed as that of determining the degree to which it is desirable to purchase valuation information through the competitive pricing process. A purchase of valuation information reduces the utilization of a public good below the levels that seem to be warranted by the direct cost of extending utilization. If the direct cost of, say, increasing the volume of traffic carried by an existing bridge is zero, it may nonetheless be *un*desirable to charge a zero price because of the indirect costs implied by zero-pricing. These indirect costs are of two kinds.

Firstly, and obviously, valuation information about the

bridge is sacrificed. (Is not valuation information one of the most important public goods?) Secondly, the alternative methods of financing the building of bridges may also lead to inefficiency, especially by degrading valuation information elsewhere. This is most easily seen by supposing that an excise tax is levied on other goods to finance bridges. Such a tax will lead to inefficiently small rates of production of these other goods (assuming competitive markets). Alternatively, the levying of an income tax will inefficiently reduce the quantities of income-generating activities undertaken by those taxed. A tax on property values, even one on rent, would tend to discourage the seeking out of more valuable uses of property. A head tax would have the least effect because it is not concentrated on particular activities. Even a head tax, one could argue, would alter a person's choice of community, and moreover, a resident who refused to pay the tax might be excluded from use of the bridge. Taxes exclude just as do prices, so that on grounds of exclusion there is not much principle to guide us. Given these indirect costs of alternative methods of financing the provision of public goods, the desirability of zero-pricing is not at all clear, especially if the cost of policing is low.

For some goods, however, it must be recognized that police cost may seem too high to allow the market to generate accurate information on social benefits economically. In these cases taxation *may* be the most practical method of finance and zoning the most practical way of establishing rights, just as subsidies, excise taxes, and government nonprice rationing may be the most practical way of coping with high exchange costs. But it must be remembered that all these devices are 'exclusionary' and have costs of their own. At best, they would be second best alternatives to a market in which police and exchange costs are small and in which there is no bias in arithmetic mistakes as between civil servants and others, for these devices are not as likely to turn up correct estimates of the social values of alternative goods.

In a world in which exchange and police cost and the cost of providing alternative political devices are all zero, reliance on the political mechanism of a smoothly run democracy will result in less efficiency than will reliance on the market. Aside from problems of monopoly in government or of errors in calculation, in a one-man, one-vote democracy, where votes are

E

not for sale, the polling place will generate information that is based on majoritarian principles rather than on maximum benefit principles. Thus, suppose some citizens prefer a stronger national defense but that a majority prefer a weaker defense. Left to a vote, the weaker defense will be our chosen policy even though the minority is willing to pay more than the additional cost required to bring defense up to the level they desire (and so, if possible, they may hire private police services). An error in the opposite direction is also possible. The majority of voters may approve of a large space effort even though they would not be able to bid high enough to acquire these resources for space in the absence of forced tax contributions. (Here, however, the minority cannot privately adjust.)

Although taxation is sometimes the most practical way of dealing with the provision of high police costs goods, there are other methods which are likely to arise in the market and which will lower the required police cost. As we have seen, extending the firm and the practice of sale-in-combination may overcome many instances of high exchange costs. These devices can also be used to reduce high police cost.

In the famous railway example, sparks from passing trains destroy some crops. The damage caused was believed to be adequate grounds for the government to take action through one or more of the political devices we have already mentioned. Direct contracting between the farmers and the railroad might take account of this side effect were it not that a bargain struck between a farmer and the railway would automatically confer benefits on all surrounding farmers by reducing spark fall-out on their land. Police costs are too high to allow benefits to be conferred on the contracting farmer without at the same time conferring them on non-contracting farmers. Therefore, it is believed that each farmer will wait for someone else to buy a reduction in spark output. (This conclusion requires two preliminary assumptions. The exchange cost of farmers getting together to submit a joint bid must be high relative to the benefits they will receive so that it is blocked by the expense it entails, and the exchange cost of their getting together to submit a joint bid must be higher than the cost of their organizing politically to lobby for antispark legislation.)

However, once the spatial aspects of the problem are admitted, we must again consider the phenomenon of differential land rent. Presumably, land rents on property adjacent to railways have been suitably depressed to allow farmers to compete with those not affected by sparks. The landowners, who find it in their interest to reduce the railroad's output of sparks, also find themselves not willing to enter into contracts through which other landowners will benefit. To some extent each would wait for the other to transact with the railway for a reduction in spark output. However, the analysis is not yet finished. The railway may realize a profit by purchasing the surrounding land at its depressed price. The purchase of a parcel of land does not confer benefits on neighbors to the same degree as would a purchase of spark curtailment so that this action would not hamper the concluding of similar contracts with other landowners as much as would the sale of a reduction in sparks. After the railroad purchases title to enough land to make it worthwhile, it could take into account the effect of its output of sparks on land values and profitably bring about an adjustment of this output to the socially optimal amount – that which maximizes the joint value of railroading and landowning. The land must, of course, be rented or resold with a contractual agreement requiring a continuance of reduced spark output. The low police cost associated with the purchase of land is substituted for the very high police cost that would be required to eliminate sparks on some land but not on other nearby land. The necessity for purchasing a reduction in spark output is obviated by substituting a purchase of land.

The extension of the firm together with the combination-sale devices that are associated with differential land rent are extremely important alternatives to government action. These devices can extend considerably the usefulness of markets for revealing and measuring the value of many side effects. The sale of land may entail much less exchange and policing cost than the direct exchange of whatever is producing the side effect. The smoke emitted from a nearby factory would, in principle, be subject to solution in the same manner. Now, of course, in many of these cases we do not observe such solutions taking place because exchange and police costs are not reduced sufficiently and because they may require too much underspecialization cost. Governmental devices, say zoning laws, may help take account of such benefits, however inaccurately, at a lower cost (in which we should include those costs imposed by

the rigidities of zoning laws). It may be, however, that both
governmental and market solutions are too costly and that the
most efficient alternative is not to attempt to take account of
some side effects.[6]

There are other indirect devices for internalizing via combination sales. The activities of labeling, branding, and advertising allow for internalization of side effects by tying in the
sale of information with other goods. Suppose persons would
like their tuna boiled longer before canning. Each canner would
find it in his interest to prepare the tuna more carefully except
that, in a world without labels, all competitors would enjoy at
no cost some of the benefits of the resulting increase in demand.
Some, therefore, wait for competitors to act. Underinvestment
in tuna boiling (or overinvestment in boiling tuna at home)
takes place and government regulations governing canning
procedures are instituted.

Suppose we allow each canner to state on the label both his
name and the minimum boiling time. The name is required to

---

[6] The ability of combination sales to take account of side benefits depends on how
closely the value of the tied-in good reflects the value of the public good. There is a
direct and exact correspondence between the value of land and the (negative to
farmers) value of spark output. A less exact correspondence between the values of
the tied goods, while not a perfect device, can nonetheless be useful for taking
account of the value of public goods.

Even the stubborn classic case of providing for the national defense is amenable
to some usable tie-in arrangements. The provision of defense again presents us with
a situation in which it is in the interest of a beneficiary to let others buy defense
since he will benefit from their purchases. Suppose, however, that instead of financing defense with taxes, the government resorts to the sale of insurance to citizens
which covers their lives and property in the event of loss arising from war. The tied
goods, insurance and defense, are substitutes, but they do not fully correspond in
value fluctuations. For a stated premium per thousand dollars of insurance and a
stated maximum, citizens would buy more insurance the more likely they thought
war and the less able they thought our defense. Those having more at stake would
buy more insurance. The premiums could then be used to finance the defense
establishment. The side effect is not fully captured, however, because your purchase of insurance, although it fully internalizes your losses in the event of war, also
decreases the likelihood of war, and, hence, reduces the amount of insurance others
would volunteer to buy. This smaller remaining public aspect of the good could be
accounted for by offering the insurance for premiums that are believed to be
subsidized.

War, as well as other events, can topple governments, so that to make the insurance credible, the government might need to offer citizens the option of cancelling
their insurance and receiving all or some of the premiums they have paid. This
cancellation option need be effective only up to the date before a war starts. The
insurance device is not without dangers. By raising the maximum purchasable
insurance (and lowering premiums), the government could induce a more aggres-
sive attitude among the citizens than is warranted by actuarial fair insurance.

establish responsibility and thereby to reduce policing cost, which is another way of saying that the cost of exercising the rights acquired by purchasers by reason of the purchase contract is reduced for the buyer. The sale of knowledge jointly with that of tuna allows the value of longer boiling to be taken into account by producers and buyers. Structural market imperfections of the monopolistic competition variety can be ruled out if both longer-boiled and less-boiled tuna have numerous producers. The demand for each producer's tuna will then be the going market price of the particular quality he produces.[7]

Still other institutional arrangements have been devised to combine extensions of the firm with the sale-in-combination device. Department stores and shopping plazas are organizational devices for overcoming high police cost. The owner of the department store or shopping plaza can provide a general environment that is conducive for shopping, such as pleasant plantings, escalators, and other customer services that merchants who owned their own land might hesitate to pay for, hoping instead that neighboring landowners would incur the necessary expenses from which all would benefit. The enclosing of the land into a single ownership entity which often undertakes to provide services usually provided by government from tax revenues, such as streets, sidewalks, refuse collection, and even police protection, allows the owner to exclude those who refuse to pay rentals which cover the cost of these services. The competition of various plazas and department stores will provide ample opportunity for merchants to select the services that they wish to buy without fearing or counting on free-loading. Apartment buildings can also be viewed in the same light, and especially the modern apartment building which combines office and recreational space with living space. The development of these institutional arrangements provides an interesting challenge to political institutions for the provision of many of the services generally presumed to be within the scope of the polling place.

The preceding discussion has taken as given the state of technical arts. The levels of exchange and police costs that are required for effective marketing and the costs of government substitute services depend on how well we master the technology

---

[7] It is not really necessary for efficiency to obtain to require that producers take the product price as given and beyond their control. See Demsetz, op. cit., n. 3.

of operating markets and governments. Attention is sometimes called to the fact that emerging technical developments will make the use of markets or governments more economic than they now are. There are surely many instances where this is true. However, our analysis suggests that technological developments can operate in the opposite direction. At the same time that technology is reducing the cost of using these alternative institutional arrangements for economizing, it is also reducing the cost of constructing parking spaces, of developing fire-resistant corn, and of mass producing automobiles. Whether or not it pays to increase the extent to which we exchange via markets, protective private property rights, or use alternative government devices depends on how much we will thereby reduce production cost and crop damage. Markets or their government alternatives should come into greater prominence only if technical developments lower the costs of these institutional arrangements more than they reduce the costs of producing parking spaces and cars and the cost of crop damage.

Essentially, we have argued in this paper that there exist no qualitative differences between side effects and what we may call 'primary' effects. The only differences are those that are implicitly based on quantitative differences in exchange and police cost. Suppose a factory invents a new, more efficient furnace which can burn a cheaper grade of coal than can existing furnaces. The burning of cheap coal, we will assume, dirties homes in the neighborhood. We label this effect as side or neighborhood or external, but its real economic implication is to reduce the wealth of nearby homeowners. If this same factory, by virtue of its new furnace, successfully forces a nearby competing firm out of business, and if the resulting decline in demand for housing reduces the wealth of neighborhood homeowners, we do not become concerned. Why the difference in our attitudes toward these two situations which have the same effect on homeowners?

The decline in wealth which results from the fall in demand for housing is more than offset by an increase in wealth elsewhere. This increase accrues primarily to other homeowners and to persons purchasing the lower-priced product produced by the factory. We accept the reallocation, I conjecture, because we feel that the existence of a smoothly operating market will insure that wealth is maximized. In the smoke case, exchange and police costs are high relative to the benefits of marketing smoke and, therefore, we do not have an existing market to rely on for the reallocation, although a potential one always stands ready. If the costs of exchanging and policing smoke contracts were zero (and if the cost of exchanging houses were zero) there would be no reason for distinguishing between the two cases insofar as 'remedial' action is concerned. We have already argued that the most efficient arrangement may, in fact, require that nothing be done to prohibit smoke and we will not go into these matters again. Our present purpose is merely to emphasize that there is nothing special or qualitatively different about any of these effects, including the effects which stem from what we ineptly call public goods, and that any special treatment accorded to them cannot be justified merely by observing their presence.

PART TWO

The Framework of State Intervention

7 Economies as an Anti-Trust Defense: The Welfare Tradeoffs

O. E. Williamson

Suppose that a merger (or other combination) is proposed that yields economies but at the same time increases market power. Can the courts and antitrust agencies safely rely, in these circumstances, on a literal reading of the law which prohibits mergers 'where in any line of commerce or any section of the country, the effect of such acquisition may be substantially to lessen competition, or to tend to create a monopoly',[1] or does this run the risk of serious economic loss? In the usual merger where both effects are insubstantial this problem is absent.[2] But

---

[1] Public Law 899, Sec. 7, 38 Stat. 731, as amended; 15 U.S.C. 18.

[2] Donald Dewey has observed in this connection that most mergers 'have virtually nothing to do with either the creation of market power or the realization of scale economies' ([12] p. 257). Jesse Markham agrees that since 1930 monopolization has not been a principal merger objective, but finds that 'some mergers have undoubtedly come about as adjustments to major innovations . . .: the first great wave of mergers followed a period of rapid railroad building, and the wave of the 1920s came with the rise of the motor car and motor truck transportation and a new advertising medium, the home radio' ([26] pp. 181–2). It might be useful briefly to summarize some of the ways in which efficiencies might result from combination. These would include miscalculation, shifts in demand, technological developments, displacement of ineffective managements, and mixtures thereof.

As an example of miscalculation consider two firms that have entered a market at an efficient plant scale but have incorrectly estimated the volume necessary to support an efficient distribution system. Combination here could lead to efficiencies but might also have some market power effects (reducing competition between the two but possibly enhancing their competitive position with respect to their rivals). A significant, persistent decline in demand might produce a condition of excess capacity in which combination would permit economies but would also have market power consequences. As discussed in section 3, an increase in demand might induce a change from job shop to assembly line type operations with vertical integration consequences. Technological developments may similarly provide opportunities for a significant reorganization of resources into more efficient configurations – the electronic digital computer being a recent example. Finally, merger may be the most expeditious way of displacing an inefficient by a more efficient management – but the benefits here may only be of a short-run variety.

Reprinted with the author's amendments from *American Economic Review*, LVIII (Mar 1968) 18–36, by kind permission of the author and of the American Economic Association.

in the occasional case where efficiency and market power consequences exist, can economies be dismissed on the grounds that
market power effects invariably dominate? If they cannot,
then a rational treatment of the merger question requires that
an effort be made to establish the allocative implications of the
scale economy and market power effects associated with the
merger.

The initial indication of the Supreme Court's view on this
question came on the occasion of the first merger case to come
before it under the 1950 amendment to Section 7 of the Clayton
Act. In a unanimous opinion, the Court took the position in
Brown Shoe that not only were efficiencies no defense, but a
showing that a merger resulted in efficiencies could be used
affirmatively in attacking the merger since small rivals could be
disadvantaged thereby ([9] p. 374). Opportunities to reconsider
this position have presented themselves since, *Procter & Gamble*
being the most recent.

Justice Douglas, in delivering the opinion of the Court,
observed that Procter & Gamble 'would be able to use its
volume discounts to advantage in advertising Clorox', and
went on to state that 'economies cannot be used as a defense to
illegality. Congress was aware that some mergers which lessen
competition may also result in economies but it struck the
balance in favor of protecting competition' ([13] pp. 1230–1).
Although reference to congressional intent may relieve the
Court of the responsiblity for making tradeoff valuations, this
does not fully dispose of the issue. What tradeoff calculus did
Congress employ that produced this result?

In a concurring opinion to the Clorox decision, Justice
Harlan provides the first hint that efficiencies may deserve
greater standing. At least with respect to conglomerate or
product-extension mergers 'where the case against the merger
rests on the probability [as contrasted, apparently, with a
certainty] of increased market power, the merging companies
may attempt to prove that there are countervailing economies

A manifestly inefficient management would, hopefully, be displaced by other
means if, by reason of the market power consequences of a combination, the merger
route were closed.

A merger can, of course, produce diseconomies as well. What I have previously
characterized as the 'control loss' phenomenon appears to be an increasing
function of firm size [35]. See also parts H and I section 2 below.

reasonably probable which should be weighed against the adverse effects' ([13] pp. 1240–1). But inasmuch as the economies in Clorox were in his opinion merely pecuniary rather than real, which distinction is of course appropriate, he concluded that Procter's efficiency defense was defective ([13] p. 1243).

Even if Justice Harlan's position were the prevailing one, it is clear that economies would be an acceptable antitrust defense for only a restricted set of structural conditions. Since the relevant economic theory, although widely available, has never been developed explicitly on this issue, such a result is not unexpected. Indeed, lacking a basis for evaluating net effects, for the Court to hold that the anticompetitive consequences of a merger outweigh any immediate efficiency advantages is only to be expected. An institution acting as a caretaker for the enterprise system does not easily exchange what it regards as long-term competitive consequences for short-term efficiency gains.

The merits of the Supreme Court's position on mergers are at the heart of the recent Bork and Bowman v. Blake and Jones debate [3] [4] [6] [7]. Although this dialogue deals directly with the critical issues, its failure to produce a consensus is at least partly due to the fact that essential aspects of the relevant economic model were not supplied. Lacking a tradeoff relation, Bork is forced to assert that 'Economic analysis does away with the need to measure efficiencies directly. It is enough to know in what sorts of transactions efficiencies are likely to be present and in what sorts anticompetitive effects are likely to be present. The law can then develop objective criteria, such as market shares, to divide transactions [into those predominantly one type or other]' ([7] p. 411). But this obviously leaves the mixed cases, which are the hard ones, unresolved. Blake and Jones, by contrast, conclude that 'claims of economic efficiency will not justify a course of conduct conferring excessive market power. The objective of maintaining a system of self-policing markets requires that all such claims be rejected' ([4] p. 427). But what are the standards for 'excessive' market power and 'self-policing' markets? And are these really absolute or do they reflect an implicit tradeoff calculation? And if it is the latter, should we (if we can) make this tradeoff explicit?

Indeed, there is no way in which the tradeoff issue can be avoided. To disallow tradeoffs altogether merely reflects a particularly severe *a priori* judgment as to net benefits. More-over, it is doubtful that a goal hierarchy scheme of the sort proposed by Carl Kaysen and Donald Turner has acceptable properties. As they formulate the problem, higher-level goals strictly dominate lower-level goals, so that only when the latter are available without sacrifice in the former is lower-level goal pursuit allowed ([19] pp. 44–5). Inasmuch as they rank efficiency and progressiveness above reductions in market power, an absolute defense would appear to obtain when, for any structural condition present or prospective, it could be shown either that economies have not yet been exhausted or that discreteness conditions (indivisibilities) would not efficiently permit a separation ([19] pp. 44–6, 58, 78). But this may be to construe their intentions too narrowly; for it is with anti-trust actions that result in *substantial* efficiency losses ([19] pp. 44, 133) and involve *too great* a sacrifice in performance ([19] p. 58) that they are especially concerned. Although these distinctions are important, they are not ones for which goal hierarchy analysis is well suited to deal. Tradeoff analysis, by contrast, is designed to cope with precisely these types of issues.

The relevant partial equilibrium model with which to characterize the tradeoffs between efficiency and price effects together with a representative set of indifference relations are developed in section 1 of this paper. A variety of essential qualifications to this naïve model are then presented in section 2. Extensions of the argument, which is developed initially in horizontal merger terms, to deal with questions of dissolution as well as vertical and conglomerate mergers, are given in section 3. The conclusions follow in section 4.

1. The Naïve Tradeoff Model

The effects on resource allocation of a merger that yields economies but extends market power can be investigated in a partial equilibrium context with the help of Fig. 7.1. The horizontal line labeled AC_1 represents the level of average costs of the two (or more) firms before combination, while AC_2 shows the level of average costs after the merger. The price before the merger is given by P_1 and is equal to k (AC_1), where k is an index of pre-merger market power and is greater than or equal to unity. The price after the merger is given by P_2 and is assumed to exceed P_1 (if it were less than P_1 the economic effects of the merger would be strictly positive).[3] Assume for our purposes here that pre-merger market power is negligible ($k = 1$).

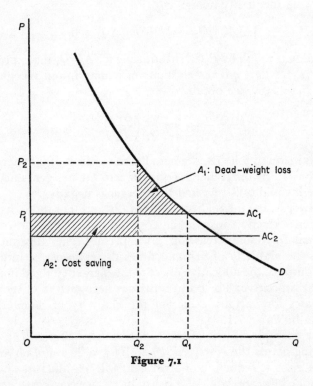

Figure 7.1

The net welfare effects of the merger are given (approximately) by the two shaded areas in the figure. The area designated A_1 is the familiar dead-weight loss that would result if price were increased from P_1 to P_2, assuming that costs remain constant. But since average costs are actually reduced by the merger, the area designated A_2, which represents cost savings, must also be taken into account. The net allocative

[3] This is a simple but basic point. It reveals that market power is only a necessary and not a sufficient condition for undesirable price effects to exist. It would be wholly irrational to regard an increase in the price to average cost ratio ($P_2/AC_2 > P_1/AC_1$) as grounds for opposing a merger if, at the same time, the post-merger price were less than the pre-merger level ($P_2 < P_1$) and the qualifications discussed in section 2 are insubstantial.

effect is given by the difference, $A_2 - A_1$, of these two areas.[4]

The area A_2 is given by $(AC_2 - AC_1)Q_2$, or $[\Delta(AC)]Q_2$, while A_1 is given approximately by $\frac{1}{2}(P_2 - P_1)(Q_1 - Q_2)$, or $\frac{1}{2}(\Delta P)(\Delta Q)$. The net economic effect will be positive if the following inequality holds:

$$[\Delta(AC)]Q_2 - 1/2(\Delta P)(\Delta Q) > 0. \tag{1}$$

Dividing through by P_1Q_1, substituting for $\Delta Q/Q_1$ the expression $\eta(\Delta P/P_1)$, where η is the elasticity of demand, and recognizing that $P_1 = AC_1$, we obtain

$$\frac{\Delta(AC)}{AC} - \frac{1}{2}\eta\frac{Q_1}{Q_2}\left(\frac{\Delta P}{P_1}\right)^2 > 0. \tag{2}$$

If this inequality holds, the net allocative effect of the merger is positive. If the difference is equal to zero the merger is neutral. If the inequality is reversed the merger is negative.

In words, the inequality shown in (2) says that if the decimal fraction reduction in average costs exceeds the square of the decimal fraction increase in price premultiplied by one-half times the elasticity of demand times the ratio of the initial to final outputs, the allocative effect of the merger (judged in naïve terms) is positive. The cost reductions necessary to offset price increases for various values of the elasticity of demand are shown in Table 7.1.

For example, if price were to increase by 20 per cent, then running across the row $[(\Delta P/P) \times 100] = 20$ we observe that if η is 2 a cost reduction of 5 per cent will be sufficient to offset the price increase, while if η is 1 only a 2 per cent cost decrease is needed to neutralize the price effect, and if η is $\frac{1}{2}$, a cost reduction of 1 per cent is sufficient. More generally it is evident that a relatively modest cost reduction is usually sufficient to offset relatively large price increases even if the elasticity of demand is as high as 2, which is probably a reasonable upper

---

[4] My use of dead-weight loss is somewhat restrictive. Inefficiency is also a dead-weight loss. For convenience of exposition, however, I refer to the Marshallian triangle as the dead-weight loss and compare this to the cost saving (efficiency) aspects of a merger. Estimating the value of consumers' surplus by the Marshallian triangle follows the common (and broadly defensible) practice of suppressing the income effects associated with a price change. The net social benefit associated with a particular cost–price configuration is defined as total revenue plus consumers' surplus less social cost, where social and private costs are assumed to be identical (externalities and producers' surplus are both assumed to be zero).

TABLE 7.1

PERCENTAGE COST REDUCTIONS $[(\Delta(AC)/AC) \times 100]$ SUFFICIENT TO
OFFSET PERCENTAGE PRICE INCREASES $(\Delta P/P \times 100)$ FOR SELECTED
VALUES OF η

$(\Delta P/P) \times 100$	η 2	1	1/2
5	0·26	0·12	0·06
10	1·05	0·50	0·24
20	4·40	2·00	0·95
30	10·35	4·50	2·10

bound. Indeed, if a reduction in average costs on the order of 5
to 10 per cent is available through merger, the merger must give
rise to price increases in excess of 20 per cent if $\eta \cong 2$, and in
excess of 40 per cent if $\eta \cong \frac{1}{2}$, for the net allocative effects to
be negative. Moreover, it should be noted, if the merger re-
duces average costs by x per cent and the post-merger price
increases by y per cent, the post-merger price to average cost
differential slightly exceeds $x + y$ per cent. Thus, expressing
price with respect to the post-merger level of average costs
yields an even greater differential than is reflected by the relations stated above. The naïve model thus supports the following
proposition: a merger which yields nontrivial real economies
must produce substantial market power and result in relatively
large price increases for the net allocative effects to be negative.

2. Qualifications

Our partial equilibrium analysis suffers from a defect common to
all partial equilibrium constructions. By isolating one sector
from the rest of the economy it fails to examine interactions
between sectors. Certain economic effects may therefore go un-
detected, and occasionally behavior which appears to yield net
economic benefits in a partial equilibrium analysis will result in
net losses when investigated in a general equilibrium context.
Such a condition has been shown to exist in an economy in
which monopoly exists in many sectors. Thus, whereas partial
equilibrium analysis indicates that an increase in the monopoly
price in any one sector invariably yields a loss, viewed more
generally such an isolated price increase may actually lead to a

desirable reallocation of resources.[5] Conceivably, therefore, a merger that has monopoly power and cost-saving consequences could yield benefits in *both* respects[6] – although it is probably rare that operational content can be supplied to this qualification. But were there no other considerations, such bias as our partial equilibrium construction produces would be to underestimate the net economic gains of combination.

This does not, however, exhaust the range of qualifications. Among the other factors that can or should be taken into account are pre-existing market power, inference and enforcement expense, timing incipiency, weighting, income distribution, extra-economic political objectives, technological progress, and the effects of monopoly power on managerial discretion.

A. *Pre-existing market power*

We continue to employ the conventional partial equilibrium welfare function; to wit, welfare is expressed as $W = (\text{TR} + S) - (\text{TC} - R)$, where, under appropriate restrictions, the terms in the first set of parenthesis reflect social benefits (total revenue plus consumers' surplus) and those in the second reflect social costs (total pecuniary costs less intramarginal rents). Assuming that R is negligible, this can be restated as $W = (\text{TR} - \text{TC}) + S$, or inasmuch, as $\text{TR} - \text{TC}$ reflects profits, as $W = \pi + S$, where π denotes profits. Any change in welfare is then given by

$$\Delta W = (\pi_2 - \pi_1) + (S_2 - S_1).$$

Let k be the pre-existing market power parameter, where $k = P_1/\text{AC}_1$. It can be shown that ΔW can be expressed as

$$\Delta(\text{AC})Q_2 - [\tfrac{1}{2}\Delta P + (k - 1)\text{AC}_1]\Delta Q. \tag{3}$$

The parallel test expression to equation (2) is whether

$$\frac{\Delta(\text{AC})}{\text{AC}_1} - \left[\frac{1}{2}k\left(\frac{\Delta P}{P_1}\right) + (k - 1)\right]\eta\,\frac{\Delta P}{P_1} \cdot \frac{Q_1}{Q_2} \tag{4}$$

is greater or less than zero.

[5] This is the familiar 'second-best' argument. For a discussion of second-best qualifications in treating the monopoly problem, and references to this literature, see Ferguson ([14] pp. 16–17, 49–51).

[6] This is more likely if (*a*) the factor markets of the industry in question are competitive, (*b*) the firms involved in the merger produce strictly for final demand, and (*c*) significant relations with sectors in which distortions exist are mainly ones of substitutability rather than complementarity.

The question now to be addressed is what values of k might reasonably obtain. Consider in this connection Joe Bain's treatment of entry barriers in the 'very high', 'substantial', and 'moderate or low' categories ([2] p. 170):

> It is hazardous to assign any absolute values to the entry barriers corresponding to these three rankings, but the very roughest guess would be as follows: (1) that in the 'very high' category, established firms might be able to elevate price 10 per cent or more above *minimal* costs while forestalling entry; (2) that with 'substantial' barriers, the corresponding percentage might range a bit above or below 7 per cent; (3) that in the 'moderate to low' category the same percentage will probably not exceed 4, and will range down to around 1 per cent. [Emphasis added.]

This suggests that k may ordinarily be expected to fall in the range 1·00 to 1·10. Table 7.2 shows the percentage cost reductions sufficient to offset various percentage price increases for selected demand elasticities (assumed to be constant in the relevant range) and values k of 1·05 and 1·10.

TABLE 7.2

PERCENTAGE COST REDUCTIONS $[(\Delta AC/AC_1) \times 100]$ SUFFICIENT TO OFFSET PERCENTAGE PRICE INCREASES $[(\Delta P/P_1) \times 100]$ FOR SELECTED VALUES OF η AND $k = 1·05$ AND $1·10$

$\Delta P/P_1 \times 100$	$\eta = 2$		$\eta = 1$		$\eta = \frac{1}{2}$	
	$k = 1·05$	$k = 1·10$	$k = 1·05$	$k = 1·10$	$k = 1·05$	$k = 1·10$
5	0·78	1·31	0·38	0·64	0·19	0·31
10	2·15	3·26	1·03	1·55	0·50	0·76
20	6·82	9·23	3·10	4·20	1·48	2·00
30	14·28	18·27	6·21	7·95	2·90	3·57

As is evident from an inspection of Tables 7.1 and 7.2, the cost savings required to offset price increases are significantly greater if pre-merger market power prevails. The enforcement agencies are thus well advised to give special scrutiny to the monopolistic subset. Still, the existence of pre-merger market power is not enough, by itself, to upset the basic conclusions of the naïve model.

B. *Inference and enforcement expense*

The relevant effects are those which take the form of real rather than pecuniary economies. Also, since evaluating a claim that economies exist will itself absorb real resources, it seems reasonable to impose a requirement that the net gain exceed some threshold value before such a defense will even be entertained. This, in conjunction with qualifications C through E below, would appear to meet Donald Turner's point that if economies are to be invoked as a defense 'the law might well require clear and convincing evidence that the particular merger would produce substantial economies that could not be achieved in other ways' ([31] p. 1328). As the tools for assessing economies are progressively refined (and the incentive to make such improvements is obvious once an efficiency defense – even in principle – is granted), this threshold level should be reduced accordingly. Still, protection for the legal process may be essential.

A four-stage program to implement an economies defense is proposed. At a minimum, the antitrust agencies and the courts should explicitly recognize the merits of an economies defense in principle, even though they may disallow it as a practical defense. This would at least forestall perverse treatment of economies before the law. The effects of even such a modest change might well be considerable. As Kaysen has pointed out, 'policy change comes about, in large part, by the way in which the enforcing agencies select cases and frame issues for courts and commissions to decide' ([21] p. 85).

Second, although an economies defense would be disallowed, it could be introduced for 'explanatory completeness'.[7] This would hopefully encourage companies to reveal the efficiency consequences of mergers more completely, so that the importance of allowing an economies defense could be better assessed. The legal process would be protected, and an idea of the magnitude of the implicit tradeoffs might begin to emerge.

A more ambitious undertaking, but one which would still provide substantial protection to the legal process, would be to allow an economies defense for certain types of mergers. Justice Harlan has suggested that an economies defense should be

---

[7] As Bork points out, the courts have, occasionally, permitted this ([8] p. 390, n. 40).

available for conglomerate or product-extension mergers ([13] pp. 1240–1). As experience is accumulated, this might be eventually extended to include other types of mergers. With respect to vertical and horizontal mergers, for example, *Merger Guidelines* could be rewritten to acknowledge a band of uncertainty within which an economies defense would be available: above a specified set of market share values, a merger would be disallowed; below a second set of values, a merger would be permitted; within the range between, an economies defense, subject to an appropriate set of threshold stipulations, would be entertained. Proceeding in a gradualist way of this sort would appear to conform to the objective proposed by Bok ([5] pp. 348–9):

> While the basic values and objectives of Section 7 should presumably remain unchanged by court or agency, the methods and standards used to achieve these ends must evolve to keep pace with developments in our knowledge concerning the nature and effects of mergers. . . . The issue . . . is fundamentally one of timing; the question is whether *at present* we stand to gain from rules which seek to capture the subtler images of reality evoked by the complexities of economic theory.

Finally, an economies defense (appropriately qualified) might be admitted quite generally. Even, however, if this last stage is never reached, the process is worth setting in motion. Stage one involves merely an immediate expression of positive regard for economies by the antitrust agencies and the courts – a step which is unambiguously desirable. There are clear benefits and no evident costs.

C. *Timing*

Significant economies will ordinarily be realized eventually through internal expansion if not by merger. Growth of demand can facilitate this internal adjustment process; the necessity for part of the industry to be displaced in order that efficient size be achieved is relieved in a growing market. Thus, although a merger may have net positive effects immediately (cost savings exceed the dead-weight loss), when allowance is made for the possibility of internal expansion these effects can become negative eventually (the cost savings persist, but these could be realized anyway, and the dead-weight loss could be avoided by prohibiting the merger).

Designating the dead-weight loss effects of the merger by $L(t)$ and the cost savings by $S(t)$, the argument would be that the value of $S(t)$ falls while $L(t)$ persists over time. Thus, taking the discounted value of net benefits (V) we have

$$V = \int_0^T [S(t) - L(t)]e^{-rt}dt \tag{5}$$

and if initially $S(t)/L(t) > 1$, but eventually $S(t)/L(t) < 1$, this can easily become negative.

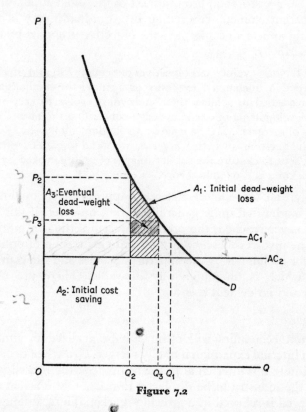

Figure 7.2

For purposes of illustration, let P_3 be the price that would obtain if the economies were realized, with a delay, by internal expansion, and define an attenuation coefficient a by the ratio $a = (P_2 - P_3)/(P_2 - AC_2)$. P_2 and AC_2 are specified; the value that a takes on thus depends on the post-expansion price P_3. If $P_3 = AC_2$, in which case $a = 1$, internal expansion results in the full attenuation of the market power effects that a merger, if permitted, would produce; no attenuation exists if $a = 0$ (since here $P_3 = P_2$); partial attenuation occurs if a falls in the interval $0 < a < 1$.

For each value that P_3 (and hence a) takes on, the question becomes: How soon must the internal expansion occur for the merger to have net negative allocative consequences? The relevant benefit and loss regions to be examined are those shown in Fig. 7.2.

Again let S be the initial cost savings of the merger (the rectangle designated as A_2) and L be the initial dead-weight loss (the triangle designated as A_1). When the internal expansion is completed and the price P_3 obtains, the dead-weight loss of the merger becomes the shaded region A_3. Let T' be the switch-over point such that, on allocative grounds, one is indifferent between going the internal expansion route or permitting the merger, and let the discount rate be 10 per cent Substituting the values $\bar{S}$, $\bar{L}$, and A_3 into equation (5), the critical values of T' are those for which the discounted value of the net benefits of the merger are equal to zero. To wit:

$$V(T') = \int_0^{T'} (\bar{S} - \bar{L})\, e^{-rt} dt - \int_{T'}^{\infty} A_3 e^{-rt} dt = 0. \tag{5}$$

Solution values of T' in this expression, for selected values of $\bar{S}/\bar{L}$ and a, require that the magnitude of the initial price increase and the elasticity of demand be specified. Assume for this purpose that demand has unit elasticity in the relevant range and that the merger gives rise to a 10 per cent price increase, which is probably a rough upper bound. The switch-over (indifference) values that obtain for selected values of $\bar{S}/\bar{L}$ and a under these assumptions are shown in Table 7.3.

The lower the value of T', the more quickly must economies be realized by internal expansion for a merger to have net negative allocative consequences. As would be expected, early internal expansion becomes more essential as the ratio of initial cost savings to the initial dead-weight loss $(\bar{S}/\bar{L})$ increases and as the attenuation coefficient (a) decreases. Roughly, the values of T' that appear on and to the right of the main diagonal are sufficiently small that one should have reasonable confidence that potential economies will be realized in the next few years

TABLE 7.3

SWITCH-OVER VALUES (T') FOR SELECTED VALUES OF $\overline{S}/\overline{L}$ AND OF
THE ATTENUATION COEFFICIENT (a)

a \\ $\overline{S}/\overline{L}$	1·5	2	3	6
0·0	0·0	0·0	0·0	0·0
0·3	7·2	4·7	3·0	1·5
0·7	11·1	7·1	4·6	2·7
1·0	12·0	7·9	5·1	3·0

for a merger to be disallowed on account of timing considerations alone.[8]

D. *Incipiency*

It is likewise vital to consider not merely the market power effects
of any single merger taken in isolation, but whether the merger
is representative of a trend. If a series of such mergers can
reasonably be expected, the judgment of whether to permit any
given combination should properly be cast in an industry
context – in which case the anticipated economy and market
power effects throughout the industry should be examined.
Since, if economies are available by combining one pair of firms
they will often be available more generally, this may frequently
be an important consideration. The notion of incipiency thus
has special relevance in administering the law on mergers
where economies are claimed.

This proposition might usefully be contrasted with that of
Bork and Bowman ([6] p. 594):

> The difficulty with stopping a trend toward a more concentrated
> condition at a very early stage is that the existence of the trend is
> prima facie evidence that greater concentration is socially desir-
> able. The trend indicates that there are emerging efficiencies or
> economies of scale – whether due to engineering and production

[8] Note that the solution values of T' depend on the choice of $\Delta P/P_1$, r, and η –
increasing as either $\Delta P/P_1$ and η increase, decreasing as r increases. My guess is
that the selected values of r and η are probably close, but that the choice of $\Delta P/P_1$
tends toward an upper bound. Hence, 'typical' values of T' will be lower than
those shown.

developments or to new control and management techniques – which make larger size more efficient. This increased efficiency is valuable to the society at large, for it means that fewer of our available resources are being used to accomplish the same amount of production and distribution. By striking at such trends in their very earliest stages the concept of incipiency prevents the realization of those very efficiencies that competition is supposed to encourage.

Their evaluation of the social desirability of a trend suggests a certain insensitivity to the relevant scale economy–market power tradeoff considerations, and they appear to read the significance of a trend somewhat too loosely; it may also indicate an emerging awareness that market power advantages might be realized through a series of combinations.[9] Moreover, whereas they seem to suggest that to disallow a merger is to prevent the realization of scale economies altogether, ordinarily it is not a question of whether economies will be realized but when and with what market power effects. Thus, while Bork and Bowman may be correct in charging that scale economy justifications have not been given sufficient weight in the recent enforcement of the merger law, they are also guilty of a certain heavy-handedness in their own treatment of the incipiency question.

E. *Weighting*

The economies that a merger produces are usually limited strictly to the combining firms. But the market power effects of a merger may sometimes result in a price increase across a wider class of firms. Where this occurs, a weighting factor should be introduced into expression (2) to reflect this condition. The criterion becomes

$$\left(\frac{Q_2}{Q_T}\right) \frac{\Delta(\text{AC})}{\text{AC}} - \frac{1}{2} \eta \frac{Q_1}{Q_2} \left(\frac{\Delta P}{P_1}\right)^2 > 0 \qquad (2')$$

where Q_2 is the output of the merging firms and Q_T is the total quantity of industry sales for which the price increase becomes effective.

---

[9] This is George Stigler's point in his treatment of 'Monopoly and Oligopoly by Merger' [28]. Bork concedes this possibility in his response to Blake and Jones ([7] p. 412); but his principal emphasis, which is probably correct, is that a trend signals emerging economies.

F. *Income distribution*

An additional qualification to our analysis involves income distribution effects. The rectangle in Fig. 7.1 bounded by P_2 and P_1 at the top and bottom respectively and O and Q_2 on the sides represents a loss of consumers' surplus (gain in monopoly profits) that the merger produces. On the resource allocation criteria for judging welfare effects advanced above, the distribution of these profits becomes a matter of indifference. For specific welfare valuations, however, we might not always wish to regard consumer and producer interests symmetrically – although since, arguably, antitrust is an activity better suited to promote allocative efficiency than income distribution objectives (the latter falling more clearly within the province of taxation, expenditure, and transfer payment activities), such income distribution adjustments might routinely be suppressed. If they are not, the tradeoff between efficiency gains and distributive losses needs explicitly to be expressed. Thus, while economies would remain a defense, any undesirable income distribution effects associated with market power would be counted against the merger rather than enter neutrally as the naïve model implies.

Inasmuch as the income redistribution which occurs is usually large relative to the size of the dead-weight loss, attaching even a slight weight to income distribution effects can sometimes influence the overall valuation significantly. Thus, expressing the dead-weight loss ($L = \frac{1}{2} (\Delta P) (\Delta Q)$) as a ratio of the income distribution effect ($I = (\Delta P)Q$), and substituting into this ratio the expression for the elasticity of demand (η), the fraction $L/I = \frac{1}{2}(\Delta P/P) \eta$ obtains. It is therefore obvious that, except where the elasticity of demand is 'high', the dead-weight loss as a fraction of the income distribution effect is relatively small – certainly less than unity. Hence if, as is probably common, the income redistribution which results when market power is increased is regarded unfavorably, an appropriate weighting of this factor will, at least occasionally, upset a net valuation which on resource allocation grounds is positive.

Note in this connection that the transfer involved could be regarded unfavorably not merely because it redistributes income in an undesirable way (increases the degree of inequality in the size distribution of income), but also because it produces social discontent. This latter has serious efficiency implications that the above analysis does not take explicitly into account.

This same point also appears to have gone unnoticed in the entire Bork and Bowman v. Blake and Jones exchange [3] [4] [6] [7]. Distinguishing social from private costs in this respect may, however, be the most fundamental reason for treating claims of private efficiency gains skeptically.

G. *Political considerations*

Combinations which involve firms that are already very large in absolute terms might be resisted on grounds that these raise extra-economic problems of political significance. There is not, however, any obvious way in which to integrate these into the analysis. Rather, although the political implications of control over wealth are a matter for serious concern, these are separable from the economic problems posed by control over markets; a different calculus is required to deal with each. The necessary political judgment, ideally, is one for Congress to make. Possibly, as Carl Kaysen has suggested, this would take the form of a prohibition against expansion by merger of the largest 50 or 100 corporations ([20] p. 37).

The issue here reaches beyond the social discontent matter raised above. Thus, whereas social discontent can be reduced, in principle at least, to efficiency-equivalent (net value product) terms, the political implications of the control over wealth involve a judgment of how the quality of life in a democracy is affected by size disparities. The latter is less easily (or even appropriately) expressed in efficiency terms. The issue is nevertheless important, and failure to deal with it may be unresponsive to the position taken by Blake and Jones. Inasmuch as several of the counterexamples that they pose in their critique of Bork and Bowman appear deliberately to have been selected from the giant firm universe ([4] pp. 425–7), possibly it is mergers within this subset that concern them most. Should economies be allowed as a defense, therefore, the rule proposed by Kaysen would limit such a defense in a way which would presumably relieve this aspect of their concern.

H. *Technological progress; and*
I. *Managerial discretion*

The highly conjectural nature of qualifications H and I makes it unclear at this time what weight ought to be assigned to them. It is at least arguable that the prevailing uncertainties are too great to give any effect to these two factors at this time. They are, nevertheless, potentially of such significance that to dismiss them may run the risk of serious error. In consideration of this potential importance, additional research which would permit us better to evaluate their actual significance would seem warranted. The manner in which each would influence the estimate of net effects is sketched out below.

Consider technological progress first. Such increases in market power that result in predictable effects on technological progress should, if they can easily, be taken into account. The present evidence, while hardly abundant, suggests that, as a general rule, the research and development expenditures of the four largest firms in an industry are neither as large proportionately nor as productive as those of their immediately smaller rivals.[10] But this fails to answer the question of what market structures most enhance progressiveness. The evidence on this latter is somewhat mixed.[11] It seems unlikely, however, that subsequent investigation will upset the basic proposition that progressiveness is promoted by at least some elements of competition at virtually every stage of an industry's development – if for no other reason than that competition tends to assure that variety in research approaches will be employed. Local or

[10] With respect to size, Mansfield found that the ratio of innovations to firm size reached a maximum at about the sixth largest firm for the petroleum and coal industries, and at a much lower rank for steel ([24] p. 566). Elsewhere Mansfield reports that the largest firms in petroleum, drugs, and glass spent somewhat less on R. & D., relative to sales, than did somewhat smaller firms; in chemicals they spent somewhat more; in steel they spent less, but the difference was not statistically significant ([25] p. 334). Scherer concludes from his study of patent behavior in a group of 448 firms selected from the Fortune list of the largest 500 industrial corporations in 1955 that 'the evidence does not support the hypothesis that corporate bigness is especially favorable to high inventive output' ([27] p. 1114). Turning to productivity, Mansfield concludes that 'in most industries, the productivity of an R. & D. program of given scale seems to be lower in the largest firms than in somewhat smaller firms' ([24] p. 338). Comanor found that diseconomies of scale in the pharmaceutical industry were encountered at even moderate firm sizes ([11] p. 190). For a recent review of this literature, see Johnson ([18] pp. 169–71).

[11] Hamburg ([16] chap. 4) and Horowitz ([17] pp. 330–1) report a positive correlation between R. & D. expenditures and industrial concentration. Scherer finds a much weaker but slightly positive association ([27] pp. 1119–21). Kendrick concludes from an examination of Terleckyj's data that there is no significant correlation between productivity changes and industrial concentration ([22] p. 179). Stigler found in an earlier study 'hints that industries with lower concentration had higher rates of technological progress' ([30] p. 278), while I, using Mansfield's data, found a negative correlation between the proportion of innovations introduced by the four largest firms and industrial concentration [34].

regional monopolies may provide partial exceptions (since here the requisite variety will be available nationally, although the rate at which innovations are implemented may nevertheless lag if competitive pressures are lacking), but monopoly, or near-monopoly, would not seem to be the perfect instrument for technical progress in industries for which the relevant market is national.

Lacking additional evidence, it would not seem injudicious to assume that mergers between relatively small-sized firms rarely have negative (and may frequently have positive) effects on progressiveness, whatever the condition of concentration. This judgment probably holds for most mergers involving lower-middle sized firms as well. Thus it is mainly in the relatively large firms, particularly those in moderately to highly concentrated national markets (which, of course, are also ones where market power effects may be important), that the effects of a merger on technological progress deserve special attention.

Whether the effects be positive or negative, the necessary extension to the model is identical. Assume therefore that a merger is proposed involving a large firm in a concentrated industry, and that while it yields economies it also predictably decreases the rate of progressiveness. Holding constant for the moment the effects on price, how large a change in the rate of technical progress would be required to offset the available economy of scale advantage? To obtain a crude estimate of this, let θ be the ratio of the immediate post-merger to pre-merger average costs (so that $1 - \theta$ is the immediate decimal fraction reduction in average costs), g_1 be the rate of productivity increase in the absence of the merger and g_2 the rate if the merger is approved (where $g_1 \geq g_2$), $Q(t)$ be the output in period t, and let r be the social discount rate. Then the merger will have neutral effects if the discounted value of costs under each condition is the same. This requires that the equality given below should hold:[12]

$$\int_0^\infty [(\mathrm{AC})Q(t)e^{-g_1 t}]e^{-rt}dt = \int_0^\infty [\theta(\mathrm{AC})Q(t)e^{-g_2 t}]e^{-rt}dt. \qquad (6)$$

[12] The argument assumes that only the yield and not the expenditures on R. & D. are affected by the combination. Although any expenditure difference could go either way, one would expect in general that the higher rate of progress would be associated with a higher expenditure stream, in which case the indicated allocative advantage associated with the more progressive structure would be correspondingly reduced.

Assuming that output increases exponentially at the rate δ, the critical value of g_2 is given by

$$g_2 = \theta g_1 - (1 - \theta)(r - \delta). \qquad (7)$$

If, for example, the values of θ, g_1, and $r - \delta$ were 0·90, 0·03, and 0·07 respectively, the critical value of g_2 would be 0·02. Were g_2 to fall below this value, an indicated economy of 10 per cent would not be sufficient to offset the cumulative productivity loss associated with the merger, to say nothing of the market power effects that the merger produces. If indeed the selected values of g_1 and $r - \delta$ are at all representative, a predictable decrease in the rate of productivity advance by one-third or more would thus be sufficient to disallow a merger for which an efficiency advantage as large as 10 per cent could be expected.[13]

Consider now the managerial discretion argument. Here the direction of the effect is not so much a matter for dispute as is its quantitative significance. The argument is that market power provides a firm with the opportunity to pursue a variety of other-than-profit objectives. Although this is an 'old' argument, its persistence at least suggests the possibility that it may not be without merit.[14] Whether qualitatively there is anything to it turns essentially on the behavioral proposition that where competition in the product market presents no significant threat to survival, the resources of the firm are absorbed in part as corporate consumption activities by those members of the firm who are knowledgeable of discretionary opportunities, powerfully situated, and disposed to be assertive [33, 36]. Its quantitative significance rests on a judgment over whether the conspicuous evidence is sufficiently strong.[15]

If indeed a predictable relaxation in the least-cost posture of a

[13] If the beneficial economies of scale are available only to the combining firms, while the negative progressiveness effects are felt throughout the industry, the above results underestimate the extent of economies necessary to produce indifference.

[14] As Arthur Hadley observed in 1897, 'The tendency of monopoly to retard the introduction of industrial improvement is . . . a more serious thing than its tendency to allow unfair rates. This aspect of the matter has hardly received proper attention. We have been so accustomed to think of competition as a regulator of prices that we have lost sight of its equally important function as a stimulus to efficiency. Wherever competition is absent, there is a disposition to rest content with old methods, not to say slack ones. In spite of notable exceptions this is clearly the rule' ([15] p. 383).

[15] This presently is the weakest part of the argument. For a recent survey of the data, see [23].

firm which has acquired market power through merger can be made, the estimated cost savings that appear in equation (5) should be adjusted accordingly. Economies which are available in theory but, by reason of market power, are not sustainable are inadmissible.

3. Extensions

Although the foregoing analysis has been concerned exclusively with horizontal mergers, the argument applies generally to problems in which market power–efficiency tradeoffs exist. Dissolution, vertical mergers, and conglomerate mergers can all be treated within this general framework.

A. *Dissolution*

The argument here is perfectly straightforward. It is simply not sufficient in a monopolization case for which dissolution is the indicated relief that (1) a persistent monopoly condition $(P_1 > AC_1)$ exist, and (2) a reduction in price following dissolution $(P_2 < P_1)$ be expected. It is necessary in addition that the gains realized by the price reduction be sufficient to offset any losses in economies that result. The relevant test is that shown in equation (3) – modified, as may be necessary, by the qualifications discussed in section 2 above.

B. *Vertical mergers*

It is important to note in dealing with vertical mergers that the conventional analysis of vertical integration, which takes a historical definition of an industry as given, often leads to incorrect results. The logical boundaries of a firm are not necessarily those which have been inherited but rather are defined by the condition that the firm be unable to arrange a transaction internally more cheaply than the market.[16] This is not something which is given once-for-all but depends both on technology and the extent of the market. Thus what may be regarded as 'vertical integration' under a historical definition of an industry might, in many instances, more accurately be

---

[16] As Ronald Coase has pointed out, 'a firm will tend to expand until the costs of organizing an extra transaction within the firm become equal to the costs of carrying out the same transaction by means of an exchange on the open market or the costs of organizing in another firm' ([10] p. 341).

characterized as a reorganization into a more efficient configuration. For example, as technology evolves processes that are
more fully automated or as demand for a commodity increases
sufficiently to warrant continuous processing techniques, com-
binatorial economies may result by serially linking activities
within a single firm that had previously been done in separate
specialty firms.[17] A transformation of this sort accomplished in
part through vertical mergers is probably common in the
production of commodities which shift from sequential job shop
to continuous assembly line type operations.

That vertical integration can produce real economies is a
result of the fact that the market does not perform its exchanges
costlessly. Going to the market involves search costs, contracting
costs, misinformation costs, delay costs, transfer costs, interface
costs, etc.,[18] and these must be balanced against the costs of
organizing a transaction internally. Where the former exceed
the latter, 'vertical integration' is indicated. But of course this
is vertical integration in only an apparent sense: in fact it
represents a rationalization of the firm into an optimum economic unit.

The historical organization of an industry can ordinarily be
presumed to reflect adequately basic efficiencies where significant market or technological developments have been lacking. And even where such recent changes have occurred, an
efficiency defense is not automatic. Furthermore, if an efficiency
defense can be supplied, any market power consequences that a
vertical merger produces need also to be considered.[19] Again
the basic tradeoff calculation is that given by equation (3) –
modified as necessary by the qualifications discussed in section
2.

[17] Stigler argues that increasing the extent of the market will often lead to dis-
integration of manufacturing processes since now the market will be sufficient to
support a specialized firm ([29] pp. 188–90). Although this may often occur,
there is also the countervailing tendency to maintain or extend integration where
coordination among the parts in the face of market uncertainties is critical – as it
often is where assembly line operations are employed. See Coase ([10] p. 337).

[18] Coase discusses some of these ([10] pp. 336–7). (For an early example in which
the costs of going to the market were examined in a common law proceeding,
see *Hadley* v. *Baxendale*.) In addition, if suppliers possess market power, going to
the market may involve pecuniary expenses that could be avoided by integrating
backward into supply activities.

[19] Stigler identifies barriers to entry that take the form of increased capital and/
or knowledge requirements as potential anticompetitive consequences of a vertical
merger ([29] p. 191).

C. *Conglomerate mergers*

The principal ways in which conglomerate mergers can produce efficiencies have been given previously by M. A. Adelman ([1] pp. 241–2] and Turner ([31] pp. 1323–39, 1358–61). The ways in which conglomerate mergers may produce market power are also discussed by Turner.[20] All that remains, essentially, is to deal with the tradeoff question. Again the rules for estimating net benefits are substantially those given above.

4. Conclusions

Most mergers produce neither significant price nor efficiency consequences, and where this is true the analysis of this paper has limited relevance. Where both occur, however, and if without merger the transition to an efficient industrial configuration is apt to be both painful and delayed, an efficiency defense deserves consideration. This does not of course mean that the mere existence of economies is sufficient to justify a merger. But since a relatively large percentage increase in price is usually required to offset the benefits that result from a 5 to 10 per cent reduction in average costs, the existence of economies of this magnitude is sufficiently important to give the antitrust authorities pause before disallowing such a merger.

There are, however, as indicated in section 2, a variety of qualifications that may upset this general conclusion in any particular case. The argument, thus, is not dispositive; a crude feel for the quantitative significance of the relevant factors is all that can be claimed.[21]

[20] For a more recent treatment of the economies and market power effects of conglomerate organization, see [37].

[21] Moreover, the argument does not pretend to be exhaustive. Product variety considerations, for example, have been suppressed: any predictable change in product variety attributable to the merger should appropriately be reflected in the welfare valuation. Inasmuch, however, as product variety changes could go either way (an increase or decrease in product variety is possible), since neither is apt to be evident *ex ante*, and as such effects as do obtain are likely to be small, it seems reasonable to proceed, for the present at least, as though product variety will remain unchanged. This is the usual, if implicit, assumption in most welfare loss valuations. For a recent contribution to the product differentiation literature that might, were the matter to be regarded as operationally significant, eventually be brought to bear on these issues, see [38].

F

REFERENCES

[1] M. A. ADELMAN, 'The Antimerger Act, 1950–60', *American Economic Review, Papers and Proceedings*, LI (May 1961) 236–44.

[2] J. BAIN, *Barriers to New Competition* (Cambridge, Mass., 1956).

[3] H. M. BLAKE and W. K. JONES, 'In Defense of Antitrust', *Columbia Law Review*, LXV (Mar 1965) 377–400.

[4] —— and ——, 'Toward a Three-Dimensional Antitrust Policy', *Columbia Law Review*, LXV (Mar 1965) 422–66.

[5] D. C. BOK, 'Section 7 of the Clayton Act and the Merging of Law and Economics', *Harvard Law Review* (Dec 1960) 226–355.

[6] R. H. BORK and W. S. BOWMAN, 'The Crisis in Antitrust', *Columbia Law Review*, LXV (Mar 1965) 363–76.

[7] R. H. BORK, 'Contrasts in Antitrust Theory: I', *Columbia Law Review*, LXV (Mar 1965) 401–16.

[8] ——, 'The Rule of Reason and the Per Se Concept: Price Fixing and Market Division, II', *Yale Law Journal* (Jan 1966) 375–475.

[9] *Brown Shoe* v. *United States*, 370 U.S. 294 (1962).

[10] R. H. COASE, 'The Nature of the Firm', *Economica*, n.s., IV (1937) 386–485. Reprinted in G. J. Stigler and K. E. Boulding (eds.) *Readings in Price Theory* (Homewood, Ill., 1952) 331–51.

[16] W. S. COMANOR, 'Research and Technical Change in the Pharmaceutical Industry', *Review of Economics and Statistics*, XLVII (May 1965) 182–90.

[12] D. DEWEY, 'Mergers and Cartels: Some Reservations about Policy', *American Economic Review, Papers and Proceedings*, LI (May 1961) 255–62.

[13] *Federal Trade Commission* v. *Procter & Gamble Co.*, 87 S. Ct. 1224 (1967).

[14] C. E. FERGUSON, *A Macroeconomic Theory of Workable Competition* (Durham, N. C., 1964).

[15] A. T. HADLEY, 'The Good and Evil of Industrial Combination', *Atlantic Monthly*, LXXIX (Mar 1897) 377–85.

[16] D. HAMBURG, *R. & D.: Essays on the Economics of Research and Development* (New York, 1966).

[17] I. HOROWITZ, 'Firm Size and Research Activity', *Southern Economic Journal*, XXVIII (Jan 1962) 298–301.

[18] R. E. JOHNSON, 'Technical Progress and Innovation', *Oxford Economic Papers*, XVIII (July 1966) 158–76.

[19] C. KAYSEN and D. F. TURNER, *Antitrust Policy: An Economic and Legal Analysis* (Cambridge, Mass., 1959).

[20] C. KAYSEN, 'The Present War on Bigness: I', in *The Impact of Antitrust on Economic Growth*, Fourth National Industrial Conference Board Conference on Antitrust in an Expanding Economy (New York, 1965) pp. 31–8.

[21] ——, 'Models and Decision-Makers: Economists and the Policy Process', *Public Interest* (summer 1968) 80–95.

[22] J. W. KENDRICK, *Productivity Trends in the United States* (Princeton, 1961).

[23] H. LEIBENSTEIN, 'Allocative Efficiency versus "X-Efficiency"', *American Economic Review*, LVI (June 1966) 392–415.

[24] E. Mansfield, 'Size of Firms, Market Structure, and Innovation', *Journal of Political Economy*, LXXI (Dec 1963) 556–76.

[25] ——, 'Industrial Research and Development Expenditures: Determinants, Prospects, and Relation to Size of Firm and Inventive Output', *Journal of Political Economy*, LXXII (Aug 1964) 319–40.

[26] J. W. Markham, 'Survey of the Evidence and Findings on Mergers', in *Business Concentration and Price Policy* (Princeton, 1955) pp. 141–82.

[27] F. M. Scherer, 'Firm Size, Market Structure, Opportunity, and the Output of Patented Inventions', *American Economic Review*, LV (Dec 1965) 1097–1125.

[28] G. J. Stigler, 'Monopoly and Oligopoly by Merger', *American Economic Review, Papers and Proceedings*, XL (May 1950) 23–4, reprinted in R. B. Heflebower and G. W. Stocking (eds.), *Readings in Industrial Organization* (Homewood, Ill., 1958) pp. 69–80.

[29] ——, 'The Division of Labor is Limited by the Extent of the Market', *Journal of Political Economy*, LIX (June 1951) 185–93.

[30] ——, 'Industrial Organization and Economic Progress', in L. D. White (ed.), *The State of the Social Sciences* (Chicago, 1956) pp. 269–82.

[31] D. F. Turner, 'Conglomerate Mergers and Section 7 of the Clayton Act', *Harvard Law Review*, LXXVIII (May 1965) 1313–95.

[32] *United States* v. *Philadelphia National Bank*, 374 U.S. 312 (1963).

[33] O. E. Williamson, *The Economics of Discretionary Behavior: Managerial Objectives in a Theory of the Firm* (Englewood Cliffs, N. J., 1964).

[34] ——, 'Innovation and Market Structure', *Journal of Political Economy*, LXXIII (Feb 1965) 67–73.

[35] ——, 'Hierarchical Control and Optimum Firm Size', *Journal of Political Economy*, LXXV (Apr 1967) 123–38.

[36] ——, 'A Dynamic-Stochastic Theory of Managerial Behavior', in A. Phillips and O. E. Williamson (eds.), *Prices: Issues in Theory, Practice and Public Policy* (Philadelphia, 1967) pp. 11–31.

[37] ——, *Corporate Control and Business Behavior* (Englewood Cliffs, N. J., 1970).

[38] J. C. G. Wright, 'Products and Welfare', *Australian Economic Papers* (Dec 1969).

8 Anti-Trust Policy: Economics versus Management Science[1]

M. A. Crew and C. K. Rowley

Neo-classical economic theory taught that the state is justified in taking action against trusts or monopolies, because they artificially raise prices and thus cause a loss to consumers.[2]

This doctrine, however, has recently been challenged, at least in its unambiguous form, by O. E. Williamson,[3] who points out that an increase in size resulting from a merger can give economies of scale, which might result in lower costs of production. Yet more recently, on the other hand, W. S. Comanor and H. Leibenstein[4] have pointed out that the loss to the welfare of the community from a monopoly might be even greater than the loss arising from higher monopoly prices because of the loss of efficiency by the monopoly due to lack of competition – what Leibenstein calls a reduction in 'X-efficiency'.[5] This concept of 'X-efficiency' is new to economics, but has long been present implicitly or explicitly in the literature of management science[6] which has always been concerned with helping firms to reduce costs by using their

[1] We are very grateful to Maxwell Stamp for his helpful suggestions which have added considerably to the clarity of the paper.

[2] Neo-classical theory always recognised the possibility of natural monopoly in which the existence of overwhelming scale economies presaged the breakdown of competition. Examples of natural monopolies include bridges and public utilities.

[3] O. E. Williamson, 'Economies as an Antitrust Defense', pp. 111–35 above.

[4] W. S. Comanor and H. Leibenstein, 'Allocative Efficiency, X-Efficiency and the Measurement of Welfare Losses', pp. 23–9 above. For a further development see M. A. Crew and C. K. Rowley, 'On Allocative Efficiency, X-Efficiency and the Measurement of Welfare Losses', *Economica*, n.s., xxxviii (May 1971) 199–203.

[5] H. Leibenstein, 'Allocative Efficiency vs. X-Efficiency', *American Economic Review*, lvi (June 1966) 392–415.

[6] A good example of the management science approach is provided by W. W. Cooper, 'A Proposal for Extending the Theory of the Firm', *Quarterly Journal of Economics*, lxv (Feb 1951) 87–109.

Reprinted from *Moorgate and Wall Street* (autumn 1970) pp. 19–34, by kind permission of the authors and of the editor.

resources more efficiently, and thus always interested in factors making for inefficiency.

This paper considers anti-trust policy in the light of these considerations. Since the values – the social priorities – of authors and readers may differ, the paper sets out the specific set of value assumptions used. This paper considers the classic case for controlling monopolies, Williamson's 'trade-off' approach, the problem of reduced efficiency in monopolies, and the problems and costs[7] of introducing and implementing alternative types of control in the light of one specific example recently before the British Monopolies Commission.[8] And finally the authors' views are outlined on a policy for controlling monopolies, near monopolies, or cartels.

One of the most difficult problems in discussing matters of this nature is to distinguish clearly between conclusions which arise out of the economic analysis and conclusions which arise out of the value judgements of the arguer. This makes life particularly difficult for non-economists who cannot be expected to be *au fait* with the intricacies of welfare economics, and partly accounts for the suspicion with which economics is regarded by the non-economist. To minimize this difficulty it is necessary to set out clearly the value judgements of the authors, so that the reader can see whether he agrees or disagrees with them, and thus whether he takes issue with the authors – if he does – on grounds of fact and interpretation or because his values are different.

The relevant value judgements in this case form a so-called 'social welfare function', which is concerned with maximizing the net gains that consumers receive together with any gains derived by producers from cost savings,[9] so that benefits received by producers are given the same importance in our

[7] For an analysis of transaction costs see H. Demsetz, 'The Exchange and Enforcement of Property Rights', pp. 88–107 above. See also H. Demsetz, 'Toward a Theory of Property Rights', *American Economic Review*, LVII (May 1967) 347–59.

[8] The Monopolies Commission, *A Report on the Proposed Merger between Barclays Bank Ltd, Lloyds Bank Ltd, and Martins Bank Ltd* (July 1968, H.C.P. 319).

[9] More precisely, the social welfare function to be maximised in this paper is $W = TR + S - TC$ where $W =$ net welfare gain, $TR =$ total revenue, $S =$ consumers' surplus, and $TC =$ total cost. This approach has been used with insight by O. E. Williamson, both op. cit. and also in 'Peak-Load Pricing and Optimal Capital under Indivisibility Constraints', *American Economic Review*, LVI (1) (Sep 1966) 810–27.

scale of desirability as benefits received by consumers. Where intervention would increase benefits received by consumers, whilst diminishing benefits received by producers (or vice versa), the net effect (appropriately valued) must determine whether or not it should be encouraged. This is a very important assumption since it implies that the income redistribution consequences of an anti-trust policy (be it as between separate consumers, or as between consumers and producers) are ignored and attention is centred only upon aggregate benefits irrespective of who receives them. Anti-trust policy is not viewed as an efficient instrument for income redistribution and for this reason the problem of income redistribution consequences of anti-trust is assumed to be resolved elsewhere within the system, presumably via the fiscal policy of central government.[10] In other words, the case for anti-trust policy is viewed exclusively in efficiency terms whilst equity aspects are suppressed. Readers who disapprove of this decision may well find themselves at odds with the policy conclusions of this paper even though they remain convinced of the validity of the analysis.

Neo-classical Economics and the Case for Anti-trust

Neo-classical theory assumes that firms aim to maximize profits in the light of a constant and known technology and that in so doing they will combine the resources which they use efficiently so that costs are minimized for any selected rate of output. On this basis, it is easy to demonstrate that social welfare (in the sense previously defined) is maximized when conditions equivalent to perfect competition are approximated in which there is no divergence between price and marginal cost.[11] For in such circumstances, there is no loss of consumer benefits which must always arise under monopoly where prices are higher than marginal cost so that some consumption is prevented because of 'artificially' high prices. Anti-trust policy

[10] See O. E. Williamson, 'Allocative Efficiency and the Limits of Antitrust', *American Economic Review*, LIX (May 1969) 108: 'Macroeconomic policy instruments (taxes, transfers, expenditures) with which to correct distributional conditions are not only available but are superior to the use of antitrust for this purpose.'

[11] For a discussion of some problems in this approach, however, see R. A. Berry, 'A Note on Welfare Comparisons between Monopoly and Pure Competition', pp. 3–22 above.

may be viewed, in such circumstances, as an unambiguously appropriate device for improving social welfare by replacing monopoly by competition. In this way, neo-classical economics provided a useful theoretical underpinning for anti-trust policy of the kind provided (at least in principle) by the U.S.A. since 1890, and constituted a standing rebuke to countries such as the United Kingdom which operated at most a half-hearted, inconsistent policy of anti-trust intervention.[12]

Scale Economies and Anti-trust: The Trade-off Approach

Professor O. E. Williamson formalized a challenge to the neo-classical approach to anti-trust policy, which was already implicit in the public policy literature, but in an imprecise and somewhat non-operational form, namely the scale economies defence against anti-trust-enforced competition. Although Williamson's argument was designed explicitly with preventive anti-trust policy (more specifically merger regulation) in mind, it has obvious extensions to the field of corrective anti-trust policy (for example dissolving existing monopolies). Williamson's model was designed to apply only to mergers which would simultaneously provide market power and scale economies for the resulting combination, i.e. to a very small minority of actual mergers almost always involving horizontal integration.

In such circumstances, Williamson demonstrated that a trade-off was required between the loss of consumer benefits resulting from the market-power-induced increase in price and the cost savings arising from the larger scale of activity of the combined unit. He clearly indicated that in the usual case the cost savings would easily outweigh the loss of consumer benefits,[13] with the implication (given the social welfare function

[12] The Sherman Act (1890) and subsequent U.S. anti-trust legislation was motivated as much by public distrust of political as of economic power, a distrust which is reflected more generally in the U.S. constitutional emphasis upon the separation of powers. For a discussion of the inconsistency of British monopoly policy during the period 1964–68 see C. K. Rowley, 'Monopoly in Britain: Private Vice but Public Virtue?', *Moorgate and Wall Street* (autumn 1968).

[13] Williamson introduced an index of pre-merger market power, K. The cost reductions necessary to offset the price increases for various values of price elasticity of demand are based on the assumption that $K = 1$, i.e. that pre-merger market power is zero. Obviously, this is not always the case, and K may often be greater than 1. Price equals $K.AC$ in the pre-merger situation.

outlined above – that a gain to the producer is as important as a gain to the consumer) that the merger should be allowed to proceed. For example, where the price elasticity of demand for the product is $\frac{1}{2}$, a 2·1 per cent reduction in costs would be sufficient to offset a price increase of 30 per cent subsequent upon the merger. Even with relatively high price elasticities of demand of the order of 1 to 2, the corresponding cost reductions for a price increase of 30 per cent would only be 4·5 per cent and 10·35 per cent respectively. This indeed is a remarkable result, for it implies that where a merger offers almost any level of scale economies with certainty it should be allowed to proceed. Anti-merger legislation is thus presented in an especially unfavourable light. Williamson himself advanced certain qualifications, however, to this strong policy conclusion.

Firstly, significant economies of scale (where available) would be realized eventually in the absence of merger at least in markets subjected to a secular growth in demand, by the internal expansion in size of individual companies without any corresponding increase in market power. In such circumstances, the 'deadweight' loss to consumers from the merger could be avoided simply by postponing the cost savings due to scale. A more complicated procedure of discounting future costs and benefits would then be required before comparing the 'deadweight' consumer loss with the cost savings due to the merger reduced by the present value of future cost savings resulting from internal expansion in the absence of merger. This qualification obviously is inappropriate in the case of a static or a declining market.

Secondly, there may in practice be time lags between the completion of the merger and the achievement of the eventual cost–benefit consequences, in which case a fully fledged discounting procedure in any event would be necessary. In so far as the price adjustments are more quickly achievable than the cost savings any positive discount rate would weaken the 'economies of scale' defence against anti-trust action. There is good reason to believe that this would be the typical case.

Thirdly, in assessing the likely degree of market power, due regard would be necessary for the possibility that the merger in question might trigger off secondary merger movements within the affected market with positive or negative market power consequences. Once again, the magnitude and timing of any such chain reaction strictly should be taken into consideration in the trade-off evaluation.

Fourthly, the impact of a merger upon technological progress in practice might be anything but neutral, and evidently this should be accounted for in the trade-off process. Such econometric evidence as is available suggests that competition is conducive to technological progress and that medium-sized firms are more progressive than giant firms in this respect. If this evidence is accepted the anti-merger case is strengthened, but more research is clearly necessary before great confidence can be placed in this particular argument.

Finally, in a brief but insightful section of his article, Williamson recognized that the management of a post-merger combination might take advantage of the market power thereby provided to pursue a variety of non-profit objectives. He failed to pursue the implications of this outcome, which is a pity since, as will be shown, they have considerable relevance for anti-trust policy, but, as the following passage illustrates, he came very close indeed to incorporating the X-inefficiency concept into his anti-trust trade-off analysis:

> If indeed a predictable relaxation in the least-cost posture of a firm which has acquired market power through merger can be made, the estimated cost savings . . . should be adjusted accordingly. Economies which are available in theory but, by reason of market power, are not sustainable are inadmissible.[14]

Once the possibility of economies of scale is admitted the economic approach to anti-trust policy is no longer unambiguous and a quite complex trade-off analysis appears necessary, at least when the relevant qualifications to Williamson's introductory model are admitted. But this is by no means the end of the story. For at this point management science offers an important contribution which disturbs the entire emphasis of Williamson's message and (oddly enough) provides countervailing support for the conclusions (though not the rationale) of neo-classical economic theory.

[14] Williamson, 'Economies as an Antitrust Defense', pp. 130–1 above.

X-Inefficiency and Anti-trust: The Contribution of Management Science

Despite Williamson's important contribution there can be little doubt that economic analysis has continued to provide an unrealistic approach to the problem of anti-trust policy, largely because it ignored the problem of technical and managerial efficiency as a basis for theoretical developments. The difference in this respect between economic and management science is highlighted by John P. Shelton's caricature:

> It is interesting to consider that this possible distortion in economic theory parallels and may help to explain the sometimes noted schism between university economics departments and business schools. The economics department tends to assume that firms operate on their most efficient production surface so the only issue is one of allocative efficiency; business schools on the other hand emphasise the need to increase efficiency within the firm.[15]

In part, no doubt, the reliance of economic theory upon the prior existence of technical and managerial efficiency is a direct product of the preoccupation of neo-classical economics with competitive markets. For competition in its keenest form ensures that the surviving firms are those which are the most efficient and have sought to maximize their profits through producing at minimum cost. In this sense, competition may be viewed as a costless policing mechanism (at least from the viewpoint of surviving firms) to ensure efficiency. However, the anti-trust problem is the problem of markets characterised by the *absence* of keen competition and it is precisely for this reason that standard neo-classical analysis is inappropriate, and that management science has been called in to the rescue. It is of some interest to note that Professor O. E. Williamson[16] himself implicitly mounted an attack on the principle of cost minimization in a 'management discretion' theory of the firm, which recognized explicitly the divorce between ownership and control in the modern industrial system.

[15] J. P. Shelton, 'Allocative Efficiency vs. X-Efficiency: Comment', *American Economic Review*, LVII (Dec 1967) 1253.

[16] O. E. Williamson, *The Economics of Discretionary Behavior: Managerial Objectives in the Theory of the Firm* (Prentice-Hall, 1964).

The concept of 'X-inefficiency·, introduced to economics by Professor Harvey Leibenstein, has provided the basis for a more thorough-going revision of the economic approach to anti-trust policy which does not require the abandonment of the profit maximization postulate of neo-classical theory.

The 'X-theory' of the firm[17] retains the profit maximization postulate but rejects the inference that costs are always mini-mized in situations of market power, on the ground that labour is not a factor input similar to capital that can be used passively in the production process. In practice, labour (both shopfloor and management) tends to seek goals, such as leisure, an easy life, security, maximum income, which are at odds with those of the enterprise which are mainly to maximize its profits. Under competitive conditions, labour is assumed to be forced to co-operate fully. But where market power exists the enterprise must decide whether or not to devote policing resources (in the guise of management consultants, works study experts, foremen and gatekeepers) as a means of improving the X-efficiency of labour. The minimum costs of neo-classical theory could never be achieved except via competition since policing costs expended have to be added to the normal costs of production and distribution. In so far as labour may tend to co-operate less as the firm's market power increases an anti-trust policy reducing that market power would tend to lower a firm's costs, and in the limit (represented by pure competition) X-inefficiency would be entirely eliminated.

The shift to competition induced by an anti-trust policy itself would take time and in the interim elements of X-inefficiency would continue to exist. Government no doubt could accelerate the process of cost reduction by such methods as redundancy payments, tariff reductions and improving the market in information. By contrast, Government policy in the recent past has been successful in increasing X-inefficiency by means of such policies as the bailing out of failing enterprises (e.g. shipbuilding) in response to regional and other pressure group considerations.

What then are the implications of X-inefficiency for anti-trust policy? The consumer net benefits from consuming would

[17] See M. A. Crew, M. Jones-Lee and C. K. Rowley, 'X-Theory versus Management Discretion Theory', *Southern Economic Journal*, xxxviii (Oct 1971) 173–84.

remain as a positive gain from an anti-trust policy and the economies of scale thereby sacrificed would remain as an off-setting loss. But cost savings derived from a reduction in X-inefficiency would provide additional reasons for an anti-trust policy and in so far as these outweighed the economies of scale the unambiguous case for an anti-trust policy which was weakened by Williamson's trade-off analysis would be re-established and, indeed, perhaps reinforced. Casual evidence of an international flavour referred to by Harvey Leibenstein[18] suggests that the possibilities of reducing costs by improvements in X-efficiency are considerable, whereas most recent evidence on the economies of scale indicates only moderate cost advantage for large-scale organization.[19] But more research is necessary before general conclusions are possible on this important trade-off problem.

The Transaction Costs of Pragmatism

At first blush, the reader may feel inclined to resort to a fully fledged trade-off approach to the problems posed by market power, perhaps of the kind adopted by the United Kingdom since 1948 when the Monopolies Commission was first constituted for this purpose, and there is little doubt about the support for this proposal that would be forthcoming from the 'cost–benefit analysis' wing of the economics profession since this indeed is their bread and butter. However, this cost–benefit approach is expensive and imprecise, and the costs of putting it into practice are likely to be heavy and have to be paid by someone. So the trade-off approach to market power and monopoly is by no means established as the most efficient means of dealing with the problem in practice.

Even if the qualifications posed by Williamson are ignored (and there is every reason why they should not be) the task of determining the extent and nature of the economies of scale and of the X-inefficiency which might be caused by a merger is monumental, not least because the measurement process almost always is hypothetical and comparative yardsticks non-existent. The information available from company accounts is almost

---

[18] Leibenstein, op. cit., pp. 397–406.

[19] See G. J. Stigler, 'The Economies of Scale', *Journal of Law and Economics*, I (Oct 1958) 54–71.

useless and yet there is probably no other alternative short of setting out upon a full-blooded model-building exercise. Such a task would be complex enough for the companies themselves, but well-nigh impossible for an outside investigating body with a roving commission and faced by hostile non-cooperation from those most able to provide assistance. Moreover, the econometric problems in identifying how much of the production of the combined organization would be demanded at various prices – the 'demand function' – would be immense; yet in the absence of such information the exact loss of consumer benefits from market power could not be estimated. There can be little doubt that the costs of a thorough efficiency audit of the kind required would far outweigh the expected benefits.[20] Yet in the absence of such an audit pragmatic investigation is a fraud, enabling the bureaucrats who man the investigatory body to indulge their own pet fantasies concerning the nature of the industrial system.

A revealing example of the practical implementation of the pragmatic approach and its inherent transaction cost limitations is provided by a brief examination of the proposed merger between Barclays Bank, Lloyds Bank and Martins Bank which was disallowed by the Board of Trade in 1968 following a contrary decision by the British Monopolies Commission.

The proposed merger would have provided a combine responsible for approximately 47 per cent of the gross deposits of the London clearing banks, but this overstates the effective market influence provided since the clearing banks accounted only for 64 per cent of total bank deposits in the United Kingdom in 1967. The Monopolies Commission felt unable to specify more precisely than this the extent to which consumer benefits might be jeopardized if the merger was allowed to proceed, though it concluded that 'the provision of finance is a more important influence throughout the whole economy than the provision of a particular material or of some individual service, because finance is an essential condition of obtaining any materials or services'.[21] On this basis, the loss of consumer benefits from the exercise of monopoly would be valued disproportionately in the trade-off analysis.

[20] For example, see C. K. Rowley, *The British Monopolies Commission* (Allen & Unwin, 1966) pp. 90–2.

[21] Op. cit., para. 216.

On the other hand, as the Commission noted, competition between clearing banks was not exactly keen at the time of investigation, partly as a result of the non-disclosure of their true profits and reserves and partly as a result of overt collusion in seeking deposits or in making advances, a limitation on price competition which was strongly supported by the Treasury, despite powerful criticism in 1967 from the National Board for Prices and Incomes.[22] In such circumstances, the precise magnitude (indeed the direction) of the market power implications of the merger could not be estimated. Hardly an auspicious start, this, to the merger inquiry!

The case in favour of the merger was centred, inevitably, upon scale economy considerations, both domestically and from an international viewpoint. The banks contended that 3,500 staff could be made redundant by the merger, whilst actually extending the geographical coverage of their combined activities, and that 475 sub-branches and 725 branches could be absorbed, together with ten years' growth of the resulting combined bank. Further cost savings were anticipated from the use of computers. The banks estimated that overall savings in running costs from these sources achievable within five to ten years would amount almost to £10 million a year. Savings of this order would be equivalent to 20 to 25 per cent of the current bank charges to customers, to some 5 per cent of the current level of income of the three banks, or to some 5 to 10 per cent of current running expenses. The basis for these estimates, as presented in the Report, was decidedly shaky.

The Commission's judgement on the scale issue predictably was one of questioning the magnitudes suggested, pruning for expected exaggeration, but providing no alternative evaluation of its own. If the reader leans to the view that this approach is the economics of religion, he has our sympathy, but what else could be expected in the time-period allotted for the inquiry? In the event, the Commission split decisively over the relevance of the scale issue, with a majority conclusion that the present value of expected cost savings was insignificant but with a substantial minority in dissent. The disagreement was one of interpretation and not one of fact.

On the other hand, the Commission in its majority report considered that competition within the clearing bank system

[22] N.B.P.I., *Bank Charges*, Report No. 34 (May 1967, Cmnd 3292).

would be weakened by the merger and that realised savings would on this account fall short of the estimated savings which, in principle, would be attainable. In this respect the Commission entirely endorsed the X-inefficiency theory of market power, as is evident from the following passage of the Report:

> More generally, the estimates of savings made possible by the mergers cannot make allowance for the possibility that the mergers might give rise to inefficiency in operations, which could persist undetected and be tolerated in the absence of strong competitive pressures impinging on the combined bank. . . . In the absence of strong competitive pressures or incentives, the tendency to defer or avoid difficult decisions which could lead to otherwise attainable savings might be expected to be present over a long period.[23]

Those (including the authors) who place any faith in the concept of X-inefficiency could scarcely deny the logic of the Commission's analysis. Unfortunately, the initial premise (that the merger would reduce competition) was in question as a result of inadequate market analysis. Indeed the minority dissent from the Commission's contrary judgement on the merger emphasized that competition within the limited range permitted by the existing system would be enhanced by the merger especially in the longer term. The Commission made no attempt to quantify the cost consequences of X-inefficiency, which perhaps is not surprising given the conflicting qualitative views of its members.

In terms of the evidence available to the Monopolies Commission a rational cost–benefit judgement on the merger clearly was impossible and the split decision was perhaps inevitable. Yet the bank merger case was one of the more efficiently researched of the Commission's merger investigations. If this was the best that a relatively well-organized, well-staffed and experienced investigatory body could produce, is there not good reason for calling into question the pragmatic approach of piecemeal investigation and substituting wherever possible rules for discretion in the approach to anti-trust policy?

A Policy Alternative

The complexity of the trade-off analysis, once scale and

[23] Op. cit., para. 251.

X-inefficiency aspects of market power are recognized, is such that the pragmatic approach to anti-trust policy almost certainly is too expensive to be economic. There are two simple alternatives worthy of consideration. ──

The first alternative is that of allowing unfettered market forces to determine the degree of market power to be accepted within the economy but of applying regulatory devices in the form of price controls to prevent excessive profits arising from monopolistic practices. In many ways, this approach is far from costless since expensive investigations into profits presumably would be required. Moreover, high profits are not only to be derived from market power, but are also a means by which resources are allocated between different claimants within a competitive market economy. (Firms which do well expand their business and bid resources away from firms which are relatively inefficient.) Resource misallocation of a serious nature may follow from indiscriminate price regulation. But even more serious is the fact that the justification for permitting price increases under a system of price control is normally an increase in costs; so an increase in X-inefficiency which leads to an increase in costs always appears to justify corresponding increases in price, unless a very detailed and expensive investigation into the firm's efficiency is undertaken. This, indeed, is almost certainly the Achilles' heel of the regulatory process.[24]

The second, and in our view preferable, alternative is to pursue a vigorous anti-trust policy in which rules for the most part replace discretionary intervention. For example, all cases of conspiracy might well be prohibited with severe penalties for transgression, on the principle that scale benefits can very rarely be significant whereas consumer losses and X-inefficiency may often be extensive. Similarly, all mergers might be prohibited which would raise the market share (properly defined) of the resulting combine above an acceptable limit (say 50 per cent). Where individual companies already enjoyed a market share in excess of 50 per cent (again properly defined) a solution would be less tractable. In growing markets, absolute limits on size might be imposed to provide for a progressive reduction through time in their market shares. Where this solution proved unsuitable improvements in market information and tariff reductions might be actively encouraged, but in

[24] See M. Kafoglis, 'Output of the Restrained Firm', pp. 206–15 below.

the last analysis residual regulation might prove essential. In the longer term, technological progress might help to erode the market power of those companies which initially escaped the full impact of the anti-trust policy.

A non-discretionary anti-trust policy of the kind here recommended would most suitably be pursued through the judicial process, since in many instances significant political consequences might flow from anti-trust decisions and it would be difficult for the Government to refrain from harmful and distorting intervention because of political exigencies if the opportunity existed. That the judiciary itself is susceptible to outside pressure cannot be denied, but it stands out as the least corruptible of all the available instruments for anti-trust enforcement and the most experienced in the implementation of non-discretionary policy.

9 The Theory of Public Utility Price – An Empty Box[1]

Jack Wiseman

Criticism of the analytical validity of public utility pricing 'rules' has resulted over a period of years in the introduction of successive modifications to the original simple (though not unambiguous) marginal-cost 'rule', culminating in advocacy of the two-part tariff and of the 'club' principle.[2] While these pricing rules have been regarded with scepticism as practical guides to public utility pricing policy,[3] however, there has perhaps been a less general appreciation of the cumulative weight of the theoretical objections to all such rules; there is still interest in the discovery of a 'right' rule, and in the estimation of the 'marginal' or other costs of particular public utility enterprises.

It will be argued in this article that no general pricing rule or

[1] I am grateful to Professor H. G. Johnson, to Mr T. Wilson, and to colleagues at the London School of Economics for reading and criticizing drafts of this article.

[2] There is a good deal of literature on this subject. For a useful first list, the reader is referred to the end of the lucid survey of the topic by Professor E. H. Phelps Borown in chap. viii of his book, *A Course in Applied Economics*. Cf. also G. F. Thirlby, 'The Ruler', *South African Journal of Economics* (Dec 1946); William Vickrey, 'Some Objections to Marginal Cost Pricing', *Journal of Political Economy*, LVI (1948); Gabriel Dessus, 'The General Principles of Rate Fixing in Public Utilities', *International Economic Papers*, no. 1 (translation of a report presented to the Congress of the Union Internationale des Producteurs et Distributeurs d'Énergie Électrique, 1949); and T. Wilson, 'The Inadequacy of the Theory of the Firm as a Branch of Welfare Economics', *Oxford Economic Papers* (Feb 1952). This list is not comprehensive.

The historical development of the 'rules' and their analytical origins is set out in two articles by Nancy Ruggles: 'The Welfare Basis of the Marginal Cost Pricing Principle' and 'Recent Developments in the Theory of Marginal Cost Pricing', *Review of Economic Studies*, nos. 42 and 43 (1949–50).

Specific references have been given in the text only where articles are of particular relevance to the issue concerned.

[3] The scepticism is by no means universal: e.g. the *Report of the Committee on National Policy for the Use of Fuel and Power Resources* (Cmd 8647, 1952; Ridley Report), considered the question of whether coal should be priced at marginal cost, and half the members of the Committee in fact favoured the use of some form of marginal-cost pricing.

Reprinted from *Oxford Economic Papers*, n.s., IX (Feb 1957) 56–74, by kind permission of the author and of the Clarendon Press.

rules can be held unambiguously to bring about an 'optimum' use of resources by public utilities, even in theory. Indeed, failing some universally acceptable theory of the public economy, the economist can offer no *general* guidance at all to a government having to decide a price policy for such utilities. To demonstrate this, it will be necessary to begin with a brief survey of the criticisms of the simple marginal-cost rule. This will provide the basis for a demonstration of the possibly less familiar (though no less decisive) analytical shortcomings of the two-part tariff rule, both in its simple form and as modified by a 'club' principle. In conclusion, the effect of uncertainty on the analysis will be examined, and the broad implications of the whole argument for public policy will be suggested.

1. The Marginal-cost Rule

Any discussion of a 'right' price presupposes criteria of the public interest against which alternative suggested prices can be judged. The criteria from which the marginal-cost rule stems are derived from the analytical model of a perfectly competitive market economy, in which entrepreneurs are assumed to have perfect foresight[4] and it is a property of the long-run equilibrium situation that, given the distribution of income between consumers, no transfer of factors between uses could increase the satisfactions of one consumer without reducing those of another. The optimum conditions of 'economic welfare' are consequently said to be fulfilled by the model. For the competitive firm, it is an incidental property of the long-run situation that marginal cost (money outlay on factors) = average cost = price of product. Consequently, this equality can be regarded as evidence of the existence of an 'ideal' situation, and pricing at marginal cost has accordingly been proposed as a general pricing rule (e.g. as the 'principle of administration' of a collectivist economy).[5] But public utility

---

[4] This assumption is of course highly unrealistic; there are also tenable arguments for the view that it is internally inconsistent (cf., e.g., J. Wiseman, 'Uncertainty, Costs, and Collectivist Economic Planning', *Economica*, May 1953, p. 120). For the purposes of this article, the model is accepted for the present and criticism is developed within its assumptions. Section 3 discusses the consequences of relaxation of the foresight assumption.

[5] For a critique of this collectivist 'rule' and of the model from which it derives, cf. Wiseman, idem.

enterprises are not perfectly competitive firms. By the usual definition, an important part of the factors they employ are not perfectly divisible; they can be obtained only in large physical units, or in a durable or specific form, or both. Also, the technically efficient production unit is large relative to the possible size of the market, and the utilities are public bodies, often with considerable powers of monopoly protected by law. In such circumstances, there may be no possible price equal both to marginal cost (the money outlay required to increase output marginally) and average cost (which includes outlays on the 'indivisible' factors excluded from marginal cost). It therefore appears to be necessary to decide whether price should be fixed equal to the one or to the other.

The argument for pricing such public utility products at average cost is, simply, that 'each tub should stand on its own bottom'; all money outlays which would have been avoided if a product had not been produced should be recovered in the price charged by the utility. But the advocates of marginal-cost pricing find this unconvincing. Some of the outlays included in average cost, they argue, are not current opportunity costs but are either payments for technically indivisible factors or past out-payments for durable and specific factors. The inclusion of these outlays in the price charged therefore prevents the achievement of the optimum welfare conditions, which (it is said) require that additional consumption of a good or service should be possible at a price not greater than the additional costs (money outlays) necessarily incurred in providing for that consumption. Accordingly, such outlays should be ignored, and the product priced a marginal cost, even though the enterprise runs at a loss as a result.

Clearly, the proposal for pricing at marginal cost requires an explanation of how the consequent losses are to be financed. Hotelling, who originated much of the discussion,[6] suggested the use of particular types of taxes. The inclusion of charges for

[6] H. Hotelling, 'The General Welfare in Relation to Problems of Taxation and of Railway and Utility Rates', *Econometrica* (1938). Hotelling's paper was stimulated by the much earlier work of Dupuit, around 1844. The relevant papers have been collected and reprinted with comments by Mario di Bernardi and Luigi Einaudi, 'De l'Utilité et de sa Mesure', in *La Riforma Sociale* (Turin, 1932). One of the most interesting papers, 'On the Measurement of Utility of Public Works', *Annales des Ponts et Chaussées* (1844), is published in translation in *International Economic Papers*, no. 2.

'overheads' (past outlays on indivisible factors) was itself, he said, of the nature of a tax. But there were other and preferable taxes (lump-sum taxes on inheritance, income taxes, &c.) which did not offend against the welfare criteria since they affected only the *distribution* and not the *size* of the national income. If such taxes were used, and public utility prices were equated with marginal cost, the optimum welfare conditions would be achieved. Later writers have been justifiably sceptical of the possibility of a tax-system that would meet Hotelling's conditions.[7] In particular, income taxes (on which he expected to have to rely) can be shown to affect the marginal welfare conditions directly. In any case, the proposal is open to an even more fundamental objection: the welfare 'ideal' relates to a *given* distribution of income, and that distribution of income must be altered by the proposed taxes (unless these fall on consumers of public utility products in proportion to their consumption, which is effectively a return to average-cost pricing). Thus to advocate marginal-cost pricing and the meeting of losses out of taxation is to advocate acceptance of income redistribution from non-consumers to consumers of public utility products. The welfare criteria provide no justification for an interpersonal comparison of this kind. In other words, any government deciding upon a pricing policy for public utilities has to take simultaneously into account the effects of its decisions upon the fulfilment of the welfare optima (and hence the size of the national product) and upon the distribution of incomes, and there is nothing in the welfare analysis that provides guidance as to the 'right' policy about the second of these.[8]

[7] Cf. (*inter alia*) J. E. Meade, 'Price and Output Policy of State Enterprise', *Economic Journal* (1944) pp. 321–8, and 'Rejoinder', pp. 337–9; P. A. Samuelson, *The Foundations of Economic Analysis*, p. 240; R. H. Coase, 'The Marginal Cost Controversy', *Economica*, n.s. (1946) pp. 169–82; H. P. Wald, 'The Classical Indictment of Indirect Taxation', *Quarterly Journal of Economics* (1945) pp. 577–97; I. M. D. Little, 'Direct *v.* Indirect Taxes', *Economic Journal* (1951) pp. 577–84.

[8] There is implicit in Hotelling's argument (and in that of writers who have supported him) the view that the welfare criteria can be extended to cover situations involving changes in the distribution of income. Some attempt has been made to support this position by reformulating the compensation principle (that a decision about a particular measure can be made only if all who would lose by it can be, and in fact are, compensated for their loss) in such a way that only the *possibility* and not the *fact* of compensation is necessary for an economic policy to be accepted as beneficial. However, it has been amply demonstrated that interpersonal comparisons cannot be avoided in this way (cf. M. W. Reder, *Studies in the Theory of Welfare Economics*; I. M. D. Little, *Critique of Welfare Economics*; W. J. Baumol, *Welfare Economics and the Theory of the State*, and the references cited therein).

The reason why marginal-cost pricing raises these difficulties is to be found in the fact that the arguments for the marginal-cost rule are logically unsatisfactory in that they attempt to apply welfare criteria derived from an analysis concerned with marginal variations in factor-use to a problem whose essence is discrete change; the whole basis of the public utility discussion is the indivisibility of the factors employed by such utilities. The results of this attempt are not only of dubious relevance to policy; they are also uncertain in themselves.

The type of indivisibility most emphasized in the discussion is that created by the durability and specificity of factors (*temporal* indivisibility).[9] It is enlightening to examine the nature of such indivisibility more closely. It has been shown that the marginal-cost 'rule' distinguishes between 'current' and 'past' opportunity-cost problems. Once the sacrifices necessary to create a durable and specific asset have been made, it is argued, no further opportunity costs are created by its later use. The opportunity costs having been borne in the past, no account should be taken of them in deciding current prices,[10] even though, as has been demonstrated, this results in losses and in income redistribution. Such an argument rests upon a dubious interpretation of the welfare criteria. The long period, from which the welfare postulates derive, is a situation in which all factors of production are considered to be perfectly mobile; this would seem to imply consideration of a time-period at least as long as the lowest common multiple of the life-span of all the factors of production concerned. If the marginal-cost rule

The debate will not be discussed in the text; all that has to be established is that the simultaneous decisions referred to therein are unavoidable, and that the welfare criteria provide guidance about only one of these decisions.

[9] The distinction between this type of indivisibility and *technical* indivisibility is not always made clear in the literature (for a clear separation, cf., e.g., Phelps Brown (op. cit.) and Coase (idem)).

In contrast with the present section, the discussion of the 'club' principle in section 2 will be conducted with reference mainly to technical indivisibility. Such indivisibility amounts to no more than the fact that the whole of a productive factor must be employed in order to obtain *any part* of the total product of that factor, so that if the factor is an economic good it must have *current* alternative uses, and therefore a price (e.g. if a railway carriage can be attached to different trains, opportunity costs are incurred in attaching it to any one train. But no opportunity costs may be incurred in allowing one more passenger to travel once the carriage is attached).

[10] Dupuit's argument against bridge tolls (op. cit.) is the *locus classicus* of this argument.

is conceived in terms of a time-period shorter than this, then not all the opportunity costs requisite to the manufacture of the product concerned can be imputed to that product, and the time-period chosen must itself be arbitrary, so that the marginal-cost rule becomes simply a statement that outlays on factors of some specified durability should be ignored in deciding prices (i.e. should be treated as 'past' outlays). The figure treated as marginal cost will thus depend upon the time-period selected.[11]

The division of outlays into 'past' and 'current' is clearly unsatisfactory, and the implications of durability and specificity become less obscure if such a division is abandoned and the problem is presented in the form of a planning process through time. All opportunity-cost decisions, taken at one moment in time, fix the use of factors during some future period of time. All factors embodied in plans implemented by entrepreneuers, that is, become durable and specific to some degree; new opportunity costs arise in respect of them only when their use can be replanned. This being so, it is not possible to separate opportunity costs into two groups, 'past' and 'current'. The most that can be said is that some kinds of factors lend themselves more readily than do others to frequent replanning. There is a difference, for example, between the extent to which factor-use will be 'fixed' over time by the implementation of a decision to build a railway bridge and by a decision to hire a railway porter. But the difference is one not of kind but of degree; it is possible to conceive of an 'ordering' of opportunity-cost decisions in accordance with the length of time for which they commit factors to particular uses (i.e. create specificity and durability), but it is not possible to divide such decisions into a group that involves a commitment over time and another group that does not.

Marginal (opportunity) cost in these circumstances is represented by a foregone revenue. The use of factors of production in the entrepreneur's selected plan excludes them from use in some other plan; marginal cost is the foregone marginal revenue from the best plan necessarily excluded because the chosen plan is selected. But the alternative uses to which factors can be put, and hence the opportunity-cost valuation imputed to them in the planning process, will depend on the time-period in terms of which the entrepreneur's plans are

[11] Cf. T. Wilson, idem.

themselves conceived; marginal cost will consequently vary according to the time-span of the production plans considered. Thus, the meaning and results of an instruction to equate marginal cost and price will be determined by the length of the planning period to which the marginal cost is intended to refer. At one extreme, the period chosen may be as long as the lowest common multiple of the life-periods of the assets required to produce the public utility product, and the marginal-cost rule would then give a price that took into account the whole of the sacrifice of alternative consumption caused by the implementation of plans to manufacture the utility product. At the other extreme, the consideration of 'current' opportunity costs only, if interpreted rigorously, would seem to require that products should be given away. Between these two extremes, there is a range of possible marginal-cost rules, differing from each other in the planning time-period chosen as appropriate and hence in the 'durable' assets they ignore and in the opportunity costs they treat as relevant to decisions about price and output.

The only time-period in which all factor-use can be clearly attributed is one as long as the lowest common multiple of the life-periods of the assets concerned; the designation of any other (shorter) time-period as the one appropriate to the rule must involve both an arbitrary decision that that period is one relevant to the computation of marginal cost and a value judgement that income should be redistributed over time towards the consumers of goods produced with relatively durable assets. The marginal-cost principle thus becomes, not the assertion of a general welfare 'ideal', *but the expression of a particular value judgement, that certain long-run opportunity costs for the community as a whole should be ignored in the interests of the greater short-run utilization by consumers of specific factors of some stated degree of durability.*[12]

The only defence offered against criticism of the marginal-cost rule on such grounds lies in the introduction of a supplementary criterion: the investment principle. This requires that marginal-cost pricing should be used to decide the selling prices of public utility products once the utilities are in existence, but that the public investment necessary to create a utility initially

---

[12] It will be appreciated that arguments based on *technical* indivisibility raise similar considerations.

should be considered justified only if a perfectly discriminating monopolist could (notionally) recover its cost by charging prices that would maximize his returns. The need for such a supplementary principle to a 'general' rule is implausible. In any case, the investment principle does not answer the criticisms. It still has to be decided which economic decisions are to be treated as 'investment' decisions and which as subject to the marginal-cost rule, and no principle has been suggested by reference to which such decisions might be made. Further, since the prices actually charged are to be determined by the marginal-cost rule, the discussion of the effects of that rule (e.g. on income distribution) is unaffected by the introduction of the supplementary principle. It is worth pointing out, further, that the investment criterion itself has redistributive implications: certainly it does not appear to meet the welfare conditions in the same fashion as would a perfectly competitive market.[13]

The foregoing criticisms of marginal-cost pricing have been fairly widely accepted, although the precise nature of the value judgements implied in the treatment of temporal indivisibility is perhaps not generally recognized. Despite this acceptance, there still seems to be considerable support for marginal-cost pricing from those who feel that policies affecting only the *distribution* of the national income both are possible and are in some sense superior to alternative policies that would also affect its *size*. In the absence of some generally acceptable basis for preference between different income distributions, it is clear that such a position cannot be supported by logic. The two issues cannot be separated, and policies desirable in terms of the welfare criteria may therefore reasonably be rejected because a government chooses to obtain a 'preferred' distribution of income even at the cost of some diminution of its total size. There

---

[13] In the competitive market case, all consumers are faced with the same system of prices: in Wicksteed's phrase, the 'terms on which alternatives are offered' are the same for all. In the other, since discrimination is admitted, each individual is considered to be faced with a different price for the purpose of deciding whether or not to make the investment. If such prices were subsequently charged, they would involve a change in the distribution of real income, and would fall under the same strictures about interpersonal comparison as the marginal-cost rule. That is, a decision taken in accordance with the investment principle might be considered as being partly concerned with the consequences for consumption of the public utility product in question of a change in the distribution of real income. But it would appear that in this respect, as with the advocacy of marginal-cost pricing, the income redistribution is treated as a problem separable from, and in some way inferior to, that of income size (as expressed in the welfare 'ideal').

is no escape from the very special value judgements that marginal-cost pricing implies.[14]

2. The Multi-part Tariff and the 'Club'

The two- (or more) part tariff is intended to avoid the anomalies of marginal-cost pricing, in that it is designed to meet the marginal 'welfare' conditions and also to avoid problems of interpersonal comparison by raising revenues large enough to cover all outlays. The essence of the proposal is that the price to be charged should be the sum of two parts:[15] a 'marginal-cost' element determined by the increase in costs necessarily incurred in providing further consumption for an individual consumer, and a 'fixed charge' to cover costs which do not vary with consumption but which must be incurred if the consumer in question is to be enabled to consume at all. In this way, total costs are covered and the payments made for additional consumption are kept equal to the extra costs of provision (marginal cost) alone. The problem appears to be solved, since the 'welfare' conditions are satisfied and no income redistribution seems to be implied.[16]

Unfortunately, multi-part pricing provides an unambiguous

[14] An illustration may help to make the point clear:

A government, having decided to build a bridge out of revenue raised by taxation, might offer the services of the bridge free and ignore the source of the initial revenues in framing subsequent tax policy. Alternatively, it might decide to charge tolls for (say) twenty years, accepting the reduction in use (i.e. in total income) in the interests of compensating those who had to make the initial sacrifice, or it might decide upon some other combination of current financing and compensation. The economist is without adequate criteria to judge between these alternatives.

[15] There could of course be more than two parts, depending upon the nature of the fixed factors. To introduce more simply adds complexity without affecting the logic of the argument.

[16] A model used by R. H. Coase (idem) gives the essentials of the argument very clearly. The model is concerned with current (technical) indivisibility only, problems of time and of common costs being abstracted therefrom. In the model, a number of roads radiate from a central market, and there is one consumer on each road. All costs are assumed to be currently incurred, and each consumer purchases a combination of the market product and the transport service necessary to deliver it. Transport units are sufficiently large to carry any one consumer's requirements. Thus, while the transport service is *indivisible*, in that extra units of product can be carried without cost, yet there are *no common costs* since one van serves only one customer and the transport cost is attributable to that consumer. In these conditions, Coase argued, the price charged should comprise a fixed charge for the transport service and a price per unit for the product. Total costs are then covered, and the additional payment for extra consumption is equal to the price of the product only (i.e. to marginal cost).

solution only if the two types of costs concerned can be clearly imputed to individual consumers. In fact, when this can be done the two 'parts' of the price can logically be treated as the prices of separate products, each capable of clear determination by a normal market process. When these conditions do not obtain, however, the situation becomes very different. This can be seen by introducing the possibility of common costs. If problems of time are disregarded, these are simply current costs that do not vary with total output, but are necessarily incurred if *any* output is to be produced at all and *are not imputable directly to individual consumers.*[17] How should these current 'fixed and common' costs be shared between consumers? In principle, limits can be set to the charges that individual consumers can and should be asked to pay, by reference to the cost of providing the indivisible service for them if other consumers ceased to consume, on the one hand, and the minimum possible cost of providing their addition to total consumption on the other.[18] But there may still remain a variety of possible methods of charging, and some non-arbitrary means of choosing between them is required if the multi-part tariff is to provide an unambiguous solution to the public utility pricing problem.[19]

There is a suggested means of meeting this common-cost problem that seems to be fairly widely accepted. This is the use of the 'club' principle. This principle is not usually stated

[17] Indivisibility need not imply the existence of such costs, though their presence must imply indivisibility.

The nature of the complications caused by common costs can be illustrated by replacing Coase's road-system (n. 16 above) by a ring road, with the market at the centre and one van serving a number of customers around the circumference, which the van can join at any point. Clearly, the pricing problem now becomes much more complex.

[18] In the conditions of the modification of the Coase model (n. 17 above), these limits (for any one consumer) would be the total cost of providing the service ('indivisible' transport cost plus cost of goods purchased), on the one hand, and the cost of the goods alone on the other. If there were also variable costs associated with the transport service (e.g. petrol cost), then the lower limit would have to be increased by the minimum cost of transport between the consumer in question and the next nearest consumer.

[19] The problem becomes even more intractable if time is introduced into the analysis, so that the 'common costs' being considered can become past outlays on *temporally* indivisible assets. This kind of question cannot suitably be discussed without relaxing the assumptions of the competitive model. The present section therefore ignores these questions of time, which are more fully treated in the following section of the article. It will be appreciated that the criticisms of the two-part tariff and the 'club' principle in the present section are in no way invalidated by this simplification.

with precision; its essence appears to be the proposition that the consumers of the utility product can be treated as a 'club', created by the consumers to arrange both the amount of the goods each individual shall consume and the amount that he shall pay for it. Then, if all 'members' (potential consumers) are asked what they would voluntarily pay as a fixed charge rather than go without the possibility of consuming a particular product at a price per unit equal to marginal cost (money outlay), and if the sum of the amounts offered would be great enough to cover the total outlays required, the service should be provided and each consumer charged that part of the common cost that he has stated his willingness to bear. It follows that the 'club' principle is likely to give rise to price discrimination, in that different individuals need not be required to pay the same amount for a similar volume of consumption. That is, the principle must imply a redistribution of real income, since consumers with given money incomes purchase a technically homogeneous product at money prices differing from one consumer to another. But, it is argued, the 'club' principle allows consumers themselves to make a voluntary decision whether to accept the good and the consequent income redistribution in preference to having neither. If they, as consumers, take the first course, then this must produce a more satisfactory situation from the point of view of consumers' choice, and the optimum 'welfare' conditions must therefore be better satisfied as a result of the use of the 'club' principle despite the consequent redistribution of income.

The 'club' principle has deficiencies serious enough to make the extent of its acceptance a matter for some surprise. The deficiencies are of two kinds. First, the value judgements being made in relation to income redistribution are difficult to justify. Second, the 'club' proposals require an unusual (and peculiar) interpretation of the concept of voluntary choice.

Income redistribution and the 'club' principle

No one suggests that the 'club' principle avoids the need for value judgements about income distribution.[20] Rather, what is

[20] The 'club' argument might indeed be stated in the form that there is some distribution of income, different from the existing one, which would induce consumers to cover the costs of the utility without the need for differential charges, and that this distribution must be superior to the existing one because consumers will 'voluntarily' bring it about if allowed to do so. This form of statement brings

implied is that 'welfare' can unambiguously be said to have been improved by a policy which meets the marginal welfare conditions, even though there is a consequent change in the distribution of income, *provided that the changed income distribution is the consequence of the 'voluntary' action of consumers*. This extension of the welfare criteria is less innocuous than might at first appear. Economic welfare, as normally defined, is concerned solely with the optimum conditions of individual choice, given the distribution of income; the objective of the public utility discussion might be described as the discovery of a pricing policy to meet those conditions, in the special circumstances of public utility production. But if a suggested principle of pricing would affect economic magnitudes other than the conditions of choice, then it becomes necessary to establish further policy criteria concerned with these other magnitudes, by reference to which the proposed principle can be assessed. In the present case, since income distribution is affected by the 'club' principle, criteria for choice between income distributions are required. Moreover, these criteria must take the form of a statement about the *income-redistributive objectives of a government*, since it has to be recognized that the public utility discussion (although itself conceived in relation to the conditions of individual choice) is concerned to recommend policies to be implemented by a government. *That is, income distribution is a question of public policy, and it is the attitude of the government to it, and not the attitude of particular groups of consumers, that is of significance for policy*. The value judgement implied in the 'club' principle is that if the members of the public utility 'club' agree to a particular redistribution of income, then the government must necessarily think such a redistribution desirable. This is not plausible; there are likely to be many cases in which the 'voluntary' redistribution would be of a kind that the government disapproved.[21] In short, once a government is committed,

---

out the similarity between the 'club' principle and the investment criterion and compensation principle (n. 8 above) discussed earlier; it is therefore not surprising to find that they have similar weaknesses.

[21] An illustration used by Phelps Brown (op. cit., p. 260) makes the point very well; poor families in an area may be willing to pay more towards the provision of a playground than richer families in the same area, but there is no presumption that a government will agree that they should. The welfare criteria provide no guidance in such cases since they offer no means of choice between income distributions.

by the creation of a utility and the existence of common costs, to a decision about income distribution, there is no reason why it should prefer public utility pricing policies that cover total costs by use of the 'club' principle to other policies which may or may not cover costs, but which accord better with its own attitude to redistribution. A government permitting utilities to use the 'club' principle in effect substitutes the authorities of the utility for itself as the final arbiter in matters of income distribution in this particular context.[22]

'*Voluntary*' *choice and the* '*club*' *principle*

The argument for the 'club' principle depends upon the fact that the charges to which it gives rise are 'voluntarily' agreed by consumers. In general, this agreement will be 'voluntary' only in the special sense that a malefactor voluntarily goes away to prison after a judge has sentenced him; he chooses the best alternative still available. To appreciate this, it is necessary to look more closely at the form these 'clubs' can take and at the nature of their 'regulations' (i.e. the powers they have to take and enforce decisions about such matters

[22] These criticisms are the more striking when the restrictive assumptions of the analysis are recalled; the 'offers' made by consumers must be quite independent, since otherwise there may be no possibility of an 'agreed' set of prices because 'club' members insist on relating their own offers to the amounts others will be expected to pay. Further, there is no *logical* reason why only one system of prices should satisfy the 'club' principle; what happens, e.g., if the amounts offered to meet standing charges are greater than the total of common costs, but only total cost is to be recovered? In these cases, where more than one set of prices would satisfy the conditions, someone will have to choose between them. Value judgements must be made in the process, and it is difficult to understand why the government should accept those of the utility as superior to its own.

The false plausibility of the argument for voluntary redistribution through the 'club' arises from the application of a logical system concerned solely with individual choice and taking no account of the existence of a government with coercive powers, to a situation where governments have to take decisions involving economic matters outside the scope of individual choice. Some attempt has indeed been made to 'fit' the behaviour of the public economy into the individual choice (welfare) analysis, by treating the whole of the economy as a 'club'. This brings out the weakness and unrealism of the 'club' argument even more forcefully than the discussion above; it leads to advocacy of an 'ethically neutral' system of government income and expenditure, such that the size of the taxes paid and the public services consumed by individuals would be determined by the free agreement of the citizens (taxpayers and consumers) themselves, and to the suggestion that those unwilling to pay such taxes should be treated as 'pathological' (see F. Benham, 'Notes on the Pure Theory of Public Finance', *Economica*, 1934, pp. 453–4, and, for a critical discussion, Musgrave, 'The Voluntary Exchange Theory of the Public Economy', *Quarterly Journal of Economics*, Nov 1949).

as the payments to be made by members). Three broad types of 'club' can be envisaged.

The first type might be called the *direct production club*: it is created and administered by the consumers themselves. Thus, if factor services are available for purchase in free competitive markets, groups of consumers may find it convenient to join together to hire certain services whose products will be consumed by all the group, although it would not be worth the while of individual consumers to hire them separately. Effectively, the consumers *ask themselves* whether it is worth their while to create a 'club' to provide the good concerned, and agree together (in deciding to create it) upon the volume of their individual consumption and upon the payments each shall make. The illustrations given of the 'club' principle are usually of this direct-production character.[23] Provided that there are alternative competing means of satisfying the demand in question without recourse to a 'club', then the possibility of forming a 'club' simply represents a widening in the range of choices made available by the competitive market, and so increases satisfactions ('welfare').[24] This is true even though members of the 'club' pay different amounts for what is technically the same service. However, such cases of direct production would seem unlikely to be of widespread importance, though there may be special instances in which the conditions are quite well satisfied.[25]

---

[23] If, for example, a man wishes to fly to Scotland to visit a sick relative, but cannot quite afford to charter an aeroplane at £30 for the trip, it may be possible to find a prospective rail traveller who is willing to pay £10 to share the air trip. The same (physical) service thus costs each traveller a different amount, but each prefers to make the payment and take the service rather than take the services to be obtained by using the market in any other way.

[24] e.g., in the illustration given (n. 23 above) the travellers could themselves decide whether to travel separately or together, could choose between a variety of competing means of transport, and could decide between various offers of aeroplanes for hire.

[25] A good example is given in part III (pp. 94–145) of R. S. Edwards, *Co-operative Industrial Research*. Here the common service is research for a group of firms with a common interest in the results. Firms can, within broad limits, control the direction of research activity, the distribution of benefits between members, and the methods by which common costs are covered. There is also a possibility of using the market as an alternative to the 'club'. But it is also not without interest, in view of the earlier argument about the role of government (see p. 161), that a decision had to be made as to whether membership should be made compulsory, because the benefits of the co-operative research are not always easily confined to members of the 'club'.

The second form that the 'club' might take is one in which the organization of production is undertaken, not by the eventual consumers, but by independent producers, who find the use of standing charges advantageous but whose freedom in deciding the charges that consumers ('members') shall be asked to pay is restricted by the presence in the market of other, similar clubs competing for the consumer's membership. An example of this type of 'club' (the *competitive producer club*) is provided by the book clubs, offering supplies of books at differential rates related to total guaranteed consumption, but with the discretion of any one club in deciding its rates circumscribed by the policies adopted (or able to be adopted) by the other book clubs, and by the ability of consumers to transfer their 'membership'. There is a case for the existence of this type of 'club' also, on grounds of economic welfare. But it must be noticed that the consumers are not now taking decisions about how much they are willing to contribute to a venture in joint production; their 'voluntary' decisions are concerned solely with the nature and amount of their personal consumption at the prices thrown up by the market. The production decisions are taken by independent producers, and the fulfilment of the welfare conditions depends upon the protection provided for the consumers by competition between these producers.[26]

The third type of 'club', *the discriminating monopoly club*, occurs when neither direct production (with factor services provided by a competitive market) nor competition between 'club'-type producers is present. Only one 'club' is in a position to provide the good or service, so that consumers must join this 'club' and pay the discriminatory charges asked, or go without the good. In such cases, where the producer has a considerable degree of monopoly power, it is difficult to see how discriminatory charges can be justified by appeal to the 'club' principle. The differential charges are fixed by the producer without reference to consumers, who must accept them as a datum when deciding how much to consume – the only 'voluntary' decision left with them. Consumers in these circumstances are protected neither by direct association with pricing and

[26] The difference between the two types of 'club' might be put in this way: in the second type, unlike the first, the members of the 'club' are not automatically members of the committee, although they are still in a strong position to influence its decisions.

production decisions nor by the existence of competition among producers of the good concerned. The distinction between this last formulation of the 'club' principle and the earlier ones is clear; it is the difference between my offer (choice) to pay two-thirds of the cost of a particular taxi shared with a friend, in preference to travelling by bus, and my choice whether or not to consume electricity at the particular set of discriminatory prices that a monopolistic electricity utility decides to apply to me. Cases of the latter type are clearly not justifiable on 'welfare' grounds; if all that is required to satisfy the 'club' principle is that some consumers should pay rather than go without, then any private discriminating monopolist might meet the conditions.

Unfortunately, it is only the last and most unsatisfactory type of 'club' that is likely to be relevant to the pricing policy of public utilities, whose products often have no close substitutes and whose monopoly power is protected by law, so that the 'club' becomes effectively a method of coercion operated by a sole producer.

In summary, there are clear arguments for a multi-part pricing rule only where the services of the indivisible factors (and therefore the 'standing charges') can be imputed directly to individual consumers. In such conditions the method avoids the need for interpersonal utility comparisons. This is not so if there are common costs, which is likely to be the general case. In these cases, the decision taken about the prices to be charged must involve a value judgement about the distribution of income, and this cannot in general be avoided by an instruction to make use of the 'club' principle.

3. The Welfare Model and Uncertainty[27]

In the simplified conditions of the competitive model so far postulated, the pricing 'rules' could be implemented simply on the basis of objective cost computations made by utility managers. The assumptions about knowledge that lie behind the model are such that it does not matter who takes the decisions about the use of factors in production, nor is there any need for

---

[27] The method of analysis adopted in this section is similar to that used by G. F. Thirlby, idem. Cf. also T. Wilson, idem, and J. Wiseman, idem.

G

economic activity concerned with the discovery of information, framing of expectations, or considering and choosing between alternative and speculative courses of action. Any departure from the 'ideal' situation in which the price of any factor (including 'entrepreneurship' as rewarded by normal profit) is equal to its value in another use or to another user must be explained solely by reference to the short-term immobility of factors of production.

A simple model of this kind is inadequate for the derivation of pricing rules intended to have relevance to practical policy. This can be seen by considering the effects of uncertainty.[28] Once uncertainty is admitted, it becomes necessary to distinguish between the process of decision-taking by which the use of resources is determined (the *ex ante* planning process), and the *ex post* distribution of factors between uses that is the consequence of that process. The opportunity-cost problems arise at the *ex ante* planning stage: costs are incurred when decisions committing factors to particular uses are taken. With uncertainty, this *ex ante* planning process must involve judgement as well as a capacity for arithmetic; there is no longer any reason why different individuals, working as they must in an atmosphere of doubt and with incomplete information, should make the same assessments or reach the same decisions even in the unlikely event of their acting on the basis of identical data. That is, the *ex post* distribution of factors between uses at any time is determined not only by factor-mobility but also by the skill of those who plan the use of those factors *ex ante*.

In these circumstances, the entrepreneurial function cannot be treated simply as a factor of production rewarded in similar fashion to other factors. The decision-taking process is concerned with the selection and implementation of the production plans which, in the view of those taking the decisions, offer combinations of riskiness and expected net revenue superior to those offered by any alternative plans considered. But the imple-

---

[28] It is not suggested that the unsatisfactory treatment of uncertainty is the only reason for objection to the perfectly competitive model and to the welfare criteria. In particular, there has been considerable and cogent criticism of the validity of the simple welfare model as an explanation of the process and nature of individual choice (cf., e.g., I. M. D. Little, op. cit., and W. J. Baumol, op. cit.). However, such criticism need not concern us here. There is still point in discussing the use of resources in terms of choice, and the logic of the 'rules' can be destroyed even accepting the conceptions of the simplest welfare analysis.

mentation of any plan at all involves a risk that the actual revenues and outlays achieved *ex post* will differ from the *ex ante* forcasts that provided a basis for action. This risk is borne by those whose resources are utilized in implementing the plan (the 'owners'). The 'owners' and the 'decision-takers' need not be identical. The possible combinations of the functions of ownership and planning control (decision-taking) are clearly very numerous, and the returns to risk-bearing and to the planning function are difficult if not impossible to separate in practice, since individuals may share both functions in varying degrees. But the separation is clear in principle.

The reward of the decision-taking function will be that part of the earnings of decision-takers that is not directly dependent upon the *ex post* success of their *ex ante* planning activities. So regarded, the return to such decision-taking can be treated, like normal profit in the competitive model, as an outlay on a productive factor. But the rewards offered to individual decision-takers will reflect the view taken by owners of their relative abilities; there can be no question of their being treated as homogeneous. The return to risk-bearing, on the one hand, cannot be treated as an outlay at all; its reward is the *ex post* (achieved) excess of revenues over outlays (net revenue) in plans actually implemented. It is in no sense a hire-payment for a factor, depending as it does upon the ability to obtain a return from the utilization of factors greater than the hire-payments that have to be made to those factors. The size of the return obtained is directly determined by the efficiency with which planning decisions are taken *ex ante* and by the attitude of risk-bearers to ventures of different degrees of riskiness.

Since net revenue is the return to the essential economic function of risk-bearing, but cannot be treated as an outlay on a factor, it follows that, if factors of production are to be ideally distributed between uses, the total revenues obtained by firms (*ex post*) should be greater than their total outlays and not equal to such outlays as in the conditions of the perfectly competitive model. Also, the 'normal profit' principle cannot be satisfactorily replaced, as a condition of the welfare 'ideal', by a requirement that the net revenues obtained by different firms should be equated *ex post*. The competitive process does provide a check on the undue divergence of the net revenues actually obtained from different kinds of productive activity, by directing activity towards avenues in which large net revenues seem likely. But even with complete freedom for potential producers to enter any market they wish there is no reason to expect that competition will, or (from the point of view of an 'ideal' factor-distribution) should, result in a general equality of achieved net revenues. Net revenue depends upon the individual skill of risk-bearers and decision-takers and upon their attitude to risk. If the abilities and risk-attitudes of these individuals differ, then net revenues must also be expected to differ. A welfare principle of net-revenue equalization, in accord with the general principle of factor-price equalization, would thus be valid only in a society in which risk-bearers and decision-takers were of precisely equal ability and took the same attitude to risk. Such a situation being unlikely, it seems better to substitute the more realistic, if less precise, formula that some net revenue must be obtained if the employment of factors of production in any use is to be justified, and that some means (such as the competitive process) is necessary to limit the extent of the divergences between the net revenue obtained from different kinds of productive activity.

If this argument is accepted, then a new dilemma arises for public utility pricing policy. The need for skill in making production plans, and the risks involved in implementing those plans, are not peculiar to one form of economic organization. They do not disappear because an industry becomes a public utility; simply, the risks are transferred from private owners to the community as a whole. In respect of decision-taking, no insuperable difficulties need arise; so long as there is a large private sector, suitable individuals can be hired at prices determined by their earnings in private industry, and their hire-prices treated as outlays. The only difficulty in this respect is the discovery of an incentive to efficient *ex ante* planning activity that will replace the association of reward with achieved net revenue generally used in private industry. But risk-payments cannot be treated in this way; they are not simply factor-outlays. If public utilities are not expected to earn some net revenue, as in the case with the 'rules' so far discussed, then factors of production will be utilized in plans that would not be implemented in private industry because the expected returns were too small. On the other hand, public utilities will often have considerable powers of monopoly, so that the competitive process is not available as a check upon the means utilized to obtain revenues. Consequently, if they are required to earn a net revenue, utilities may do so simply by using their monopoly power to raise prices. Some increase in *ex ante* planning efficiency may (but need not) also be stimulated, by the need to reach a more difficult target. Thus there would appear to be some justification for the view that if a public utility, required to achieve a specified net revenue, did so solely by exercise of its monopoly power over prices, yet the need to raise the revenue might serve a useful 'welfare' purpose by checking the over-expansion of the public utility enterprise relative to enterprises in private industry of a similar degree of riskiness. But there seems to be no 'right' net revenue that all utilities should be required to earn in all circumstances, since public utilities differ both in riskiness and in the extent of their monopoly power.

The introduction of considerations of uncertainty also draws attention to the problems that would arise for utility managers concerned with interpreting and administering 'rules' of the type so far discussed. These problems are particularly important in the case of rules that do not require costs to be covered. For example, the investment principle, interpreted in *ex ante* planning terms, requires that managers, when deciding whether or not to create an asset, should base their revenue estimate upon the system of prices (discriminatory or not) that they would expect to maximize such revenues. The asset should be created if any plan shows a potential (*ex ante*) excess of revenues over outlays. But if no charge is made for the use of the asset once created, then the plans that prompted its creation will never be implemented. There will therefore be no means of checking upon the efficiency with which the investment decisions are made. This position will be aggravated by the fact that once charges for the use of durable assets cease to be made, no guidance can be obtained from the success of *ex post* (implemented) plans when considering newly current (*ex ante*) plans, since the revenues obtained from implemented plans are not an indication of the valuations placed upon the durable factors by consumers. It is difficult to believe that such a situation would be conducive to efficiency in planning the use of factors and hence in the *ex post* (achieved) distribution of factors between uses. Similar problems arise with the marginal-cost rule.

The marginal-cost–price relationship becomes a manager's opinion about the results of a marginal increase in factor-use in the alternative *ex ante* plans considered by him.[29] There is consequently no possibility of any outside authority checking upon whether a general instruction to implement the marginal-cost rule is being followed, quite apart from the other short-comings of such a policy. Considered together with the proposition advanced earlier, that what is treated as marginal cost must depend upon the length of the planning period specified, this suggests that the marginal-cost rule could only be made intelligible in an environment of uncertainty if the general rule were replaced by specific individual directions to managers. Such directions would take the form of an instruction to ignore the estimated replacement costs of particular specified durable assets when deciding price policy, which should otherwise aim at the recovery of all outlays. But this would amount to the replacement of the marginal-cost rule by average-cost (or multi-part) pricing, associated with a specific subsidy.

Summary and Conclusions

It must be concluded that the welfare criteria give rise to no unambiguous general rule for the price and output policy of public utilities, such that for the given distribution of income to which the welfare model refers, obedience to that rule must achieve an ideal use of resources by the utility. An instruction to price at marginal cost, if it was to be intelligible, would need to be supplemented by a specific statement of what costs were to be ignored when fixing prices, in the case of each utility, so that the general 'rule' would effectively be replaced by average-cost (or multi-part) pricing and specific subsidies decided separately for each utility. Furthermore, value judgements about income distribution are unavoidable with marginal-cost pricing. Average-cost or multi-part pricing can solve some of the problems, but only if there are no important common costs, or if the 'club' principle can be justified in individual cases. In any case, any policy 'rule' adopted would need adjustment to take account of uncertainty; an optimum use of resources

---

[29] For further discussion of this cf. T. Wilson, idem, and 'Price and Outlay Policy of State Enterprise', *Economic Journal* (Dec 1945); G. F. Thirlby, idem; and J. Wiseman, idem.

requires that utilities should earn an excess of revenues over outlays, and there is no simple principle by reference to which the appropriate net revenue to be earned on account of the risk-factor can be decided. Failure to require an excess of revenues over outlays encourages the use of resources by utilities that could be better employed elsewhere, but a net revenue requirement may be met by the exploitation of the monopolistic position of the utility concerned. Consequently, uncertainty considerations also require the abandonment of general 'rules' and the separate determination of pricing policy in respect of each individual utility.

These negative conclusions have an important positive aspect. The failure to establish general pricing rules does not mean that the government need take no pricing decisions. Rather, given the existence of public utilities, it has to consider each utility individually, and decide policy in respect of some or all of the following matters in respect of each one:

1. The net revenue that the utility should be expected to earn.
2. Whether it is considered desirable explicitly to encourage the short-period use of particular durable and specific factors and, if so, what form the requisite subsidization shall take.[30]
3. The nature and extent of the discriminatory pricing to be permitted. That is, if there are common costs, whether these can be satisfactorily allocated by the free use of a 'club' principle without this implying a compulsory and undesirable redistribution of income by the utility managers. If the 'club' principle is not appropriate, then a decision has to be taken as to what system of charges would best accord with the government's general policy in regard to income distribution.
4. Whether, quite apart from the considerations at (2) and (3), the industry concerned is thought suitable for use as a means of redistributing income, as a part of the general system of indirect taxes and subsidies. In this regard, of course, public utilities differ from other industries only in

---

[30] In general the desire of governments to give this type of encouragement seems likely to be greater the longer the relevant planning period and the more random and imprecise the distribution of the benefits and losses concerned.

An example of a suitable case might be a change of a permanent nature in the geographical environment, as through the diversion of a river.

that they are more likely to become the subject of government policy for other reasons,[31] and in that they provide a
convenient method of achieving those 'indirect' income
redistributions that some economists consider must be one
of the purposes of public finance.[32]

Clearly, the decisions taken in the case of each utility must
be a reflection of the particular attitude of the government
concerned. It would therefore appear that, failing some universally acceptable theory of the *public* economy by reference to
which policy could be decided (and the possibility of such a
theory is doubtful), economists would find their efforts better
rewarded if they ceased to seek after general pricing rules and
devoted attention to the examination of the policies actually
adopted by governments, in order to discover their effects and
make clear to the government and to the electorate the nature
and consequences of the policies actually being pursued. That
is, the economists' *general* recommendations need to be concerned not with general pricing rules, but rather with the availability of information about policy and with the methods
adopted to keep that policy under review.[33]

---

[31] A question of this type inevitably arises, e.g., when a utility ceases to be able
to cover costs at its present size as a consequence of changes in the economic environment, so that a decision has to be taken as to whether it should be subsidized, or
should simply cease to be treated as a public utility at all, and competition allowed
to determine its future size and operations. This is perhaps a not unrealistic way of
describing the current position of the British railway industry.

[32] Cf., e.g., J. Margolis, 'A Comment on the Pure Theory of Public Expenditures',
Review of Economics and Statistics (Nov 1955).

[33] The preceding analysis would appear to furnish sound arguments, for example,
for treating British public utility pricing policy as part of indirect tax policy, and
(possibly) for providing opportunity for review and discussion of the policies of
important utilities along with the rest of tax policy at the time of the annual
budget.

10 Why Regulate Utilities?[1]

Harold Demsetz

Current economic doctrine offers to its students a basic relationship between the number of firms that produce for a given market and the degree to which competitive results will prevail. Stated explicitly or suggested implicitly is the doctrine that price and output can be expected to diverge to a greater extent from their competitive levels the fewer the firms that produce the product for the market. This relationship has provided the logic that motivates much of the research devoted to studying industrial concentration, and it has given considerable support to utility regulation.[2]

In this paper, I shall argue that the asserted relationship between market concentration and competition cannot be derived from existing theoretical considerations and that it is based largely on an incorrect understanding of the concept of competition or rivalry. The strongest application of the asserted relationship is in the area of utility regulation since, if we assume scale economies in production, it can be deduced that only one firm will produce the commodity. The logical validity or falsity of the asserted relationship should reveal itself most clearly in this case.

Although public utility regulation recently has been criticized because of its ineffectiveness or because of the undesirable indirect effects it produces,[3] the basic intellectual argu-

[1] The author is indebted to R. H. Coase, who was unconvinced by the natural monopoly argument long before this paper was written, and to George J. Stigler and Joel Segall for helpful comments and criticisms.

[2] Antitrust legislation and judicial decision, to the extent that they have been motivated by a concern for bigness and concentration, *per se*, have also benefited from the asserted relationship between monopoly power and industry structure.

[3] Cf. George J. Stigler and Claire Friedland, 'What Can Regulators Regulate? The Case of Electricity', Journal of Law and Economics, v (1962) 1; H. Averch and L. Johnson, 'The Firm under Regulatory Constraint', *American Economic Review*, LII (1962) 1052; Armen Alchian and Reuben Kessel, 'Competition, Monopoly, and the Pursuit of Pecuniary Gain', in *Aspects of Labor Economics* (1962) p. 157.

Reprinted from *Journal of Law and Economics*, XI (Apr 1968) 55–65, by kind permission of the author and of the editor.

ments for believing that truly effective regulation is desirable have not been challenged. Even those who are inclined to reject government regulation or ownership of public utilities because they believe these alternatives are more undesirable than private monopoly, implicitly accept the intellectual arguments that underlie regulation.[4]

The economic theory of natural monopoly is exceedingly brief and, we shall see, exceedingly unclear. Current doctrine is reflected in two recent statements of the theory. Samuelson writes:

> Under persisting decreasing costs for the firm, one or a few of them will so expand their q's as to become a significant part of the market for the industry's total Q. We would then end up (1) with a single monopolist who dominates the industry; (2) with a few large sellers who together dominate the industry . . . or (3) with some kind of imperfection of competition that, in either a stable way or in connection with a series of intermittent price wars, represents an important departure from the economist's model of 'perfect' competition wherein no firm has any control over industry price.[5]

Alchian and Allen view the problem as follows:

> If a product is produced under cost conditions such that larger rates . . . [would] mean lower average cost per unit, . . . only one firm could survive; if there were two firms, one could expand to reduce costs and selling price and thereby eliminate the other. In view of the impossibility of more than one firm's being profitable, two is too many. But if there is only one, that incumbent firm may be able to set prices above free-entry costs for a long time. Either resources are wasted because too many are in the industry, or there is just one firm, which will be able to charge monopoly prices.[6]

At this point it will be useful to state explicitly the interpretation of natural monopoly used in this paper. If, because of

---

[4] Thus, Milton Friedman, while stating his preference for private monopoly over public monopoly or public regulation, writes: 'However, monopoly may also arise because it is technically efficient to have a single producer or enterprise. . . . When technical conditions make a monopoly the natural outcome of competitive market forces, there are only three alternatives that seem available: private monopoly, public monopoly, or public regulation.' (*Capitalism and Freedom*, 1962, p. 28.)

[5] Paul A. Samuelson, *Economics*, 6th rev. ed. (1964) p. 461.

[6] Armen Alchian and William R. Allen, *University Economics*, 1st ed. (1964) p. 412.

production scale economies, it is less costly for one firm to produce a commodity in a given market than it is for two or more
firms, then one firm will survive; if left unregulated, that firm
will set price and output at monopoly levels; the price–output
decision of that firm will be determined by profit-maximizing
behavior constrained only by the market demand for the
commodity.

The theory of natural monopoly is deficient for it fails to
reveal the logical steps that carry it from scale economies in
production to monopoly price in the market place. To see this
most clearly, let us consider the contracting process from its
beginning.

Why must rivals share the market? Rival sellers can offer to
enter into contracts with buyers. In this bidding competition,
the rival who offers buyers the most favorable terms will obtain
their patronage; there is no clear or necessary reason for *bidding*
rivals to share in the *production* of the goods and, therefore, there
is no clear reason for competition in bidding to result in an
increase in per-unit *production* costs.

Why must the unregulated market outcome be monopoly
price? The competitiveness of the bidding process depends
very much on such things as the number of bidders, but there is
no clear or necessary reason for *production* scale economies to
decrease the number of *bidders*. Let prospective buyers call for
bids to service their demands. Scale economies in servicing
their demands in no way imply that there will be one bidder
only. There can be many bidders and the bid that wins will be
the lowest. The existence of scale economies in the production
of the service is irrelevant to a determination of the number of
rival bidders. If the number of bidders is large or if, for other
reasons, collusion among them is impractical, the contracted
price can be very close to per-unit production cost.[7]

The determinants of competition in market negotiations
differ from and should not be confused with the determinants of
the number of firms from which production will issue after
contractual negotiations have been completed. The theory of
natural monopoly is clearly unclear. Economies of scale in
production imply that the bids submitted will offer increasing

[7] I shall not consider in this paper the problem of marginal cost pricing and the
various devices, such as multi-part tariffs, that can be used to approximate
marginal cost pricing.

quantities at lower per-unit costs, but production scale economies imply nothing obvious about how competitive these prices will be. If one bidder can do the job at less cost than two or more, because each would then have a smaller output rate, then the bidder with the lowest bid price for the entire job will be awarded the contract, whether the good be cement, electricity, stamp vending machines, or whatever, but the lowest bid price need not be a monopoly price.[8]

The criticism made here of the theory of natural monopoly can be understood best by constructing an example that is free from irrelevant complications, such as durability of distributions systems, uncertainty, and irrational behavior, all of which may or may not justify the use of regulatory commissions but none of which is relevant to the theory of natural monopoly; for this theory depends on one belief only – price and output will be at monopoly levels if, due to scale economies, only one firm succeeds in producing the product.

Assume that owners of automobiles are required to own and display new license plates each year. The production of license plates is subject to scale economies.

The theory of natural monopoly asserts that under these conditions the owners of automobiles will purchase plates from one firm only and that firm, in the absence of regulation, will charge a monopoly price, a price that is constrained only by the demand for and the cost of producing license plates. The logic of the example does dictate that license plates will be purchased from one firm because this will allow that firm to offer the plates at a price based on the lowest possible per-unit cost. But why should that price be a monopoly price?

There can be many bidders for the annual contract. Each will submit a bid based on the assumption that if its bid is lowest it will sell to all residents, if it is not lowest it sells to none. Under these conditions there will exist enough independently acting bidders to assure that the winning price will differ insignificantly from the per-unit cost of producing license plates.

[8] The competitive concept employed here is not new to economics although it has long been neglected. An early statement of the concept, which was known as 'competition *for* the field' in distinction to 'competition *within* the field', is given by Edwin Chadwick, 'Results of Different Principles of Legislation and Administration in Europe; of Competition for the Field, as compared with the Competition within the Field of Service', *Journal of the Royal Statistical Society*, XXII (1859) 381.

If only one firms submits the lowest price, the process ends, but if two or more firms submit the lowest price, one is selected according to some random selection device or one is allowed to sell or give his contracts to the other. There is no monopoly price although there may be rent to some factors if their supply is positively sloped. There is no regulation of firms in the industry. The price is determined in the bidding market. The only role played by the government or by a consumers' buying cooperative is some random device to select the winning bidder if more than one bidder bids the lowest price.

There are only two important assumptions: (1) The inputs required to enter production must be available to many potential bidders at prices determined in open markets. This lends credibility to numerous rival bids. (2) The cost of colluding by bidding rivals must be prohibitively high. The reader will recognize that these requirements are no different than those required to avoid monopoly price in any market, whether production in that market is or is not subject to scale economies.

Moreover, if we are willing to consider the possibility that collusion or merger of all potential bidding rivals is a reasonable prospect, then we must examine the other side of the coin. Why should collusion or merger of *buyers* be prohibitively costly if an infinite or large number of bidding rivals can collude successfully? If we allow buyers access to the same technology of collusion, the market will be characterized by bilateral negotiations between organized buyers and organized sellers. While the outcome of such negotiations is somewhat uncertain with respect to wealth distribution, there is no reason to expect inefficiency.

Just what is the supply elasticity of bidders and what are the costs of colluding are questions to be answered empirically since they cannot be deduced from production scale economies. There exist more than one firm in every public utility industry and many firms exist in some public utility industries. And this is true even though licensing restrictions have been severe; the assertion that the supply of potential *bidders* in any market would be very inelastic if licensing restrictions could be abolished would seem difficult to defend when producing competitors exist in nearby markets. The presence of active rivalry is clearly indicated in public utility history. In fact, producing competitors, not to mention unsuccessful bidders, were so plentiful that one begins to doubt that scale economies characterized the utility industry at the time when regulation replaced market competition. Complaints were common that the streets were too frequently in a state of disrepair for the purpose of accommodating competing companies. Behling writes:

> There is scarcely a city in the country that has not experienced competition in one or more of the utility industries. Six electric light companies were organized in the one year of 1887 in New York City. Forty-five electric light enterprises had the legal right to operate in Chicago in 1907. Prior to 1895, Duluth, Minnesota, was served by five electric lighting companies, and Scranton, Pennsylvania, had four in 1906. . . . During the latter part of the nineteenth century, competition was the usual situation in the gas industry in this country. Before 1884, six competing companies were operating in New York City. . . . Competition was common and especially persistent in the telephone industry. According to a special report of the Census in 1902, out of 1051 incorporated cities in the United States with a population of more than 4,000 persons, 1002 were provided with telephone facilities. The independent companies had a monopoly in 137 of the cities, the Bell interests had exclusive control over communication by telephone in 414 cities, while the remaining 451, almost half, were receiving duplicated service. Baltimore, Chicago, Cleveland, Columbus, Detroit, Kansas City, Minneapolis, Philadelphia, Pittsburgh, and St. Louis, among the larger cities, had at least two telephone services in 1905.[9]

It would seem that the number of potential bidding rivals and the cost of their colluding in the public utility industries are likely to be at least as great as in several other industries for which we find that unregulated markets work tolerably well.

The natural monopoly theory provides no logical basis for monopoly prices. The theory is illogical. Moreover, for the general case of public utility industries, there seems no clear evidence that the cost of colluding is significantly lower than it is for industries for which unregulated market competition seems to work. To the extent that utility regulation is based on the fear of monopoly price, *merely because one firm will serve each market*, it is not based on any deductible economic theorem.

The important point that needs stressing is that *we have no*

[9] Burton N. Behling, *Competition and Monopoly in Public Utility Industries* (1938) pp. 19–20.

theory that allows us to deduce from the observable degree of concentration in a particular market whether or not price and output are competitive. We have as yet no general theory of collusion and certainly not one that allows us to associate observed concentration in a particular market with successful collusion.[10]

It is possible to make some statements about collusion that reveal the nature of the forces at work. These statements are largely intuitive and cannot be pursued in detail here. But they may be useful in imparting to the reader a notion of what is meant by a theory of collusion. Let us suppose that there are no special costs to competing. That is, we assume that sellers do not need to keep track of the prices or other activities of their competitors. Secondly, assume that there are some costs of colluding that must be borne by members of a bidders' cartel. This condition is approximated least well where the government subsidizes the cost of colluding – for example, the U.S. Department of Agriculture. Finally, assume that there are no legal barriers to entry.

Under these conditions, new bidding rivals will be paid to join the collusion. In return for joining they will receive a *pro rata* share of monopoly profits. As more rivals appear the *pro rata* share must fall. The cartel will continue paying new rivals to join until the *pro rata* share falls to the cost of colluding. That is, until the cartel members receive a competitive rate of return for remaining in the cartel. The next rival bidder can refuse to join the cartel; instead he can enter the market at a price below the cartel price (as can any present member of the cartel who chooses to break away). If there is some friction in the system, this rival will choose this course of action in preference to joining the cartel, for if he joins the cartel he receives a competitive rate of return; whereas if he competes outside the cartel by selling at a price below that of the cartel he receives an above-competitive rate of return for some short-run period. Under the assumed conditions the cartel must eventually fail and price and output can be competitive even though only a few firms actually produce the product. Moreover, the essential ingredient to its eventual failure is only that the private per-firm cost of colluding exceeds the private per-firm cost of competing.

Under what conditions will the cost of colluding exceed the

---

[10] However, see George J. Stigler, 'A Theory of Oligopoly', *Journal of Political Economy*, LXXII (1964) 44.

cost of competing? How will these costs be affected by allowing coercive tactics? What about buyer cartels? What factors affect how long is 'eventually'? Such questions remain to be answered by a theory of collusion. Until such questions are answered, public policy prescriptions must be suspect. A market in which many firms produce may be competitive or it may be collusive; the large number of firms merely reflects production scale diseconomies; large numbers do not necessarily reflect high or low collusion costs. A market in which few firms produce may be competitive or it may be collusive; the small numbers of firms merely reflects production scale economies; fewness does not necessarily reflect high or low collusion costs. Thus, an economist may view the many retailers who sell on 'fair trade' terms with suspicion and he may marvel at the ability of large numbers of workers to form effective unions, and, yet, he may look with admiration at the performance of the few firms who sell airplanes, cameras, or automobiles.

The subject of monopoly price is necessarily permeated with the subject of negotiating or contracting costs. A world in which negotiating costs are zero is a world in which no monopolistic inefficiencies will be present, simply because buyers and sellers both can profit from negotiations that result in a reduction and elimination of inefficiencies. In such a world it will be bargaining skills and not market structures that determine the distribution of wealth. If a monopolistic structure exists on one side of the market, the other side of the market will be organized to offset any power implied by the monopolistic structure. The organization of the other side of the market can be undertaken by members of that side or by rivals of the monopolistic structure that prevails on the first side. The co-existence of monopoly *power* and monopoly *structure* is possible only if the costs of negotiating are differentially positive, being lower for one set of sellers (or buyers) than it is for rival sellers (or buyers). If one set of sellers (or buyers) can organize those on the other side of the market more cheaply than can rivals, then price may be raised (or lowered) to the extent of the existing differential advantage in negotiating costs; this extent generally will be less than the simple monopoly price. In some cases the differential advantage in negotiating costs may be so great that price will settle at the monopoly (monopsony) level. This surely cannot be the general case, but the likelihood of it surely increases as the costs imposed on potential rivals increase; legally restricting entry is one way of raising the differential disadvantages to rivals; the economic meaning of restricting entry *is* increasing the cost of potential rivals of negotiating with and organizing buyers (or sellers).

The public policy question is which groups of market participants, *if any*, are to receive governmentally sponsored advantages and disadvantages, not only in the subsidization or taxation of production but, also, in the creation of advantages or disadvantages in conducting negotiations.

At this juncture, it should be emphasized that I have argued, not that regulatory commissions are undesirable, but that economic theory does not, at present, provide a justification for commissions insofar as they are based on the belief that observed concentration and monopoly price bear any necessary relationship.

Indeed, in utility industries, regulation has often been sought because of the inconvenience of competition. The history of regulation is often written in terms of the desire to prohibit 'excessive' duplication of utility distribution systems and the desire to prohibit the capture of *windfall* gains by utility companies. Neither of these aspects of the utility business are necessarily related to scale economies. Let us first consider the problem of excessive duplication of facilities.

Duplication of Facilities

Communities and not individuals own or control most of the ground and air rights-of-way used by public utility distribution systems. The problem of excessive duplication of distribution systems is attributable to the failure of communities to set a proper price on the use of these scarce resources. The right to use publicly owned thoroughfares is the right to use a scarce resource. The absence of a price for the use of these resources, a price high enough to reflect the opportunity costs of such alternative uses as the servicing of uninterrupted traffic and unmarred views, will lead to their overutilization. The setting of an appropriate fee for the use of these resources would reduce the degree of duplication to optimal levels.

Consider that portion of the ground controlled by an individual and under which a *utility's* distribution system runs.

Confront that individual with the option of service at a lower price from a company that is a rival to the present seller. The individual will take into consideration the cost to him of running a trench through his garden and the benefit to him of receiving the service at lower cost. There is no need for excessive duplication. Indeed, there is no need for any duplication of facilities if he selects the new service, provided that one of two conditions holds. If the *individual* owns that part of the distribution system running under his ground he could tie it in to whatever trunk line serves him best; alternatively, once the new company wins his patronage, a rational solution to the use of that part of the distribution system would be for the utility company owning it to sell it to the utility company now serving the buyer.

There may be good reasons for using community property rather than private property to house the main trunk lines of some utility distribution systems. The placement of such systems under or over streets, alleyways, and sidewalks, resources already publicly owned (a fact taken as datum here), may be less costly than routing them through private property. The failure of communities to charge fees for the use of public property, fees that tend to prevent excessive use of this property, can be explained in three ways:

(1) There was a failure to understand the prerequisites for efficient resource use. Some public officer must be given the incentives to act as a rational conservator of resources when these resources are scarce.
(2) The disruption of thoroughfares was not, in fact, costly enough to bother about.
(3) The setting of fees to curtail excessive use of thoroughfares by utility companies was too costly to be practical.

The first two explanations, if true, give no support to an argument for regulating utility companies. The third explanation may give support to some sort of regulation, for it asserts that the economic effects that are produced by the placing of distribution systems are such that it is too costly to economize through the use of a price system. The costs of taking account of these effects through some regulatory process must be compared with the benefits of realigning resource use, and if the benefits are worth the costs some regulation may be desirable. Note clearly: scale economies in serving a market are not at issue. To see this, imagine that electrical distribution systems are thin lines of a special conducting paint. The placing of such systems causes no difficulties. They are sprayed over either public or private property. Nonetheless, suppose that the use of each system is subject to scale economies. Clearly, the desire to regulate cannot now be justified by such problems as traffic disruption, even though scale economies are present. 'Excess' duplication is a problem of externalities and not of scale economies.

Let us suppose that it is desirable to employ some sort of regulation because it is too costly to use the price system to take account of the disruptive effects of placing distribution systems. Regulation comes in all sizes and shapes, and it is by no means clear what type of regulation would be most desirable.

A franchise system that allows only a limited number of utility companies to serve a market area was employed frequently. A franchise system that awarded the franchise to that company which seemed to offer the best price–quality package would be one that allowed market competition between bidding rivals to determine that package. The restraint of the market would be substituted for that of the regulatory commission.

An alternative arrangement would be public ownership of the distribution system. This would involve the collection of competing bids for installing the distribution system. The system could then be installed by the bidder offering to do the specified job at the lowest price. This is the same process used by communities to build highways and it employs rival bidding and not commissions to determine that price. The community could then allow its distribution system to be used by that utility company offering to provide specified utility services at lowest cost to residents. Again the market is substituted for the regulatory commission. Public ownership of streets may make public ownership of distribution systems seem desirable, but this does not mean that the use of regulatory commissions is desirable.

The Problem of Windfalls

We must now consider a last difficulty that has sometimes been marshalled to support the regulation of utilities. This argument is based on the fact that events in life are uncertain. The application of this observation to the utility business goes like this. After a buyer enters into an agreement with a utility company for supplying utility service, there may be changes in technology and prices that make the agreed-upon price obsolete. In such cases, it is asserted, the price should be changed to reflect the current cost of providing utility services. The regulation by commission of prices on the basis of current costs is needed in the utilities industries because of the durability of original investments in plant and distribution systems. This durability prohibits the use of recontracting in the market place as a method for bringing about appropriate changes in price.

Problems of uncertainty create a potential for positive or negative windfalls. If market negotiations have misjudged the development of a better technology and if there is some cost to reawarding contracts to other producers once they are agreed upon, then an unexpected improvement in the technology used by those who are awarded the contracts may generate a price that is higher than per-unit cost, but higher by an amount no greater than the cost of reawarding contracts. In such cases, the firms now holding the contracts may collect a positive windfall for a short-run period. Or, if input prices increase by more than is expected, these same firms may suffer from a negative windfall. But the same thing is true of all markets. If a customer buys eggs today for consumption tomorrow, he will enjoy a positive windfall if the price of eggs is higher tomorrow and a negative windfall if the price is lower. The difference in the two cases is that, where long-term contracts are desirable, the windfalls may continue for longer periods. In such cases it *may* be desirable to employ a cost-plus regulatory scheme or to enter a clause that reserves the right, for some fee, to renegotiate the contract.

The problem faced here is what is the best way to cope with uncertainty. Long-term contracts for the supply of commodities are concluded satisfactorily in the market place without the aid of regulation. These contracts may be between retailers and appliance producers, or between the air lines and aircraft companies, all of whom may use durable production facilities. The rental of office space for ninety-nine years is fraught with uncertainty. I presume that the parties to a contract hire experts to provide relevant guesses on these matters and that the contract concluded resolves these issues in a way that is satisfactory to both parties. Penalties for reopening negotiations at a later date can be included in the contract. I presume that buyers and sellers who agree to contract with each other have handled the problem of uncertainty in a mutually satisfactory way. The correct way to view the problem is one of selecting the best type of contract. A producer may say, 'If you agree to buy from me for twenty-five years, I can use facilities that are expected to produce the service at lower costs; if you contract five years, I will not invest much in tooling-up, and, hence, I will need a higher price to cover higher per-unit costs; of course, the longer-run contract allows more time for the unexpected, so let us include an escape clause of some kind.' The buyer and seller must then agree on a suitable contract; durability of equipment and longer-term commitments can be sacrificed at the cost of higher per-unit costs, but there is no reason to expect that the concluded contract will be biased as to outcome or nonoptimal in other respects.

Cost-plus rate regulation is one way of coping with these problems, but it has great uncertainties of its own. Will the commission be effective? Does a well defined cost-plus arrangement create an inappropriate system of incentives to guide the firm in its investment and operating policies? Do the continual uncertainties associated with the meaning of cost-plus lead to otherwise avoidable difficulties in formulating investment plans? Rate regulation by commissions rather than by market rivalry may be more appropriate for utility industries than for other industries, but the truth of this assertion cannot be established deductively from existing economic theory. We do not know whether regulation handles the uncertainty–rent problem better or worse than the market.

The problem of coping with windfalls must be distinguished from the problem of *forecastable* rents. Suppose that it is known that buyers will incur considerable recontracting cost if they decide to change sellers after they are part way through an awarded contract. It would appear that the seller who wins the initial contract will be able to collect a rent as large as this recontracting cost. But this is not true if this recontracting cost is forecastable, that is, if it is not a windfall. The bidding for the initial contract will take account of the forecastable rent, so that if the bidding is competitive the rent will be forfeited by the lower bid prices to which it gives rise.

To what degree should legislation and regulation replace the market in the utilities or in other industries and what forms should such legislation take? It is not the objective of this paper to provide answers to such questions. My purpose has been to question the conventional economic arguments for the existing legislation and regulation. An expanded role for government can be defended on the empirical grounds of a documented general superiority of public administration in these industries or by a philosophical preference for mild socialism. But I do not see how a defense can be based on the formal arguments considered here; these arguments do not allow us to deduce from their assumptions either the monopoly problem or the administrative superiority of regulation.

In the case of utility industries, resort to the rivalry of the market place would relieve companies of the discomforts of commission regulation. But it would also relieve them of the comfort of legally protected market areas. It is my belief that the rivalry of the open market place disciplines more effectively than do the regulatory processes of the commission. If the managements of utility companies doubt this belief, I suggest that they re-examine the history of their industry to discover just who it was that provided most of the force behind the regulatory movement.

11 On the Regulation of Industry: A Note[1]

L. G. Telser

The revival of interest in the old controversies about natural monopoly and whether such things exist and, if they exist, whether they should be regulated, inspires this note.[2] My purpose is to present an example to show that in those cases for which the example is relevant, some kind of direct regulation is necessary, both for efficiency and for the best public service. In my example, competition does not lead to the beneficial results often associated with a *laissez-faire* policy. In fact, competition leads to Chamberlin's tangency solution of monopolistic competition. At the end of this note I offer some suggestions for overcoming the difficulties. These suggestions are derived from the theory of the core.

My example is an exercise in spatial economics. Although it must omit many details, it is intended to preserve the crucial elements responsible for the difficulties encountered in unfettered competition. Those readers who wish to deny the relevance of my example for the real world can rest secure in their belief about the efficacy of competition, even if they agree

[1] I am grateful to H. Demsetz, Z. Griliches, H. Johnson, and P. Pashigian for helpful comments and criticisms. I assume responsibility for all errors. The financial support of the National Science Foundation is gratefully acknowledged.
[2] Among the recent articles that apparently deny the existence of such a thing as a natural monopoly are those of Demsetz (1968a, 1968b). The roots of the present controversy center on the elegant analysis of Lerner (1944) and Hotelling (1938, 1939a, 1939b). Coase's analysis (1946) advocates marginal cost pricing by means of a multi-part tariff. This proposal is fully in accord with those of Lerner and Hotelling despite Coase's claim to the contrary. In the Hotelling example of a bridge, the running expense is zero and the main problem is to determine how to share the overhead cost among the populace. This is equivalent to a two-part price in which the first part is a fixed fee independent of the rate of use of the product and the second part is proportional to the rate of use in order to cover the marginal running cost. However, since the running cost is zero, it is only necessary to determine the amount of the first part, a far from trivial problem.

Reprinted with author's amendments from *Journal of Political Economy*, LXXVII (Nov–Dec 1969) 937–52, by kind permission of the author and of the University of Chicago Press.

that my analysis is correct. However, I hope this example succeeds in returning the debate to the relevant issues. For the sake of clarity and rigor, I have cast the example in mathematical form.

At the outset I wish to consider the simplest example of a natural monopoly. Consider Fig. 11.1. In this figure a firm is

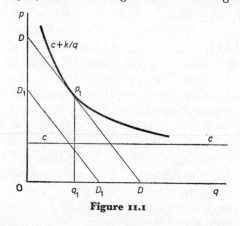

Figure 11.1

assumed to have decreasing average cost, which approaches the horizontal line, cc, asymptotically. Algebraically, its total cost is $k + cQ$ for any positive output, Q. The overhead cost is k and the variable cost is cQ. With this cost, at most one firm can supply the demand efficiently. Let the demand schedule be D_1D_1. The firm must be prevented from charging a monopoly price, because this would waste social resources. That is, it must be prevented from offering an output where marginal cost equals marginal revenue, because the latter is below the marginal social benefit. Hotelling (1938) and Lerner (1944) would advocate marginal cost pricing in this case such that the price per unit is set equal to c and the overhead cost, k, is somehow shared among the customers in such a way as to be independent of the amount they purchase. If the consumers do not value the product enough to be willing to pay for the overhead expense, then the product should not be provided at all. The most difficult problem is to discover how much consumers are willing to pay for having the product rather than going without. Closely related to this is the problem of how the cost is to be shared among the users. For example, should those who do not contribute at all to the overhead cost be allowed to purchase the product? Hotelling (1938) discusses these issues in connection with the building of a bridge, where he assumes the running expense is zero $(c = 0)$ so that his entire discussion focuses on the appropriate measure of the benefit from the bridge and on how the bridge should be financed. The latter becomes a problem of taxation.

In all of this discussion, the issues center on marginal cost pricing and not on the firm's rate of return. It does a disservice to equate efficiency with competitive rates of return. The most elementary example shows that a firm may obtain a competitive rate of return while charging a monopoly price. This can happen if it purchases a concern from the original monopolist. In a recent article, Demsetz (1968b) leaves readers with the impression that he is content with a situation in which the firm is prevented from obtaining a monopoly return and he does not raise the question of efficiency. Hence he implies that direct regulation of an industry subject to decreasing average cost is unnecessary if it is prevented from obtaining a monopoly return and that there are no natural monopolies. This misses the point. The controversy concerns regulation to secure efficiency and to promote public welfare. It does not concern the rate of return.[3]

In the simple form presented in Fig. 11.1, the problem becomes involved with questions about the relevant demand for the product, how to measure consumer surplus, and methods of sharing the overhead expense among the populace. To avoid some of these problems, my example concerns the optimum location of plants on a road of finite length.

Description of the Problem[4]

Let there be a straight road of finite length S on which plants

---

[3] See Demsetz (1968b).

[4] Both Hotelling (1952) and Smithies (1941) study competition in terms of spatial economics. Hotelling assumes a uniform distribution of demand along a finite road such that the demand at every point is perfectly inelastic. In Smithies (1941), there is also a uniform distribution of demand along a finite road, but the demand is not perfectly inelastic. Thus, my example corresponds to that of Smithies. There is an important difference between Smithies's and Hotelling's cases, because, as Smithies points out, in his case sellers will not locate so close together. This is because, as sellers approach each other toward the center of the road, say, they lose sales at their hinterland due to the rise of the delivered price. This has interesting implications about the nature of political parties which these writers point out.

are located. At every point on the road there is the same demand function for the product given as follows:

$$q = \varphi(p^*) \tag{1}$$

where p^* denotes the delivered price per unit at a point s units from the plant of purchase and q denotes the corresponding quantity demanded. The quantity demanded varies inversely with the delivered price, and the demand function is neither perfectly elastic nor perfectly inelastic. Hence

$$-\infty < \frac{\partial \varphi}{\partial p^*} < 0. \tag{2}$$

The delivered price is the price at the customer's door, including the cost of transport. Without loss of generality, it is convenient to assume that the customers pay the shipping cost. I shall also assume that all customers pay the same price at the plant. Hence it is impossible or prohibitively costly for the sellers to identify their customers' points of origin.

I assume uniform transportation costs that are constant per unit of product and proportional to distance. Hence the cost of shipping q units a distance s is given by aqs, where a is the unit transportation cost. Let p denote the f.o.b. price, the price at the plant. Hence the delivered price is $p^* = p + as$.

Plants are located on the road, and all plants have identical production costs. Let Q denote the total output of a plant. Its total production cost is $k + cQ$ if $Q > 0$ and 0 if $Q = 0$. Therefore, k is the overhead cost per plant and c is the marginal production cost for $Q > 0$. I assume the overhead cost is a given constant. For this cost function, average production cost is a decreasing function of Q and approaches c asymptotically. There is no minimum average cost for any finite output. In a more general analysis, one could assume that c and k vary inversely, so that plants with a larger fixed cost have a smaller running cost. However, in that case I would add the condition that c approaches infinity as k approaches zero. In my example, one may wish to assume that k is the smallest feasible amount.

Let there be n plants. To minimize the transportation costs, the given n plants should be equispaced and each should locate at the midpoint of its territory. Hence the n plants should be at the following points on the road: $S/2n$, $3S/2n$, . . . , $[1 - (1/2n)]S$. Hence each plant serves a market of length S/n. I shall not dwell on a proof of these assertions, which are a consequence of the uniform distribution of demand along the road. From now on, I assume that any given set of n plants is efficiently spaced.

The total cost of serving all the customers on the road is the sum of the total production cost and the total transportation cost. Assuming efficient location of the plants, the more plants there are, the less is the transportation cost and the greater is the aggregate overhead cost. Were overhead costs zero and c finite, then placing a plant at every point on the road would result in zero transportation cost. Positive overhead cost explains why sellers are not so densely located on the real roads to which my example applies. In my example, the commodity is a joint product requiring both a production and a transportation input. Hence, there is a problem of determining the efficient combination of these two inputs. Given n efficiently located plants, the total cost is as follows:

$$G = n\left(cQ + k + 2a \int_0^{S/2n} sq\ ds\right) \tag{3}$$

where

$$Q = 2 \int_0^{S/2n} q\ ds \tag{4}$$

is the output per plant and

$$T = 2a \int_0^{S/2n} sq\ ds \tag{5}$$

is the total transport cost of the shipments from each plant.[5] Let $\bar{G}$ denote the total cost per plant. Then

$$G = n\bar{G} \quad \text{and} \quad \bar{G} = cQ + k + T. \tag{6}$$

The Necessary Conditions for Efficiency

Let X denote the total output so that

$$X = nQ. \tag{7}$$

To produce and ship a given total output X efficiently means

[5] From now on, where the limits of integration are omitted, they are understood to run from zero to $S/2n$.

that the *total* cost G of the given *total* output X is as small as possible. Provided we are willing to assume that the number of plants is continuously divisible, this is a standard problem in elementary calculus. To account for the fact that n is an integer would complicate the mathematics without introducing any new principles. Form the Lagrangian function as follows:

$$L(n, Q) + G = \lambda(X - nQ) \qquad (8)$$

where λ denotes a Lagrangian multiplier. For efficiency it is necessary that $\partial L/\partial Q = \partial L/\partial n = 0$. Hence

$$\frac{\partial G}{\partial Q} - \lambda n = 0; \quad \frac{\partial G}{\partial n} - \lambda Q = 0. \qquad (9)$$

Therefore, for efficiency it is necessary that n and Q satisfy

$$\frac{1}{n}\frac{\partial G}{\partial Q} = \frac{1}{Q}\frac{\partial G}{\partial n} = \lambda \qquad (10)$$

and that λ be positive. The Lagrangian multiplier λ may be interpreted as the marginal cost of X. There is another way to derive this result that illuminates the problem.

Let X be given. Then

$$dX = n\, dQ + Q\, dn = 0 \qquad (11)$$

$$dG = \frac{\partial G}{\partial Q}\, dQ + \frac{\partial G}{\partial n}\, dn = 0 \qquad (12)$$

is necessary for an efficient combination of Q and n. Eliminating dQ from (12) by means of (11) yields the result that

$$dG = Q\left[\frac{1}{Q}\frac{\partial G}{\partial n} - \frac{1}{n}\frac{\partial G}{\partial Q}\right] dn = 0 \qquad (13)$$

for all $dn \neq 0$. This result is equivalent to (10).

For efficiency, it is also necessary that the common marginal costs of the inputs n and Q are positive. Hence the necessary conditions for efficiency are as follows:

$$\frac{\partial G}{\partial Q} = n\frac{\partial \bar{G}}{\partial Q} = nc + n\frac{\delta T}{\delta Q} \geq 0 \qquad (14)$$

$$\frac{\partial G}{\partial n} = \bar{G} + n\frac{\partial \bar{G}}{\partial n} + \bar{G} + n\frac{\delta T}{\delta n} \geq 0.[6] \tag{15}$$

Now the problem as stated makes G an explicit function of n and p, the f.o.b. price. Thus (4) and (5) imply that

$$Q = f(p, n) \tag{16}$$

$$T = g(p, n). \tag{17}$$

It follows that p is an implicit function of Q and n by means of (16). Hence

$$dp = \left(\frac{\partial f}{\partial p}\right)^{-1}\left(dQ - \frac{\partial f}{\partial n}dn\right). \tag{18}$$

Thus, by solving (16) for p in terms of Q and n, one obtains

$$p = h(Q, n) \tag{19}$$

so that (17) becomes

$$T = g[h(Q, n), n]. \tag{20}$$

It follows that

$$\frac{\delta T}{\delta Q} = \frac{\partial g}{\partial p}\frac{\partial p}{\partial Q} = \frac{\partial g}{\partial p}\left(\frac{\partial f}{\partial p}\right)^{-1} \tag{21}$$

and

$$\frac{\delta T}{\delta n} = \frac{\partial g}{\partial p}\frac{\partial p}{\partial n} + \frac{\partial g}{\partial n} = \left[\frac{\partial g}{\partial n} - \frac{\partial g}{\partial p}\frac{\partial f}{\partial n}\left(\frac{\partial f}{\partial p}\right)^{-1}\right]. \tag{22}$$

Thus, to determine whether these conditions for efficiency are satisfied, it is necessary to determine the signs of the expressions given in (14), (15), (21), and (22). We now investigate these matters.

Consider first the terms on the right-hand side of (21).

$$\frac{\partial f}{\partial p} = 2\int\frac{\partial q}{\partial p}ds < 0 \tag{23}$$

[6] The δ notation is designed to convey the notion of a partial derivative of a function with respect to a variable that holds another variable constant by means of a compensating change of a third variable. Thus, $\delta T/\delta Q$ is the partial derivative of transport cost with respect to output per plant that keeps the number of plants constant by means of a compensating change in p, the f.o.b. price at the plant. It is necessary to calculate the partial derivatives in this way because the demand function enters total cost.

because of (2) and $p^* = p + as$. Similarly,

$$\frac{\partial g}{\partial p} = 2a \int s \, \frac{\partial q}{\partial p} \, ds < 0. \tag{24}$$

It follows that $\delta T / \delta Q > 0$, so that in (14), since $c > 0$, $\partial G / \partial Q > 0$.

Next consider the sign of $\partial G / \partial n$. Obviously, if $\delta T / \delta n \geq 0$, then marginal cost with respect to n must also be nonnegative. However, this is not the only possibility. A rise in the number of plants has two effects such that one reduces and the other increases T so that the net effect on T of a change in n can be either positive or negative. Clearly, an increase in n requires the plants to be more closely spaced so that on average the customers are nearer to plants. This tends to reduce the delivered

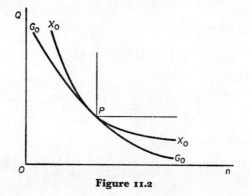

Figure 11.2

price on average, which in turn implies an increase in total quantity sold per plant. If the rise in Q resulting from a rise in n is large enough, it results in a positive $\delta T / \delta n$. However, if the demand is sufficiently elastic, then Q does not rise enough to offset the negative effect on T resulting from a rise in n, so that $\delta T / \delta n < 0$. Nevertheless, even in this case, since $\bar{G}/n \geq T/n \geq \delta T / \delta n$, it follows that $\partial G / \partial n \geq 0$. Hence, regardless of the sign of $\delta T / \delta n$, the marginal cost of G with respect to n must be nonnegative as required.[7]

---

[7] The conditions sufficient for the existence of an efficient allocation of the inputs n and Q to produce a given total X are most easily described in geometric terms. Consider Fig. 11.2. The constraint of producing a given total output X_0 with the inputs n and Q gives rise to a rectangular hyperbola as shown in the figure. The

The Marginal Social Benefit

Most economists would agree that this analysis of efficiency is correct. Thus, for efficiency, it is necessary that n and Q satisfy (10) and that the marginal cost of the total output is positive. In my example the nonnegativity conditions for efficiency are satisfied. However, these conditions do not determine the optimum total of X. The optimum amount of X depends on the marginal social benefit of X. Hence society can set λ equal to whatever value it decides is the appropriate measure of the marginal social benefit, and this will determine the best total amount of X. Given X, it is then possible to allocate n and Q efficiently to produce X at the least possible total cost. The controversy is not about (10); it is over the determination of the optimum total quantity X. Let us analyze some proposals that have been offered to determine the best total output.

The first criterion for the social benefit uses the concept of consumer surplus. Consider the customers of a given plant. All of the customers who are s units distant from the plant pay the same delivered price, $p^* = p + as$. Hence they obtain a consumer surplus measured by the expression as follows:

$$F(p, s) = \int_{p + as}^{\infty} \varphi(p^*) \, dp^* + p^* \cdot \varphi(p^*). \qquad (25)^8$$

In order to obtain the consumer surplus of all the customers of a given plant, it is necessary to integrate F over the interval

---

combinations of n and Q that have a constant cost are shown by the locus $G_0 G_0$. For an efficient allocation, it is sufficient that the isocost locus $G_0 G_0$ be less sharply curved than a rectangular hyperbola. More precisely, this means that a 1 per cent decrease in one input, say Q, accompanied by a 1 per cent increase in the other, say n, which maintains a given total output X, causes a more than 1 per cent increase in G. Whether in fact this condition is satisfied in a particular instance depends on the shape of the demand function (1) and on the size of c. There are demand functions and c's for which sufficient conditions can be satisfied, for instance, linear demand relations. However, there are also demand relations and c's for which the sufficient conditions are not satisfied, for instance, linear demand relations.

[8] I am grateful to Professor Robert M. Solow for pointing out an error in the definition of consumer surplus given in the original published version. The error consists in omitting the term $p^* \cdot \varphi(p^*)$ which leads to counting costs twice in the measure of the net surplus.

$(0, S/2n)$. This gives consumer surplus of all customers of a given plant as follows:

$$\bar{\psi} = 2 \int F(p, s)\, ds. \tag{26}$$

Finally, the total consumer surplus summed over all the plants is given by $\psi = n\bar{\psi}$.

The optimum number of plants and the optimum output per plant, according to consumer surplus measure of the social benefit, is that pair (Q, n) which maximizes $\psi - G$, the net surplus. There is another way of looking at this problem that parallels the analyses of efficiency. Given the total output $X = nQ$, choose n and Q to maximize ψ. To solve this problem we introduce the Lagrangian function as follows: $\psi + \lambda(X - nQ)$. If a maximum exists, then n and Q must satisfy the following equations: $\partial \psi/\partial Q = \lambda n$ and $\partial \psi/\partial n = \gamma Q$, so that

$$\frac{1}{n} \frac{\partial \psi}{\partial Q} = \frac{1}{Q} \frac{\partial \psi}{\partial n} = \lambda \tag{27}$$

where the Lagrangian multiplier λ is the marginal social benefit. This brings out the analogy between (10) and (27). Now

$$\frac{1}{n} \frac{\partial \psi}{\partial Q} = \frac{\partial \bar{\psi}}{\partial Q} = \frac{\partial \bar{\psi}}{\partial p} \Big/ \frac{\partial f}{\partial p}$$

$$\frac{1}{Q} \frac{\partial \psi}{\partial n} = \frac{1}{Q}\Big(\bar{\psi} + n \frac{\partial \bar{\psi}}{\partial n}\Big). \tag{28}$$

With the consumer surplus measure of the social benefit, the solution of the problem is that pair (Q, n) which makes the marginal social benefit equal to the marginal social cost. This is given by the solution of the following pair of equations:

$$\frac{\partial \psi}{\partial Q} = \frac{\partial G}{\partial Q} \quad \text{and} \quad \frac{\partial \psi}{\partial n} = \frac{\partial G}{\partial n}. \tag{29}$$

Of course, the pair (Q, n) determines the f.o.b. price, p, as well. Moreover, it follows from (14) in the preceding section that in general the f.o.b. price must exceed c.

It is possible to give a more explicit expression for the marginal social benefit in this case. First, let us calculate $\partial \bar{\psi}/\partial p$:

$$\frac{\partial \bar{\psi}}{\partial p} = 2 \int_0^{S/2n} \frac{\partial F}{\partial p}\, ds.$$

Since $\partial F/\partial p = q + p^* \partial \varphi/\partial p - \varphi^*$, it follows that

$$\frac{\partial \bar{\psi}}{\partial p} = 2 \int p^* \frac{\partial \varphi}{\partial p} \, ds. \tag{30}$$

Hence the marginal social benefit satisfies

$$\lambda = \frac{1}{n} \frac{\partial \psi}{\partial Q} = p + \frac{\delta T}{\delta Q} \tag{31}$$

as a consequence of (21) and (23). In conjunction with (10) and (14) we obtain

$$p = c. \tag{32}$$

Therefore, by the criterion of maximizing the net consumer surplus,

$$p^* = c + as \tag{33}$$

which is marginal cost pricing.

Next let us examine the second equation of (28). Since $\partial \bar{\psi}/\partial n = -S/n^2 \, F(p, S/2n)$, it follows that

$$\lambda = \frac{1}{Q} \frac{\partial \psi}{\partial n} = \frac{1}{Q} [\bar{\psi} - F(p, S/2n)(S/n)]. \tag{34}$$

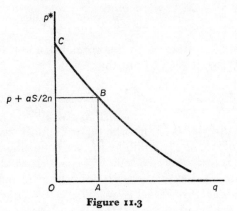

Figure 11.3

$F(p, S/2n)$ is proportional to the area $OABC$ shown in Fig. 11.3. On this interpretation, F is proportional to the consumer surplus obtained by those customers who live farthest from the given plant. Also, F has another interpretation. It is proportional to the additional quantity that would be sold by

H

a given plant if the number of plants were adjusted so that the highest delivered price coincided with the price that intersects the p^* axis. Under these conditions the customers living farthest from the plant would obtain no consumer surplus at all.

Other criteria have been proposed which ignore the demand conditions altogether. One deserving our attention proposes to set λ equal to the minimum average cost.[9] Admittedly, under some conditions this criterion would satisfy demand. For instance, this would be true in the textbook example of an industry for which the long-run supply is perfectly elastic. But this criterion leads to strange results in the present case.

The minimum average cost occurs for that output where average and marginal costs are equal. Hence it is determined by the conditions as follows:

$$G/X = \frac{1}{n}\frac{\partial G}{\partial Q} = \frac{1}{Q}\frac{\partial G}{\partial n} = \lambda. \tag{35}$$

Therefore, $\bar{G}/Q = \partial\bar{G}/\partial Q$ and $\bar{G}/Q = \bar{G}/Q + (n/Q)(\delta T/\delta n)$. For the latter conditions to be satisfied, it is necessary and sufficient that

$$\frac{n}{Q}\frac{\delta T}{\delta n} = 0. \tag{36}$$

It can be shown that, except for special demand functions, for (36) to be zero, it is sufficient that

$$\frac{n}{Q}\frac{\partial f}{\partial n} = 0. \tag{37}$$

But (37) will be true under one of two conditions. Either n is infinite or $q[p^*(S/2n)] = 0$. The former condition is impossible as long as k is positive and S is finite, because it would make total costs infinite. It does make sense for a road of infinite length, and I consider this case below. The latter condition would require a delivered price at the boundary of every plant's territory high enough to reduce the quantity sold at these

---

[9] The claim that the minimum average cost represents 'efficiency' is an implication of the argument by Chamberlin (1932) that the tangency solution is inefficient because it occurs at the point where average cost is decreasing. Similarly, Dewey's argument about the efficiency of monopolistic competition seems to equate minimum average cost and efficiency (see Dewey, 1958).

boundary points to zero. Thus at the points $0, S/n, \ldots, S$, the quantity sold would be zero.

It is difficult to defend the proposition that this is socially optimal. Surely there are demand conditions such that the minimum average cost criterion is harmful. Thus, suppose the demand function given in (1) has the property that people would be willing to buy a quantity $0q_1$ at a price p_1 that equals the average cost of producing this quantity. The situation is illustrated in Fig. 11.1. It follows that there is enough demand at every one of the points on the road, $0, S/n, 2S/n, \ldots, S$ to support a plant. Why then leave unsatisfied the demand at these points for the sake of minimizing the average cost? This possibility is enough to show that the minimum average cost criterion is unacceptable due to its neglect of the demand conditions. However, a more general criticism can be levied against this criterion.

Given the pricing scheme I have postulated, which consists of a common f.o.b. price at every plant and a c.i.f. price, $p^* = p + as$, private enterprise would be willing to supply the demand only if total receipts at every plant were at least sufficient to pay the total cost. Thus, in my example, a sufficient condition for the viability of private enterprise to supply the demand is that

$$pQ \geq cQ + k \qquad (38)$$

for some market territory. More precisely, there must exist an $m > 0$ such that

$$\int_0^m p \, q \, ds \geq c \int_0^m q \, ds + k. \qquad (39)$$

Hence, by the mean value theorem there is an m' with $0 < m' < m$ such that

$$\int_0^m (p - c)q \, ds = (p - c) \, q(m') \, m \geq k.$$

The value of m gives the smallest size of market that is viable under free enterprise. It follows that a region of size m surrounding the points where nothing would be sold by the minimum average cost criterion could support a plant. It is in this sense that the minimum average cost criterion is neglectful of the demand conditions.

The remaining case to consider is a road of infinite length. This allows an infinite number of plants, because although the aggregate overhead cost would be infinite, the aggregate total revenue would also be infinite. To study this case, let S be finite initially and then consider the consequences as S approaches infinity. The preceding discussion is now relevant. Suppose that the demand at a given point is not large enough to support one plant. This is illustrated by D_1D_1 in Fig. 11.1. Suppose there exists a market of size m that has an aggregate demand large enough to bring the demand relation up to a point of tangency with the average cost. Hence, $m = S/n$, and, given S, this determines n. This argument determines the largest number of plants that can survive on the road. Now let S approach infinity. If n also approaches infinity in such a way that m remains constant, then, in the limit, the aggregate output X would be such as to minimize average cost, G/X. This is because, with n infinite, $\partial f/\partial n = 0 \Rightarrow \partial g/\partial n = 0$, so that by (22), $\delta T/\delta n = 0$, which implies that (37) is satisfied. These results show that the criterion of choosing an output that minimizes the average cost can be consistent with the necessary condition of efficiency for a road of finite length.

Some Positive Economics

Let the cost and demand functions be as described above and assume the road is of finite length. Let there be free entry on the road. This means that anyone may establish a plant and sell to the customers on the road. Also assume that a seller cannot identify customers according to their points of origin. This implies that sellers cannot practice price discrimination according to customer location, so that all buyers at a given plant pay the same f.o.b. price and themselves bear the cost of transport. To prove that the f.o.b. price is the same at all plants, it is necessary to show that the spatial distribution of the plants is optimal. First, it is clear that firms compete for sales with their nearest neighbor at the boundary of the market territories. However, the f.o.b. price at two neighboring plants would be equal only if the market territories are of equal size and if the plants are located at the midpoints of their respective territories. This can be shown by contradiction. Thus, suppose the plants are inefficiently located; then it would pay an entrepreneur to purchase all the existing plants and relocate them efficiently. Nevertheless, the free entry of firms to the road would prevent such an entrepreneur from obtaining a monopoly return. Therefore, there would be that number of plants in business on the road such that each firm maximizes its net revenue with respect to the quantity it sells, and the value of the maximum net revenue would be zero. The first condition is equivalent to

$$\frac{\partial(pQ)}{\partial Q} = c \tag{40}$$

and the second is equivalent to

$$pQ = cQ + k. \tag{41}$$

Together these two conditions constitute Chamberlin's well-known tangency solution.[10] In general it is *not* possible to show that this solution is efficient in the sense of making $(1/n)(\partial G/\partial Q) = (1/Q)(\partial G/\partial n) = \lambda$.

Now suppose that entry is restricted by the following device. The state offers to sell a franchise to the highest bidder. The franchise gives the exclusive right to operate plants on the road. Hence, the franchise holder will have a monopoly. However, competition among firms for the privilege of obtaining the franchise will drive its price up to the point where the successful bidder can obtain only a competitive rate of return. Although there is a competitive rate of return, there is a monopoly f.o.b. price. Moreover, it will not generally be in the interest of the monopolist to produce the given monopoly output at the least possible *total* cost, because this will be generally incompatible with maximum net revenue. These surprising assertions are the result of the fact that the monopoly 'inputs', n and Q, not only affect the cost but also affect the demand. A formal analysis is helpful. Let

$$M = R - G \tag{42}$$

---

[10] Chamberlin (1932), however, did not call his analysis in the specific context of spatial economics, although his work (sixth edition) contains an appendix on the Hotelling model (1952). An article by Dewey (1958) does use a spatial exercise to analyze monopolistic competition, but it is not a satisfactory attempt. It is interesting to note that with an integral number of plants one would not obtain the exact tangency solution except by accident. In general, a fractional number of plants would be necessary for tangency. Thus, it is ironic, in view of Chamberlin's insistence on the importance of indivisibilities, that continuity is necessary for the tangency solution.

denote the net monopoly return. The monopolist chooses n and Q to maximize M. If a maximum exists, it must satisfy $\partial M/\partial Q = \partial M/\partial n = 0$. Hence, $\partial R/\partial n = \partial G/\partial n$ and $\partial R/\partial Q = \partial G/\partial Q$, so that

$$\bar{R} + n\frac{\partial \bar{R}}{\partial n} = \bar{G} + n\frac{\partial \bar{G}}{\partial n} \quad \text{and} \quad \frac{\partial \bar{R}}{\partial Q} = \frac{\partial \bar{G}}{\partial Q}. \tag{43}$$

In this case there is a tangency solution in the sense that max $M = 0$, because the cost of the franchise is bid up to the point where only a competitive return is possible. However, the equilibrium differs from that of monopolistic competition. With monopoly we have $R = G$, because to the monopolist the cost includes the price of the franchise, but we do not have $\bar{R} = \bar{G}$ as under monopolistic competition. For the latter to be true, it would be necessary to assume that the price of the franchise is proportional to the number of plants. Under monopoly, the first condition of (43) implies that

$$p - c - \frac{k}{Q} = n\left(\frac{\partial f}{\partial p}\right)^{-1}\left(\frac{\partial f}{\partial n}\right) > 0 \tag{44}$$

so that the tangency solution of monopolistic competition is not satisfied. Moreover, with a monopoly it will not be true that

$$\frac{1}{n}\frac{\partial R}{\partial Q} = \frac{1}{Q}\frac{\partial R}{\partial n} \tag{45}$$

as is required by the necessary condition for efficiency.

A more direct argument of the inefficiency of monopoly is possible in this case. Thus, assume that the total output is fixed at the monopoly level. Does it follow from this that the monopolist would have an incentive to produce the given output at the lowest total cost? This could be true only if the revenue did not depend on the composition of the inputs which are n and Q. Thus, given X, it does not follow that the maximum net revenue M occurs for that combination of inputs n and Q which makes the given output X available at the least possible total cost G. The difficulty stems from the fact that R depends on n and Q. This point is worth further consideration.

Consider the textbook monopolist who produces an output y by means of two inputs, x_1 and x_2, via a production function as follows: $y = f(x_1, x_2)$. Let the inputs be available at given prices per unit, w_1 and w_2. Given y, the monopolist would choose inputs x_1 and x_2 to minimize the total cost given by $w_1 x_1 + w_2 x_2$. This leads to the standard solution that $w_1(\partial f / \partial x_1) = w_2(\partial f / \partial x_2) = \lambda$, where the Lagrangian multiplier λ is the marginal cost. The monopolist determines his total output by setting λ equal to marginal revenue. But the marginal revenue depends only on the total amount of y; the demand does not depend directly on the composition of inputs. In contrast, in my example this is not true. The total demand does depend on the inputs n and Q directly.

To meet the criticism that under monopoly an inefficient combination of inputs would emerge, one might urge the criterion of awarding the franchise to the firm which offers to make the product available at the lowest cost. That is, the state could solicit bids which stipulate a cost schedule giving the total cost for each level of total output. The contract for operating the enterprise could then be awarded to that firm which provides the lowest total cost schedule. Hence the successful bidder would produce efficiently. However, this procedure would not determine the total output, because it remains necessary to fix the price. Moreover, there is the possibility that one bidder might offer a lower cost schedule for one range of total output while another bidder is more efficient at another range of output. Clearly, who should be awarded the contract depends on the desired total output, which, in turn, depends on the marginal social benefit. Hence this method does not avoid the need for price regulation.[11]

Conclusions

My example shows that free entry leads to Chamberlin's tangency solution, which is generally inefficient. A franchise system, equivalent to monopoly, also leads to the tangency solution and is subject to the same criticism. Hence in my example the market forces appropriate to these two cases cannot be relied upon to promote the social welfare. Nor is the criterion of minimum average cost acceptable, because it

[11] This is the only interpretation I can offer to make sense of the proposal by Demsetz (1968*b*). The answer to the question he poses in the title of his previous article (Demsetz, 1968*a*) is yes as this note shows.

neglects the demand conditions if the road is of finite length. However, for an infinite road the minimum average cost criterion can be, but is not necessarily, consistent with efficiency and satisfy the demand. If one accepts the measure of the marginal social benefit given in equation (34), which depends on the demand conditions, then some direct price control would be necessary if the industry were privately owned.

The main elements in my example responsible for these results are the existence of positive overhead cost, which makes the average production cost at every plant a decreasing function of its output, the externalities among plants which is brought about by the competition for customers at the boundaries of their markets, and the demand condition which relates the quantity demanded to the delivered price. The nature of production costs requires a single plant within each road segment. The externalities make the optimum size of the firm one that encompasses all of the plants, so that it becomes a monopoly which must be regulated. The demand conditions imply that the total output will not lead to an efficient allocation of output per plant and number of plants unless the firm is regulated.

In a more general case, I would assume that k and c vary inversely such that as k approaches zero, c approaches infinity. Even in the cases I consider, it may be that there is no efficient allocation of n and Q for certain levels of total output. This can happen even for the mundane example of a linear demand function. *A fortiori* efficient allocations may not exist in more complicated situations. Analysis of such cases is beyond the scope of this note.

There is another approach to the problems considered in this note based on the recent theory of the core. In this theory, one abandons the conventional distinction between producers and consumers. It is assumed that inhabitants along the road would combine in temporary associations, called coalitions, such that each individual would join that coalition which offers him the best terms. Thus the coalitions are equivalent to a system of contracts. If all possible coalitions are free to form, they determine a set of equilibrium conditions compatible with maximum social welfare. Increasing returns would pose no special obstacle. However, it might require joint action by a large number, possibly all, of the inhabitants along the road. However, as far as I know, the theory may not be capable of specifying precisely the principles which ought to govern the sharing of the overhead cost among the inhabitants. A full analysis with this approach is another story I cannot pursue here.[12]

REFERENCES

E. H. CHAMBERLIN, *The Theory of Monopolistic Competition* (Cambridge, Mass.: Harvard University Press, 1932).

R. H. COASE, 'The Marginal Cost Controversy', *Economica*, n.s., XIII (Aug 1946) 169–82.

H. DEMSETZ, 'Do Competition and Monopolistic Competition Differ?', *Journal of Political Economy*, LXXVI (Feb 1968) 146–8. (*a*)

——, 'Why Regulate Utilities?', *Journal of Law and Economics*, XI (Apr 1968) 55–65. (*b*)

D. DEWEY, 'Imperfect Competition No Bar to Efficient Production', *Journal of Political Economy*, LXVI (Feb 1958) 24–33.

HAROLD HOTELLING, 'Stability in Competition', *Journal of Political Economy*, (Mar 1929) 41–57. Reprinted in *A.E.A. Readings in Price Theory*, ed. G. Stigler and K. Boulding (Chicago: Irwin, 1952).

——, 'The General Welfare in Relation to Problems of Taxation and of Railway and Utility Rates', *Econometrica*, VI (Jan 1938) 242–69.

——, 'The Relation of Prices to Marginal Costs in an Optimum System', *Econometrica*, VII (Jan 1939) 151–5. (*a*)

——, 'A Final Note', *Econometrica*, VII (Jan 1939) 158–60 (*b*)

A. P. LERNER, *The Economics of Control* (New York: Macmillan, 1944).

ARTHUR SMITHIES, 'Optimum Location in Spatial Competition', *Journal of Political Economy*, XLIX (Feb 1941) 423–39. Reprinted in *A.E.A. Readings in Price Theory*, ed. G. Stigler and K. Boulding (Chicago: Irwin, 1952).

L. G. TELSER, 'Applications of Core Theory to Market Exchange', Report of the Center for Mathematical Studies in Business and Economics (University of Chicago, 1968). Mimeographed.

[12] See Telser (1968) for an account along these lines.

12 Output of the Restrained Firm[1]

M. Z. Kafoglis

This paper examines the price and output behavior of the restrained monopoly firm. H. Averch and L. Johnson [1] have examined the impact of a regulatory restraint on the behavior of the monopoly firm whose management has a preference for profits. Models describing firms which voluntarily restrain profits have been developed by O. Williamson [6] under the assumption of a managerial preference for expense and by W. Baumol [2] under the assumption of revenue preference. As one would suspect, these alternative formulations of the restrained firm reveal wide variations in price and output behavior. However, they do not reveal the range of possibilities when costs are increasing, when the firm seeks to maximize output or scale of operations, or when the firm employs price discrimination. Under these circumstances the output of the restrained monopoly may exceed that predicted by existing models and may even be pushed beyond optimum (in the Paretian sense) as a result of sales at prices below marginal cost. This prediction of excess monopoly output, even in restrained or regulated situations, is the opposite of what we generally expect.

1. Single Market Model

We consider a simple monopoly firm subject to a maximum earnings restraint calculated according to a 'cost of capital' rule.[2] The elements of the problem are summarized in

[1] The author wishes to express appreciation to the Ford Foundation for financial assistance and to William J. Baumol for helpful criticisms.

[2] Though this is the general model of earnings regulation, the earnings restraint in practice may be defined and measured in a number of ways – as a markup per unit, as a percent of sales or cost or as a fixed sum of dollars – to mention but a few. The effect of the restraint will vary depending on the technique employed in any particular industry.

Reprinted from *American Economic Review*, LIX (Sep 1969) 583–9, by kind permission of the author and of the American Economic Association.

Fig. 12.1, in which the allowable level of earnings is included in the cost function, AC, as an opportunity cost to the firm. Over ranges of output where the demand curve, D, lies above AC, the firm has slack or excess profits and may be confronted with an order to reduce rates in order to satisfy the 'break-even' condition required by the restraint. The possible reactions of the firm in the presence or in anticipation of such surpluses will vary depending on the preferences of management. We wish to examine briefly, and in simplified form, two well-known

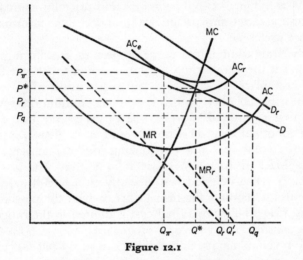

Figure 12.1

behavioral hypotheses (expense preference and revenue preference) and to set forth a third (output preference) which seems plausible but which has been overlooked.

A Williamson type of expense preference model assumes that surplus profits will be used up so as to maximize a managerial 'staff and emoluments' utility function. In this case, the output decision will be made in a '. . . conventional profit-maximizing fashion by equating marginal gross revenues to the marginal costs of production' ([6] p. 53). Thus, the firm will select the profit-maximizing output $Q\pi$, and will incur increased expenditures for staff and emoluments until excess profits are eliminated at the higher level of cost, AC_e.[3] This formulation is

---

[3] If the increased expenditures on staff have a positive impact on demand, output will be expanded somewhat beyond $Q\pi$ and the increased revenue will be absorbed through additional expenditures on staff and emoluments resulting in an equilibrium at a level of cost somewhat in excess of AC.

consistent with the view that regulated monopolies accumulate excessive staff and managerial perquisites while continuing to restrict output.

The significant characteristics of the expense preference model (profit-maximizing price and output coupled with excessive nonproduction costs) disappear under the alternative assumption of revenue preference. Under a revenue preference hypothesis, price reductions and advertising expenditures will be combined in an attempt to maximize dollar sales ([2] pp. 59–61). Thus, output is greater and price lower under the assumption of revenue preference than under the assumption of expense preference.

Some important implications of revenue maximization are revealed if the equilibrium output is defined with production costs and price as variables, but with advertising expense temporarily excluded. In this simplified situation the revenue-maximizing output is Q_r (Fig. 12.1) where the price, P_r, is below marginal cost. This novel result is implied in Baumol's description of the revenue-maximizing equilibrium as requiring $MC > MR$. If $MC > MR$, it follows that $MC > P$ is a possibility when demand is sufficiently elastic. However, since the restraint requires the firm to break even the possibility of sales at prices below marginal cost is limited to the range over which marginal cost exceeds average cost.

The revenue-maximizing equilibrium at output Q_r contains surplus or excess profits which may be absorbed by staff and emoluments as suggested by Williamson, by advertising as suggested by Baumol, or by price reductions as might be suggested by the regulatory agency. The introduction of advertising and sales promotion which are necessary for a more complete model will lead to shifts in the cost and demand relations, say to AC_r and D_r, which define the full revenue-maximizing equilibrium at the larger output, Q_r'. However, the proposition that price may be below marginal cost remains intact. The revenue maximizer must combine advertising expense and production expense so that the marginal contribution to revenue per dollar of additional production cost ($\partial R/\partial C$) is equated to the marginal contribution to revenue per dollar of additional advertising expense ($\partial R/\partial A$). The optimum combination obviously will vary depending on the relative elasticities of these relationships. If increases in output must be made in the face of inelastic demand, $\partial R/\partial C$ will be negative and advertising expense will be selected. As demand elasticity increases and production expense is selected, the price below marginal cost effect will come into play and may dominate over ranges in which $\partial R/\partial C > \partial R/\partial A$, as, for example, when the impact of advertising is limited and/or demand is quite elastic. Thus, revenue maximization in either its simple or complex form may lead firms to sell at prices below marginal cost.

A second characteristic of revenue maximization which has not been recognized is that revenue maximization is not necessarily consistent with a preference for output or physical size of the firm. Consider, for example, the choices confronting the firm when it is in the revenue-maximizing position, Q'_r. If the management prefers to trade sales revenue for a larger output or scale of operations, it may abandon revenue maximization in favor of increased output at lower prices. The firm which has a pure preference for output will expand production to Q_q where price is equated with average cost (including allowable profit). If marginal cost exceeds average cost in this equilibrium, the output will be sold at a price below marginal cost.

The recognition of a potential conflict between the preference for revenue and the preference for output adds an important dimension to the original revenue-maximizing hypothesis. The performance of firms frequently is measured directly in terms of physical output with revenue occupying a secondary position. This is particularly the case with respect to public service enterprises where measures of output like kilowatt hours, or number of customers served, may dominate revenue or dollar sales as yardsticks of performance. Thus, output or quantity maximization merits consideration as a distinct and separate hypothesis which enhances the possibility of sales at prices below marginal cost.

Precise comparisons of the three models of the restrained firm that have been described are difficult to make, because the introduction of expenditure on advertising and sales promotion affects revenue and cost functions and there is no clear-cut way to select that set of revenue–cost relationships which is consistent with a welfare maximum. However, if it is assumed that the cost and revenue functions in Fig. 12.1 represent the set appropriate to Pareto-optimal output, i.e. that AC includes no more than the social cost[4] of capital and that advertising expenditures beyond those embodied in D and AC will not be made, it is possible to make a few limited but straightforward price–output comparisons:

1. Restrained revenue and output maximizers will have lower prices and larger outputs than profit-maximizing firms or firms which have a pure preference for expense.
2. The restrained revenue maximizer will have a smaller output, Q_r, than the restrained output maximizer Q_q if demand elasticity is less than unity in the range of restraint. If demand elasticity exceeds unity in the range of restraint both firms will produce the same output.
3. In the case of increasing cost, Pareto-optimal output, Q^*, will be exceeded by the output-maximizing firm and if demand elasticity exceeds unity in the range of restraint, by the revenue-maximizing firm. Under these conditions both firms will sell at a price below marginal cost.
4. The reader may verify for himself that (a) under constant cost, Pareto-optimal price and output are attained by the output-maximizing firm, and if demand elasticity exceeds unity in the range of restraint, by the revenue-maximizing firm, and (b) under decreasing cost, the output of both revenue maximizers and output maximizers will be suboptimal, the divergence being greater in the case of the revenue maximizer where demand elasticity falls short of unity.

Though these comparisons are based on the simplification that firms are subject to identical earnings restraints and pursue identical advertising policies, they (a) reveal the significance of managerial objectives, (b) establish the possibility of excess monopoly output implemented through sales at prices below marginal cost, and (c) introduce output maximization as a distinct and separate hypothesis.

The findings may be contrasted with those of Averch and Johnson ([1] pp. 1056–8) that regulated firms will restrict output in single markets and will sell at prices below marginal cost only in the multi-market case. Revenue and output maximization suggest less restriction and lower prices including

---

[4] It is assumed that AC reflects constant input prices and is, therefore, exclusive of rent to fixed factors.

the possibility of sales at prices below marginal cost in single markets. Since Averch and Johnson base their conclusions on the assumption that the permitted rate-of-return is excessive while ours derives from assumptions concerning managerial preferences, the findings are not contradictory in a formal sense. The Averch and Johnson analysis also predicts a bias for capital which encourages inefficient combination of factors. However, Baumol ([2] pp. 55–6) has shown that revenue (and output) maximization require efficient factor combination for any given level of resource outlay. Thus, the revenue and output preference models predict a larger output and more efficient factor combination than the Averch–Johnson model.

2. The Discriminating Firm

The results developed in the preceding section are altered when the analysis is extended to the restrained firm which discriminates in price. The relevant relationships are summarized in Fig. 12.2 in which R is a total revenue schedule drawn on the assumption of identical prices in all markets and C is a total cost schedule which includes the allowable return. Under the assumption of constant cost, optimal output is Q^*. However, if the management is permitted to develop the rate structure, there is no reason to believe that it will select the nondiscriminatory revenue schedule represented by R which would, assuming appropriate regulation in other respects, yield Q^*. At least two of the infinite number of possible revenue schedules may be specified uniquely. If the firm is able to practice perfect price discrimination, i.e. sell each unit at its maximum demand price, the revenue schedule will shift to R_d (assuming zero income effects). If the firm practices third-degree discrimination, i.e. equalizes marginal revenue in each market, the revenue schedule will be R_e.[5] Actually, the firm may design a structure of rates which will yield a revenue schedule anywhere in the

---

[5] It is possible for R and R_e to have a point of tangency. If there are two markets and a point is reached where the demand elasticities are the same, total revenue will be the same under simple monopoly as under third-degree price discrimination. These relationships have been carefully examined by Joan Robinson ([5] chap. 15). The revenue relationships summarized in Fig. 12.2 assume that at no point are the demand elasticities identical and that the elasticity relations are such as to lead the discriminating monopolist to produce more than the simple monopolist. As suggested by Mrs Robinson ([5] p. 201), these are the most plausible relationships.

area bounded by R_d and R depending on its ability to develop workable customer classes, block rate schedules and quantity discounts.[6] Rightward movements along any particular revenue schedule are accompanied by price reductions, but only in the case of R do these reductions apply to all units and all markets. We wish to compare the price and output policies which will emerge under our three alternative hypotheses concerning the objectives of the firm.

If a managerial preference for nonproduction expense is assumed, and if perfect price discrimination is possible, the firm will maximize profits at output Q^* and will incur nonproduction expense which will shift the cost schedule to C' where surplus profits are eliminated.[7] Lesser degrees of discrimination will shift the revenue schedule downward (from R_d) and will be accompanied by corresponding reductions in output.

Though the expense preference model does not provide any significant new insights, it is worth noting that the existence of a profit restraint enhances the possibilities of 'waste' and this may be related to the degree of price discrimination that exists in the structure of rates.

If the managerial preference for expense is replaced by a preference for revenue, price will be reduced and output expanded so long as marginal revenue is positive and surplus profits exist. Since discriminatory revenue schedules will generally lie above R over all ranges of output, the discriminating revenue maximizer will have a larger output than the revenue maximizer who sells at a single price. If the perfectly discriminatory revenue structure R_d is selected, revenue is maximized (and the profit restraint fulfilled) at output Q_d. If R_e is selected, output will be Q_e and, if the profit restraint is not met at this output, the firm may exhaust unabsorbed profits by incurring additional expense for staff, emoluments and advertising, as suggested earlier. If expansion is not halted by the restraint or inelastic demand, output of the revenue maximizer will be expanded beyond Q^*. In this event, at least some output

---

[6] The significance of block rate design to output has been noted by J. M. Buchanan in an analysis of peak load pricing [3].

[7] Under perfect price discrimination coupled with zero income effects the demand curve becomes the marginal revenue curve of the monopolist. Thus, Pareto-optimal output defined at $P = MC$ will coincide with profit-maximizing output defined at $MR = MC$.

will be sold at prices below marginal cost. Whereas the non-discriminating revenue maximizer may sell at a price below marginal cost only in increasing cost situations, the discriminating revenue maximizer may do so regardless of cost conditions unless halted by the restraint or inelastic demand.

The discriminating firm which seeks to maximize output will produce more than an optimal output (the range being between Q^* and Q_d in Fig. 12.2) over all ranges of restraint in constant

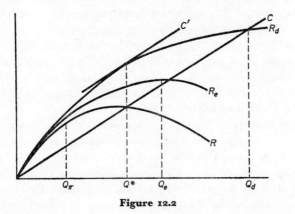

Figure 12.2

and increasing cost situations. Output may or may not exceed optimum in decreasing cost situations. The basic difference between revenue and quantity maximizers is that the former must develop a revenue structure so that marginal revenue remains positive while the latter is not restricted in this manner. Price and sales promotion policy will be evaluated by the revenue maximizer in terms of their effect on revenue and by the quantity maximizer in terms of their effects on output. The quantity maximizer will never sell at a price above that of the revenue maximizer and he will never expend more than the revenue maximizer on sales promotion and advertising.

Whereas the possibility of excessive monopoly output implemented through sales at prices below marginal cost is limited to increasing cost situations in the case of the single market model (Fig. 12.1), this possibility exists regardless of cost conditions in the case of the discriminating firm (Fig. 12.2). Prices in all markets could be below marginal cost provided the price in at least one market exceeds average cost. These conclusions, of course, apply only to restrained revenue and output maximizers.[8]

3. Some Implications

Models based on revenue or output maximization as direct objectives of the restrained firm predict less monopolistic restriction than traditional models. Viewed in this perspective, our results seem sanguine. However, the expansion of restrained firms may occur through entry into new markets and through increased penetration of existing markets at prices below marginal cost which, as we have shown, is a possibility even in the absence of price discrimination. Thus, profit restraints may enhance the possibility of 'overexpansion' and 'destructive competition'. The ability to discriminate in price dramatically increases these possibilities.

Predictions about the level of resource use will vary depending on the managerial 'preference function', the degree of price discrimination and other factors not examined fully in this paper. In any case, identical earnings restraints may be consistent with output decisions ranging from the restricted monopoly output in the expense preference model to output in excess of the Pareto-optimal quantity in the output and revenue preference models. Restrained firms which administer their own price structures have a built-in mechanism which may provide expanded output at prices below marginal cost while redistributing income and output from one class of customer to the other. Regulatory agencies which adhere primarily to a fair rate of return criterion may fail to evaluate adequately the consequences to efficiency and income distribution of rate structures designed to reflect the preferences of management. If the income redistributions are favorable, if the expanded output yields external economies at the margin, and if the impact on competition is not deleterious, the results may be judged favorably. On the other hand, unfavorable results are possible.

Finally, the analysis suggests behavioral classifications which may shed some light on the wide variety of conduct and per-

---

[8] W. Baumol's comments on this paper point out that the distinction between revenue and output maximization will be blurred in the case of the multi-product or diversified firm where there is no single measure of aggregate output.

formance that characterize big business in the United States. Empirical investigation of the performance of large firms suggests that managements '. . . pursue goals quite different than owners' and that the assumption of profit maximization is '. . . considerably less applicable in the case where the firm is controlled by management' ([4] p. 442). Where there is an effective separation of ownership and control, models based on voluntary profit restraints and managerial preference functions may have considerable predictive power.

REFERENCES

[1] H. AVERCH and L. JOHNSON, 'Behavior of the Firm under Regulatory Constraint', *American Economic Review*, LII (Dec 1962) 1052–69.

[2] W. J. BAUMOL, *Business Behavior, Value and Growth*, rev. ed. (New York, 1967).

[3] J. M. BUCHANAN, 'Peak Loads and Efficient Pricing: Comments', *Quarterly Journal of Economics*, LXXX (Aug 1966) 463–71.

[4] R. J. MONSEN, J. S. CHIU and D. E. COOLEY, 'The Effect of Separation of Ownership and Control on the Performance of the Large Firm', *Quarterly Journal of Economics*, LXXXII (Aug 1968) 435–51.

[5] J. ROBINSON, *Economics of Imperfect Competition* (London, 1961).

[6] O. WILLIAMSON, *The Economics of Discretionary Behavior: Managerial Objectives in a Theory of the Firm* (Englewood Cliffs, N. J., 1964).

PART THREE

Invention and the State:
A Study in Controversy

13 Economic Welfare and the Allocation of Resources for Invention[1]

K. J. Arrow

Invention is here interpreted broadly as the production of knowledge. From the viewpoint of welfare economics, the determination of optimal resource allocation for invention will depend on the technological characteristics of the invention process and the nature of the market for knowledge.

The classic question of welfare economics will be asked here: to what extent does perfect competition lead to an optimal allocation of resources? We know from years of patient refinement that competition insures the achievement of a Pareto optimum under certain hypotheses. The model usually assumes, among other things, that (1) the utility functions of consumers and the transformation functions of producers are well-defined functions of the commodities in the economic system, and (2) the transformation functions do not display indivisibilities (more strictly, the transformation sets are convex). The second condition needs no comment. The first seems to be innocuous but in fact conceals two basic assumptions of the usual models. It prohibits uncertainty in the production relations and in the utility functions, and it requires that all the commodities relevant either to production or to the welfare of individuals be traded on the market. This will not be the case when a commodity for one reason or another cannot be made into private property.

We have then three of the classical reasons for the possible failure of perfect competition to achieve optimality in resource allocation: indivisibilities, inappropriability, and uncertainty. The first problem has been much studied in the literature under the heading of marginal-cost pricing and the second under that

[1] I have benefited greatly from the comments of my colleague, William Capron. I am also indebted to Richard R. Nelson, Edward Phelps, and Sidney Winter of the RAND Corporation for their helpful discussion.

Reprinted from R. R. Nelson (ed.), *The Rate and Direction of Inventive Activity: Economic and Social Factors* (Princeton University Press, 1962) pp. 609–28, by kind permission of the author and of the Princeton University Press.

of divergence between social and private benefit (or cost), but
the theory of optimal allocation of resources under uncertainty
has had much less attention. I will summarize what formal
theory exists and then point to the critical notion of information,
which arises only in the context of uncertainty. The economic
characteristics of information as a commodity and, in particular,
of invention as a process for the production of information are
next examined. It is shown that all three of the reasons given
above for a failure of the competitive system to achieve an
optimal resource allocation hold in the case of invention. On
theoretical grounds a number of considerations are adduced
as to the likely biases in the misallocation and the implications
for economic organization.[2]

Resource Allocation under Uncertainty

The role of the competitive system in allocating uncertainty
seems to have received little systematic attention.[3] I will first
sketch an ideal economy in which the allocation problem can
be solved by competition and then indicate some of the devices
in the real world which approximate this solution.

Suppose for simplicity that uncertainty occurs only in production relations. Producers have to make a decision on inputs
at the present moment, but the outputs are not completely
predictable from the inputs. We may formally describe the
outputs as determined by the inputs and a 'state of nature'
which is unknown to the producers. Let us define a 'commodity-
option' as a commodity in the ordinary sense labeled with a
state of nature. This definition is analogous to the differentiation
of a given physical commodity according to date in capital
theory or according to place in location theory. The production

[2] For other analyses with similar points of view, see R. R. Nelson, 'The Simple
Economics of Basic Scientific Research', *Journal of Political Economy* (1959) pp.
297–306; and C. J. Hitch, 'The Character of Research and Development in a
Competitive Economy', p. 1297 (RAND Corporation, May 1958).

[3] The first studies I am aware of are the papers of M. Allais and myself, both
presented in 1952 to the Colloque International sur le Risque in Paris; see M.
Allais, 'Généralisation des théories de l'équilibre économique général et du rende-
ment social au cas du risque', and K. J. Arrow, 'Rôle des valeurs boursiéres pour
la répartition la meilleure des risques', both in *Économétrie*, Colloques Internationaux
du Centre National de la Recherche Scientifique, vol. XL (Paris: Centre National
de la Recherche Scientifique, 1953). Allais's paper has also appeared in
Econometrica (1953) pp. 269–90. The theory has received a very elegant generali-
zation by G. Debreu in *Theory of Values* (New York; Wiley, 1959) chap. vii.

of a given commodity under uncertainty can then be described as the production of a vector of commodity-options.

This description can be most easily exemplified by reference to agricultural production. The state of nature may be identified with the weather. Then, to any given set of inputs there corresponds a number of bushels of wheat if the rainfall is good and a different number if rainfall is bad. We can introduce intermediate conditions of rainfall in any number of alternative states of nature; we can increase the number of relevant variables which enter into the description of the state of nature, for example by adding temperature. By extension of this procedure, we can give a formal description of any kind of uncertainty in production.

Suppose – and this is the critical idealization of the economy – we have a market for all commodity-options. What is traded on each market are contracts in which the buyers pay an agreed sum and the sellers agree to deliver prescribed quantities of a given commodity *if* a certain state of nature prevails and nothing if that state of nature does not occur. For any given set of inputs, the firm knows its output under each state of nature and sells a corresponding quantity of commodity-options; its revenue is then completely determined. It may choose its inputs so as to maximize profits.

The income of consumers is derived from their sale of supplies, including labor, to firms and their receipt of profits, which are assumed completely distributed. They purchase commodity-options so as to maximize their expected utility given the budget restraint imposed by their incomes. An equilibrium is reached on all commodity-option markets, and this equilibrium has precisely the same Pareto-optimality properties as competitive equilibrium under certainty.

In particular, the markets for commodity-options in this ideal model serve the function of achieving an optimal allocation of risk bearing among the members of the economy. This allocation takes account of differences in both resources and tastes for risk bearing. Among other implications, risk bearing and production are separated economic functions. The use of inputs, including human talents, in their most productive mode is not inhibited by unwillingness or inability to bear risks by either firms or productive agents.

But the real economic system does not possess markets for

commodity-options. To see what substitutes exist, let us first consider a model economy at the other extreme, in that no provisions for reallocating risk bearing exist. Each firm makes its input decisions; then outputs are produced as determined by the inputs and the state of nature. Prices are then set to clear the market. The prices that finally prevail will be a function of the state of nature.

The firm and its owners cannot relieve themselves of risk bearing in this model. Hence any unwillingness or inability to bear risks will give rise to a nonoptimal allocation of resources, in that there will be discrimination against risky enterprises as compared with the optimum. A preference for risk might give rise to misallocation in the opposite direction, but the limitations of financial resources are likely to make underinvestment in risky enterprises more likely than the opposite. The inability of individuals to buy protection against uncertainty similarly gives rise to a loss of welfare.

In fact, a number of institutional arrangements have arisen to mitigate the problem of assumption of risk. Suppose that each firm and individual in the economy could forecast perfectly what prices would be under each state of nature. Suppose further there were a lottery on the states of nature, so that before the state of nature is known any individual or firm may place bets. Then it can be seen that the effect from the viewpoint of any given individual or firm is the same as if there were markets for commodity-options of all types, since any commodity-option can be achieved by a combination of a bet on the appropriate state of nature and an intention to purchase or sell the commodity in question if the state of nature occurs.

References to lotteries and bets may smack of frivolity, but we need only think of insurance to appreciate that the shifting of risks through what are in effect bets on the state of nature is a highly significant phenomenon. If insurance were available against any conceivable event, it follows from the preceding discussion that optimal allocation would be achieved. Of course, insurance as customarily defined covers only a small range of events relevant to the economic world; much more important in shifting risks are securities, particularly common stocks and money. By shifting freely their proprietary interests among different firms, individuals can to a large extent bet on the different states of nature which favor firms differentially.

This freedom to insure against many contingencies is enhanced by the alternatives of holding cash and going short.

Unfortunately, it is only too clear that the shifting of risks in the real world is incomplete. The great predominance of internal over external equity financing in industry is one illustration of the fact that securities do not completely fulfill their allocative role with respect to risks. There are a number of reasons why this should be so, but I will confine myself to one, of special significance with regard to invention. In insurance practice, reference is made to the moral factor as a limit to the possibilities of insurance. For example, a fire insurance policy cannot exceed in amount the value of the goods insured. From the purely actuarial standpoint, there is no reason for this limitation; the reason for the limit is that the insurance policy changes the incentives of the insured, in this case, creating an incentive for arson or at the very least for carelessness. The general principle is the difficulty of distinguishing between a state of nature and a decision by the insured. As a result, any insurance policy and in general any device for shifting risks can have the effect of dulling incentives. A fire insurance policy, even when limited in amount to the value of the goods covered, weakens the motivation for fire prevention. Thus, steps which improve the efficiency of the economy with respect to risk bearing may decrease its technical efficiency.

One device for mitigating the adverse incentive effects of insurance is coinsurance; the insurance extends only to part of the amount at risk for the insured. The device is used, for example, in coverage of medical risks. It clearly represents a compromise between incentive effects and allocation of risk bearing, sacrificing something in both directions.

Two exemplifications of the moral factor are of special relevance in regard to highly risky business activities, including invention. Success in such activities depends on an inextricable tangle of objective uncertainties and decisions of the entrepreneurs and is certainly uninsurable. On the other hand, such activities should be undertaken if the expected return exceeds the market rate of return, no matter what the variance is.[4] The existence of common stocks would seem to solve the allocation problem; any individual stockholder can reduce his risk by

---

[4] The validity of this statement depends on some unstated assumptions, but the point to be made is unaffected by minor qualifications.

buying only a small part of the stock and diversifying his portfolio to achieve his own preferred risk level. But then again the actual managers no longer receive the full reward of their decisions; the shifting of risks is again accompanied by a weakening of incentives to efficiency. Substitute motivations, whether pecuniary, such as executive compensation and profit sharing, or nonpecuniary, such as prestige, may be found, but the dilemma of the moral factor can never be completely resolved.

A second example is the cost-plus contract in one of its various forms. When production costs on military items are highly uncertain, the military establishment will pay, not a fixed unit price, but the cost of production plus an amount which today is usually a fixed fee. Such a contract could be regarded as a combination of a fixed-price contract with an insurance against costs. The insurance premium could be regarded as the difference between the fixed price the government would be willing to pay and the fixed fee.

Cost-plus contracts are necessitated by the inability or unwillingness of firms to bear the risks. The government has superior risk-bearing ability and so the burden is shifted to it. It is then enabled to buy from firms on the basis of their productive efficiency rather than their risk-bearing ability, which may be only imperfectly correlated. But cost-plus contracts notoriously have their adverse allocative effects.[5]

This somewhat lengthy digression on the theory of risk bearing seemed necessitated by the paucity of literature on the subject. The main conclusions to be drawn are the following: (1) the economic system has devices for shifting risks, but they are limited and imperfect; hence, one would expect an underinvestment in risky activities; (2) it is undoubtedly worthwhile to enlarge the variety of such devices, but the moral factor creates a limit to their potential.

Information as a Commodity

Uncertainty usually creates a still more subtle problem in resource allocation; information becomes a commodity.

---

[5] These remarks are not intended as a complete evaluation of cost-plus contracts. In particular, there are, to a certain extent, other incentives which mitigate the adverse effects on efficiency.

Suppose that in one part of the economic system an observation has been made whose outcome, if known, would affect anyone's estimates of the probabilities of the different states of nature. Such observations arise out of research but they also arise in the daily course of economic life as a by-product of other economic activities. An entrepreneur will automatically acquire a knowledge of demand and production conditions in his field which is available to others only with special effort. Information will frequently have an economic value, in the sense that anyone possessing the information can make greater profits than would otherwise be the case.

It might be expected that information will be traded in, and of course to a considerable extent this is the case, as is illustrated by the numerous economic institutions for transmission of information, such as newspapers. But in many instances, the problem of an optimal allocation is sharply raised. The cost of transmitting a given body of information is frequently very low. If it were zero, then optimal allocation would obviously call for unlimited distribution of the information without cost. In fact, a given piece of information is by definition an indivisible commodity, and the classical problems of allocation in the presence of indivisibilities appear here. The owner of the information should not extract the economic value which is there, if optimal allocation is to be achieved; but he is a monopolist, to some small extent, and will seek to take advantage of this fact.

In the absence of special legal protection, the owner cannot, however, simply sell information on the open market. Any one purchaser can destroy the monopoly, since he can reproduce the information at little or no cost. Thus the only effective monopoly would be the use of the information by the original possessor. This, however, will not only be socially inefficient, but also may not be of much use to the owner of the information either, since he may not be able to exploit it as effectively as others.

With suitable legal measures, information may become an appropriable commodity. Then the monopoly power can indeed be exerted. However, no amount of legal protection can make a thoroughly appropriable commodity of something so intangible as information. The very use of the information in any productive way is bound to reveal it, at least in part. Mobility of personnel among firms provides a way of spreading information. Legally imposed property rights can provide only a partial barrier, since there are obviously enormous difficulties in defining in any sharp way an item of information and differentiating it from other similar-sounding items.

The demand for information also has uncomfortable properties. In the first place, the use of information is certainly subject to indivisibilities; the use of information about production possibilities, for example, need not depend on the rate of production. In the second place, there is a fundamental paradox in the determination of demand for information; its value for the purchaser is not known until he has the information, but then he has in effect acquired it without cost. Of course, if the seller can retain property rights in the use of the information, this would be no problem, but given incomplete appropriability, the potential buyer will base his decision to purchase information on less than optimal criteria. He may act, for example, on the average value of information in that class as revealed by past experience. If any particular item of information has differing values for different economic agents, this procedure will lead both to a nonoptimal purchase of information at any given price and also to a nonoptimal allocation of the information purchased.

It should be made clear that from the standpoint of efficiently distributing an existing stock of information, the difficulties of appropriation are an advantage, provided there are no costs of transmitting information, since then optimal allocation calls for free distribution. The chief point made here is the difficulty of creating a market for information if one should be desired for any reason.

It follows from the preceding discussion that costs of transmitting information create allocative difficulties which would be absent otherwise. Information should be transmitted at marginal cost, but then the demand difficulties raised above will exist. From the viewpoint of optimal allocation, the purchasing industry will be faced with the problems created by indivisibilities; and we still leave unsolved the problem of the purchaser's inability to judge in advance the value of the information he buys. There is a strong case for centralized decision making under these circumstances.

Invention as the Production of Information

The central economic fact about the processes of invention and research is that they are devoted to the production of information. By the very definition of information, invention must be a risky process, in that the output (information obtained) can never be predicted perfectly from the inputs. We can now apply the discussion of the preceding two sections.

Since it is a risky process, there is bound to be some discrimination against investment in inventive and research activities. In this field, especially, the moral factor will weigh heavily against any kind of insurance or equivalent form of risk bearing. Insurance against failure to develop a desired new product or process would surely very greatly weaken the incentives to succeed. The only way, within the private enterprise system, to minimize this problem is the conduct of research by large corporations with many projects going on, each small in scale compared with the net revenue of the corporation. Then the corporation acts as its own insurance company. But clearly this is only an imperfect solution.

The deeper problems of misallocation arise from the nature of the product. As we have seen, information is a commodity with peculiar attributes, particularly embarrassing for the achievement of optimal allocation. In the first place, any information obtained, say a new method of production, should, from the welfare point of view, be available free of charge (apart from the cost of transmitting information). This insures optimal utilization of the information but of course provides no incentive for investment in research. In an ideal socialist economy, the reward for invention would be completely separated from any charge to the users of the information.[6] In a free enterprise economy, inventive activity is supported by using the invention to create property rights; precisely to the extent that it is successful, there is an underutilization of the information. The property rights may be in the information itself, through patents and similar legal devices, or in the intangible assets of the firm if the information is retained by the firm and used only to increase its profits.

[6] This separation exists in the Soviet Union, according to N. M. Kaplan and R. H. Moorsteen of the RAND Corporation (verbal communication).

✓ The first problem, then, is that in a free enterprise economy the profitability of invention requires a nonoptimal allocation of resources. But it may still be asked whether or not the allocation of resources to inventive activity is optimal. The discussion of the preceding section makes it clear that we would not expect this to be so; that, in fact, a downward bias in the amount of resources devoted to inventive activity is very likely. Whatever the price, the demand for information is less than optimal for two reasons: (1) since the price is positive and not at its optimal value of zero, the demand is bound to be below the optimal; (2) as seen before, at any given price, the very nature of information will lead to a lower demand than would be optimal.

As already remarked, the inventor will in any case have considerable difficulty in appropriating the information produced. Patent laws would have to be unimaginably complex and subtle to permit such appropriation on a large scale. Suppose, as the result of elaborate tests, some metal is discovered to have a desirable property, say resistance to high heat. Then of course every use of the metal for which this property is relevant would also use this information, and the user would be made to pay for it. But, even more, if another inventor is stimulated to examine chemically related metals for heat resistance, he is using the information already discovered and should pay for it in some measure; and any beneficiary of his discoveries should also pay. One would have to have elaborate distinctions of partial property rights of all degrees to make the system at all tolerable. In the interests of the possibility of enforcement, actual patent laws sharply restrict the range of appropriable information and thereby reduce the incentives to engage in inventive and research activities.

These last considerations bring into focus the interdependence of inventive activities, which reinforces the difficulties in achieving an optimal allocation of the results. Information is not only the product of inventive activity, it is also an input – in some sense, the major input apart from the talent of the inventor. The school of thought that emphasizes the determination of invention by the social climate as demonstrated by the simultaneity of inventions in effect emphasizes strongly the productive role of previous information in the creation of new information. While these interrelations do not create any new difficulties in principle, they intensify the previously established ones.

To appropriate information for use as a basis for further research is much more difficult than to appropriate it for use in producing commodities; and the value of information for use in developing further information is much more conjectural than the value of its use in production and therefore much more likely to be underestimated. Consequently, if a price is charged for the information, the demand is even more likely to be suboptimal.

Thus basic research, the output of which is only used as an informational input into other inventive activities, is especially unlikely to be rewarded. In fact, it is likely to be of commercial value to the firm undertaking it only if other firms are prevented from using the information obtained. But such restriction on the transmittal of information will reduce the efficiency of inventive activity in general and will therefore reduce its quantity also. We may put the matter in terms of sequential decision making. The *a priori* probability distribution of the true state of nature is relatively flat to begin with. On the other hand, the successive *a posteriori* distributions after more and more studies have been conducted are more and more sharply peaked or concentrated in a more limited range, and we therefore have better and better information for deciding what the next step in research shall be. This implies that, at the beginning, the preferences among alternative possible lines of investigation are much less sharply defined than they are apt to be later on and suggests, at least, the importance of having a wide variety of studies to begin with, the less promising being gradually eliminated as information is accumulated.[7] At each stage the decisions about the next step should be based on all available information. This would require an unrestricted flow of information among different projects which is incompatible with the complete decentralization of an ideal free enterprise system. When the production of information is important, the classic economic case in which the price system replaces the detailed spread of information is no longer completely applicable.

To sum up, we expect a free enterprise economy to under-

[7] The importance of parallel research developments in the case of uncertainty has been especially stressed by Burton H. Klein; see his 'A Radical Proposal for R. and D.', *Fortune* (May 1958) p. 112 ff.; and Klein and W. H. Meckling, 'Application of Operations Research to Development Decisions', *Operations Research* (1958) pp. 352–63.

invest in invention and research (as compared with an ideal) because it is risky, because the product can be appropriated only to a limited extent, and because of increasing returns in use. This underinvestment will be greater for more basic research. Further, to the extent that a firm succeeds in engrossing the economic value of its inventive activity, there will be an underutilization of that information as compared with an ideal allocation.

Competition, Monopoly, and the Incentive to Innovate

It may be useful to remark that an incentive to invent can exist even under perfect competition in the product markets though not, of course, in the 'market' for the information contained in the invention. This is especially clear in the case of a cost-reducing invention. Provided only that suitable royalty payments can be demanded, an inventor can profit without disturbing the competitive nature of the industry. The situation for a new product invention is not very different; by charging a suitable royalty to a competitive industry, the inventor can receive a return equal to the monopoly profits.

I will examine here the incentives to invent for monopolistic and competitive markets, that is, I will compare the potential profits from an invention with the costs. The difficulty of appropriating the information will be ignored; the remaining problem is that of indivisibility in use, an inherent property of information. A competitive situation here will mean one in which the industry produces under competitive conditions, while the inventor can set an arbitrary royalty for the use of his invention. In the monopolistic situation, it will be assumed that only the monopoly itself can invent. Thus a monopoly is understood here to mean barriers to entry; a situation of temporary monopoly, due perhaps to a previous innovation, which does not prevent the entrance of new firms with innovations of their own, is to be regarded as more nearly competitive than monopolistic for the purpose of this analysis. It will be argued that the incentive to invent is less under monopolistic than under competitive conditions but even in the latter case it will be less than is socially desirable.

We will assume constant costs both before and after the invention, the unit costs being c before the invention and $c' < c$

afterward. The competitive price before invention will therefore be c. Let the corresponding demand be x_c. If r is the level of unit royalties, the competitive price after the invention will be $c' + r$, but this cannot of course be higher than c, since firms are always free to produce with the old methods.

It is assumed that both the demand and the marginal revenue curves are decreasing. Let $R(x)$ be the marginal revenue curve. Then the monopoly output before invention, x_m, would be defined by the equation

$$R(x_m) = c.$$

Similarly, the monopoly output after invention is defined by

$$R(x'_m) = c'.$$

Let the monopoly prices corresponding to outputs x_m and x'_m, respectively, be p_m and p'_m. Finally, let P and P' be the monopolist's profits before and after invention, respectively.

What is the optimal royalty level for the inventor in the competitive case? Let us suppose that he calculates p'_m, the optimal monopoly price which would obtain in the post-invention situation. If the cost reduction is sufficiently drastic that $p'_m < c$, then his most profitable policy is to set r so that the competitive price is p'_m, i.e. let

$$r = p'_m - c'.$$

In this case, the inventor's royalties are equal to the profits a monopolist would make under the same conditions, i.e. his incentive to invent will be P'.

Suppose, however, it turns out that $p'_m > c$. Since the sales price cannot exceed c, the inventor will set his royalties at

$$r = c - c'.$$

The competitive price will then be c, and the sales will remain at x_c. The inventor's incentive will then be $x_c(c - c')$.

The monopolist's incentive, on the other hand, is clearly $P' - P$. In the first of the two cases cited, the monopolist's incentive is obviously less than the inventor's incentive under competition, which is P', not $P' - P$. The preinvention monopoly power acts as a strong disincentive to further innovation.

The analysis is slightly more complicated in the second case.

The monopolist's incentive, $P' - P$, is the change in revenue less the change in total cost of production, i.e.

$$P' - P = \int_{xm}^{x'm} R(x) \, dx - c' \, x'_m + c \, x_m.$$

Since the marginal revenue $R(x)$ is diminishing, it must always be less than $R(x_m) = c$ as x increases from x_m to x'_m, so that

$$\int_{xm}^{x'm} R(x) \, dx < c \, (x'_m - x_m)$$

and

$$P' - P < c \, (x'_m - x_m) - c' \, x'_m + c \, x_m = (c - c')x'_m.$$

In the case being considered, the postinvention monopoly price, p'_m, is greater than c. Hence, with a declining demand curve, $x'_m < x_c$. The above inequality shows that the monopolist's incentive is always less than the cost reduction on the postinvention monopoly output, which in this case is, in turn, less than the competitive output (both before and after invention). Since the inventor's incentive under competition is the cost reduction on the competitive output, it will again always exceed the monopolist's incentive.

It can be shown that, if we consider differing values of c', the difference between the two incentives increases as c' decreases, reaching its maximum of P (preinvention monopoly profits) for c' sufficiently large for the first case to hold. The ratio of the incentive under competition to that under monopoly, on the other hand, though always greater than 1, decreases steadily with c'. For c' very close to c (i.e. very minor inventions), the ratio of the two incentives is approximately x_c/x_m, i.e. the ratio of monopoly to competitive output.[8]

[8] To sketch the proof of these statements quickly, note that, as c' varies, P is a constant. Hence, from the formula for $P' - P$, we see that

$$d(P' - P)/dc' = dP'/dc' = R(x'_m)(dx'_m/dc') - c'(dx'_m/dc') - x'_m = -x'_m$$

since $R(x'_m) = c'$. Let $F(c')$ be the difference between the incentives to invent under competitive and under monopolistic conditions. In the case where $p'_m \leqslant c$, this difference is the constant P. Otherwise,

$$F(c') = x_c(c - c') - (P' - P)$$

so that

$$dF/dc' = x'_m - x_c.$$

For the case considered, we must have $x'_m < x_c$, as seen in the text. Hence, $dF/dc' \leqq 0$, so that $F(c')$ increases as c' decreases.

The only ground for arguing that monopoly may create superior incentives to invent is that appropriability may be greater under monopoly than under competition. Whatever differences may exist in this direction must, of course, still be offset against the monopolist's disincentive created by his preinvention monopoly profits. ✔

The incentive to invent in competitive circumstances may also be compared with the social benefit. It is necessary to distinguish between the realized social benefit and the potential social benefit, the latter being the benefit which would accrue under ideal conditions, which, in this case, means the sale of the product at postinvention cost, c'. Clearly, the potential social benefit always exceeds the realized social benefit. I will show that the realized social benefit, in turn, always equals or exceeds the competitive incentive to invent and, *a fortiori*, the monopolist's incentive.

Consider again the two cases discussed above. If the invention is sufficiently cost-reducing so that $p'_m < c$, then there is a consumers' benefit, due to the lowering of price, which has not been appropriated by the inventor. If not, then the price is unchanged, so that the consumers' position is unchanged, and all benefits do go to the inventor. Since by assumption all the producers are making zero profits both before and after the invention, we see that the inventor obtains the entire realized social benefit of moderately cost-reducing inventions but not of more radical inventions. Tentatively, this suggests a bias against major inventions, in the sense that an invention, part of whose costs could be paid for by lump-sum payments by consumers without making them worse off than before, may not be profitable at the maximum royalty payments that can be extracted by the inventor.

Let $G(c')$ be the ratio of the incentive under competition to that under monopoly. If $P'_m \leqslant c$, then

$$G(c') = P'/(P' - P)$$

which clearly decreases as c' decreases. For $p'_m > c$, we have

$$G(c') = x_c(c - c')/(P' - P).$$

Then

$$dG/dc' = [-(P' - P)x_c + x_c(c - c')x'_m]/(P' - P)^2.$$

Because of the upper bound for $P' - P$ established in the text, the numerator must be positive; the ratio decreases as c' decreases.

Finally, if we consider c' very close to c, $G(c')$ will be approximately equal to the ratio of the derivatives of the numerator and denominator (L'Hôpital's rule), which is $x/c x'_m$, and which approaches x_c/x_m as c' approaches c.

Alternative Forms of Economic Organization in Invention

The previous discussion leads to the conclusion that for optimal allocation to invention it would be necessary for the government or some other agency not governed by profit-and-loss criteria to finance research and invention. In fact, of course, this has always happened to a certain extent. The bulk of basic research has been carried on outside the industrial system, in universities, in the government, and by private individuals. One must recognize here the importance of nonpecuniary incentives, both on the part of the investigators and on the part of the private individuals and governments that have supported research organizations and universities. In the latter, the complementarity between teaching and research is, from the point of view of the economy, something of a lucky accident. Research in some more applied fields, such as agriculture, medicine, and aeronautics, has consistently been regarded as an appropriate subject for government participation, and its role has been of great importance.

If the government and other nonprofit institutions are to compensate for the underallocation of resources to invention by private enterprise, two problems arise: how shall the amount of resources devoted to invention be determined, and how shall efficiency in their use be encouraged? These problems arise whenever the government finds it necessary to engage in economic activities because indivisibilities prevent the private economy from performing adequately (highways, bridges, reclamation projects, for example), but the determination of the relative magnitudes is even more difficult here. Formally, or course, resources should be devoted to invention until the expected marginal social benefit there equals the marginal social benefit in alternative uses, but in view of the presence of uncertainty, such calculations are even more difficult and tenuous than those for public works. Probably all that could be hoped for is the estimation of future rates of return from those in the past, with investment in invention being increased or decreased accordingly as some average rate of return over the past exceeded or fell short of the general rate of return. The difficulties of even *ex post* calculation of rates of return are formidable though possibly not insuperable.[9]

The problem of efficiency in the use of funds devoted to research is one that has been faced internally by firms in dealing with their own research departments. The rapid growth of military research and development has led to a large-scale development of contractual relations between producers and a buyer of invention and research. The problems encountered in assuring efficiency here are the same as those that would be met if the government were to enter upon the financing of invention and research in civilian fields. The form of economic relation is very different from that in the usual markets. Payment is independent of product; it is governed by costs, though the net reward (the fixed fee) is independent of both. This arrangement seems to fly in the face of the principles for encouraging efficiency, and doubtless it does lead to abuses, but closer examination shows both mitigating factors and some explanation of its inevitability. In the first place, the awarding of new contracts will depend in part on past performance, so that incentives for efficiency are not completely lacking. In the second place, the relation between the two parties to the contract is something closer than a purely market relation. It is more like the sale of professional services, where the seller contracts to supply not so much a specific result as his best judgment. (The demand for such services also arises from uncertainty and the value of information.) In the third place, payment by results would involve great risks for the inventor, risks against which, as we have seen, he could hedge only in part.

There is clear need for further study of alternative methods of compensation. For example, some part of the contractual payment might depend on the degree of success in invention. But a more serious problem is the decision as to which contracts to let. One would need to examine the motivation underlying government decision making in this area. Hitch has argued that there are biases in governmental allocation, particularly against risky invention processes, and an excessive centralization, though the latter could be remedied by better policies.[10]

One can go further. There is really no need for the firm to be

[9] For an encouraging study of this type, see Z. Griliches, 'Research Costs and Social Returns: Hybrid Corn and Related Innovations', *Journal of Political Economy* (1958) pp. 419–31.

[10] Op. cit.

the fundamental unit of organization in invention; there is plenty of reason to suppose that individual talents count for a good deal more than the firm as an organization. If provision is made for the rental of necessary equipment, a much wider variety of research contracts with individuals as well as firms and with varying modes of payment, including incentives, could be arranged. Still other forms of organization, such as research institutes financed by industries, the government, and private philanthropy, could be made to play an even livelier role than they now do.

14 Information and Efficiency: Another Viewpoint*

Harold Demsetz

The importance of bringing economic analysis to bear on the problems of efficient economic organization hardly requires comment, but there is a need to review the manner in which the notion of efficiency is used in these problems. The concept of efficiency has been abused frequently because of the particular approach used by many analysts. My aim is to examine the mistakes and the vagueness associated with this approach. I shall focus attention on the problem of efficiently allocating resources to the production of information because in this case the issues stand out clearly. Since Kenneth J. Arrow's paper 'Economic Welfare and the Allocation of Resources for Invention'[1] has been most influential in establishing the dominant viewpoint about this subject, my commentary necessarily is a critique of Arrow's analysis.

The view that now pervades much public policy economics implicitly presents the relevant choice as between an ideal norm and an existing 'imperfect' institutional arrangement. This *nirvana* approach differs considerably from a *comparative institution* approach in which the relevant choice is between alternative real institutional arrangements. In practice, those who adopt the nirvana viewpoint seek to discover discrepancies between the ideal and the real and if discrepancies are found, they deduce that the real is inefficient. Users of the comparative institutions approach attempt to assess which alternative real institutional arrangement seems best able to cope with the economic problem; practitioners of this approach may use an

---

[1] Kenneth J. Arrow, 'Economic Welfare and the Allocation of Resources for Invention', pp. 219–36 above.

Reprinted from *Journal of Law and Economics*, xi (Apr 1969) 1–22, by kind permission of the author and of the editor.

* The author wishes to thank the Lilly Endowment for financial aid received through a grant to the University of California at Los Angeles for the study of property rights.

ideal norm to provide standards from which divergences are assessed for all practical alternatives of interest and select as efficient that alternative which seems most likely to minimize the divergence.[2]

The nirvana approach is much more susceptible than is the comparative institution approach to committing three logical fallacies – *the grass is always greener fallacy, the fallacy of the free lunch,* and *the people could be different fallacy.* The first two fallacies are illustrated in a general context in part i of what follows; in part ii, they and the third fallacy arise in contexts more specific to the economics of knowledge. Part iii is a discussion of Arrow's conclusion about the role of monopoly in the production of knowledge, and part iv offers a general criticism of the nirvana approach.

I

The grass is always greener fallacy can be illustrated by the following two quotations from Arrow's paper.

> To sum up, we expect a free enterprise economy to underinvest in invention and research (as compared with an ideal) because it is risky, because the product can be appropriated only to a limited extent, and because of increasing returns in use. This under-investment will be greater for more basic research. Further, to the extent that a firm succeeds in engrossing the economic value of its inventive activity, there will be an underutilization of that information as compared with an ideal allocation.[3]

> The previous discussion leads to the conclusion that for optimal allocation to invention it would be necessary for the government or some other agency not governed by profit-and-loss criteria to finance research and invention.[4]

An examination of the correctness of the premise is the main task of this paper, but for present purposes the premise contained in the first quotation can be assumed to be correct. It is clear from both quotations and from the text in which these quotations are imbedded that Arrow is claiming that free

---

[2] A practitioner of the nirvana approach sometimes discusses and compares alternative institutional arrangements. But if all are found wanting in comparison with the ideal, all are judged to be inefficient.

[3] Arrow, op. cit., pp. 229–30 above.

[4] Ibid., p. 234 above.

enterprise does not result in an ideal allocation of resources to the production of knowledge. From this premise he draws the general conclusion, given in the second quotation, that optimal allocation requires that the government or other nonprofit agency should finance research and invention.

Whether the free enterprise solution can be improved upon by the substitution of the government or other nonprofit institutions in the financing of research cannot be ascertained solely by examining the free enterprise solution. The political or nonprofit forces that are substituted for free enterprise must be analyzed and the outcome of the workings of these forces must be compared to the market solution before any such conclusions can be drawn. Otherwise, words such as 'government' and 'nonprofit' are without analytical content and their use results in confusion. Since Arrow does not analyze the workings of the empirical counterparts of such words as 'governments'[5] and 'nonprofit', his conclusion can be clarified by restating it as follows: 'The previous discussion leads to the conclusion that for optimal allocation to invention it would be necessary to remove the nonoptimalities.' The same charge, of course, can be levied against those who derive in a similar way the opposite policy conclusion, one that calls for a reduction in the role played by government.[6]

Given the nirvana view of the problem, a deduced discrepancy between the ideal and the real is sufficient to call forth perfection by incantation, that is, by committing the grass is always greener fallacy. This usually is accomplished by invoking an unexamined alternative. Closely associated in practice with this fallacy is the fallacy of the free lunch. An example of the latter is given in Arrow's discussion of the difficulties posed for the competitive system by uncertainty:

> I will first sketch an ideal economy in which the allocation problem can be solved by competition and then indicate some of

[5] This is a slight exaggeration. Arrow, in the last few paragraphs of his paper, does discuss some problems in substituting the government for the market. The important point, however, is that Arrow is not led to reconsider his allegation of inefficiency in the market place by his short discussion of some of the difficulties of resorting to government.

[6] But for economists at least, the charge of committing the grass is always greener fallacy must be less severe in this case. The economist who suggests that we resort to the market because of unsatisfactory experience with government at least can claim professional knowledge of how the market can be expected to allocate resources. See pp. 257–9 below.

the devices in the real world which approximate this solution.

Suppose for simplicity that uncertainty occurs only in production relations. Producers have to make a decision on inputs at the present moment, but the outputs are not completely predictable from the inputs. . . . [T]he outputs [are] determined by the inputs and a 'state of nature'. Let us define a 'commodity-option' as a commodity in the ordinary sense labeled with a state of nature. . . .

Suppose – and this is the critical idealization of the economy – we have a market for all commodity-options. What is traded on each market are contracts in which buyers pay an agreed sum and the sellers agree to deliver prescribed quantities of a given commodity *if* a certain state of nature prevails and nothing if that state of nature does not occur. For any given set of inputs, the firm knows its output under each state of nature and sells a corresponding quantity of commodity-options; its revenue is then completely determined. It may choose its inputs so as to maximize profits. . . .

An equilibrium is reached on all commodity-option markets, and this equilibrium has precisely the same Pareto-optimality properties as competitive equilibrium under uncertainty.

In particular, the markets for commodity-options in this ideal model serve the function of achieving an optimal allocation of risk bearing among the members of the economy. . . .

But the real economic system does not possess markets for commodity-options.[7]

Here I must raise an objection, for there is nothing in principle that prohibits the sale of commodity-options. The real economic system does, in fact, allow exchange of commodity-options.[8] Arrow continues:

[If commodity options are unavailable] the firm and its owners cannot relieve themselves of risk bearing in this model. Hence any unwillingness or inability to bear risks will give rise to a non-

[7] Arrow, op. cit., pp. 221–2 above.

[8] A labor contract with an adjustment for changes in the Consumer Price Index is a commodity-option. Such a contrast specifies one wage rate if nature reveals one price level and another wage rate conditional upon the appearance of a different price level. Insurance premiums often contain deduction provisions if nature helps the driver avoid an accident. Firms often will sell products to other firms with the price conditional on delivery date, product quality, and prices that are being paid by other firms at the time of delivery. The American housewife is persistently offered a money back guarantee conditional on quality and sometimes independent of quality. Numerous other examples of commodity-options can be cited, such as limit orders to buy or sell that specify reservation prices, but there is no need here for a survey of the great variety of contractual relationships that exist.

optimal allocation of resources, in that there will be discrimination against risky enterprises as compared with the optimum.[9]

Arrow here has slipped into the fallacy of the free lunch. The word 'nonoptimal' is misleading and ambiguous. Does it mean that free enterprise can be improved upon? Let me suppose that the cost of marketing commodity options exceeds the gain from the adjustment to risk. This would account for their presumed absence. Can it then be said that free enterprise results in a nonoptimal adjustment to risk? To make this assertion is to deny that scarcity is relevant to optimality, a strange position for an economist. In suggesting that free enterprise generates incomplete adjustments to risk, the nirvana approach, by comparing these adjustments with the ideal, is led further to equate incomplete to nonoptimal. This would be correct only if commodity-options or other ways of adjusting to risk are free. In this way, the nirvana approach relies on an implicit assumption of nonscarcity, but since risk shifting or risk reduction cannot generally be accomplished freely the demonstration of nonoptimality is false.

II

Arrow calls attention to three problem areas in the production of knowledge and invention, risk-aversion, indivisibilities, and inappropriability. These are discussed in this section. In his analysis of risk-aversion, Arrow recognizes three major substitutes for commodity-option contracts: insurance, common stock, and cost-plus contracts. He finds that each of these fails to completely eliminate the discrepancy between optimal allocation in his ideal norm and allocation in a free enterprise system:

> (1) the economic system has devices for shifting risks, but they are limited and imperfect; hence, one would expect an underinvestment in risky activities; (2) it is undoubtedly worthwhile to enlarge the variety of such devices, but the moral factor creates a limit to their potential.[10]

The route by which he reaches these conclusions is revealed by his discussion of the adjustment to risk provided by insurance:

[9] Arrow, op. cit., pp. 222–3 above.
[10] Ibid., p. 224 above.

Suppose that each firm and individual in the economy could forecast perfectly what prices would be under each state of nature. Suppose further there were a lottery on the state of nature, so that before the state of nature is known any individual or firm may place bets. Then it can be seen that the effect . . . is the same as if there were markets for commodity-options of all types. . . .

References to lotteries and bets may smack of frivolity, but we need only think of insurance to appreciate that the shifting of risks through what are in effect bets on the state of nature is a highly significant phenomenon. If insurance were available against any conceivable event, it follows . . . that optimal allocation would be achieved. . . .

Unfortunately, it is only too clear that the shifting of risks in the real world is incomplete. There are a number of reasons why this should be so, but I will confine myself to one, of special significance with regard to invention. In insurance practice, reference is made to the moral factor as a limit to the possibilities of insurance. . . . The insurance policy changes the incentive of the insured [in the case of fire insurance], creating an incentive for arson or at the very least for carelessness. . . . As a result, any insurance policy and in general any device for shifting risks can have the effect of dulling incentives. . . .

The moral factor [is] of special relevance in regard to highly risky business activities, including invention. . . . [S]uch activities should be undertaken if the expected return exceeds the market rate of return, no matter what the variance is. The existence of common stocks would seem to solve the allocation problem; any individual stockholder can reduce his risk by buying only a small part of the stock and diversifying his portfolio to achieve his own preferred risk level. But then again the actual managers no longer receive the full reward of their decisions; the shifting of risks is again accompanied by a weakening of incentives to efficiency. Substitute motivations whether pecuniary . . . or nonpecuniary . . . may be found, but the dilemma of the moral factor can never be completely resolved.[11]

My dissatisfaction with Arrow's approach can be explained by first referring to one sentence in the above quotation. '[S]uch activities should be undertaken if the expected return exceeds the market rate of return, no matter what the variance is.'[12]

[11] Ibid., pp. 222–4 above.
[12] In the original text, Arrow places a footnote here – 'The validity of this statement depends on some unstated assumptions, but the point to be made is unaffected by minor qualifications.' The reader perhaps may be able to guess what is meant here and how it would affect my criticism.

This statement would certainly be false for a Robinson Crusoe economy. Suppose that the expected rate of return on one project equals the expected rate of return on a second project. If the variances of the expected returns differ, and if Crusoe is risk-averse, there is good economic reason for Crusoe to prefer the less risky project. Reduction of risk is by hypothesis an economic good for Crusoe and he should be willing to pay a positive price, such as a lower expected return, in order to acquire this good. It is clear in this simple case that the economist has no more reason for saying that Crusoe should be indifferent between these projects that he has for saying that Crusoe should be risk-neutral.

Once it is admitted that risk reduction is stipulated to be an economic good, the relevant question for society is what real institutional arrangements will be best suited to produce risk reduction or risk shifting. We no longer delude ourselves into thinking that the world would be a more efficient place if only people were not risk-averse; the taste for risk reduction must be incorporated into the concept of efficiency.

Given the fact of scarcity, risk reduction is not achievable at zero cost, so that the risk-averse efficient economy, as we have already noted, does *not* produce 'complete' shifting of risk but, instead, it reduces or shifts risk only when the economic gain exceeds the cost. Once we seek to compare different institutional arrangements for accomplishing this, it is difficult to keep scarcity from entering our calculations so that it becomes obviously misleading and incorrect to assert that an economy, free enterprise or otherwise, is inefficient if it fails to economize on risk as it would if it were costless to shift or reduce risk.

Two types of adjustment to risk seem possible: pooling independent activities so that the variance in expected return is reduced and facilitating the assumption of risk by those who are less risk-averse. The market is an institutional arrangement that encourages both types of adjustment by rewarding those who successfully reduce or shift risk. Thus, future contracts provide a method whereby much risk is shifted to speculators.[13] Conditional contracts of the commodity-option type already

[13] It is not yet clear from available empirical studies whether speculators are in fact compensated, and it has been argued either that they are not risk-averse or that they enjoy the sport so much that they are willing to bear risk without pay.

discussed also can be purchased for a premium. And even with risk pooling, some risk remains to be borne by sellers of insurance, so that a payment for risk bearing is in order.

Moral hazard is identified by Arrow as a unique and irremedial cause of incomplete coverage of all risky activities by insurance. But in truth there is nothing at all unique about moral hazard and economizing on moral hazard provides no special problems not encountered elsewhere. Moral hazard is a relevant cost of producing insurance; it is not different from the cost that arises from the tendency of men to shirk when their employer is not watching them. And, just as man's preference for shirking and leisure are costs of production that must be economized, so moral hazard must be economized in shifting and reducing risk. A price can be and is attached to the sale of all insurance that includes the moral hazard cost imposed by the insured on insurance companies. And this price is individualized to the extent that other costs, mainly cost of contracting, allow. The moral hazard cost is present, although in differing amounts, no matter what percentage of the value of the good is insured.

The moral hazard problem is no different than the problem posed by any cost. Some iron ore is left unearthed because it is too costly to bring to the surface. But we do not claim ore mining is inefficient merely because mining is not 'complete'. Some risks are left uninsured because the cost of moral hazard is too great and this may mean that self-insurance is economic. There is no special dilemma associated with moral hazard, but Arrow's concentration on the divergence between risk shifting through insurance and risk shifting in the ideal norm, in which moral hazard presumably is absent, makes it appear as a special dilemma. While it may cost nothing to insure risky enterprises in the world of the ideal norm, it does in this world, if for no other reason than the proclivity of some to commit moral hazards. Arrow's approach to efficiency problems has led him directly to 'the people could be different' fallacy.

Payment through insurance premiums for the moral hazard cost imposed on insurance sellers brings into play the usual price mechanism for economizing. The fact that not everything is insured is irrelevant to the question of efficiency. The absence of insurance, especially when moral hazard is important, merely is evidence of the unwillingness to shift all risk to others at premium levels that cover the cost imposed on sellers of insurance by these moral hazards.[14]

Clearly, efficiency requires that moral hazards be economized. Otherwise we implicitly assert that the loss of assets that accompanies the realization of a moral hazard imposes no cost on society. One way of economizing on moral hazards is to allow self-insurance. If the size of the premium that is required to get others to accept moral hazard cost is higher than people wish to pay, it is appropriate to reduce the loss of assets that would accompany moral hazard by allowing prospective buyers of such insurance to self-insure.

Do we shift risk or reduce moral hazards efficiently through the market place? This question cannot be answered solely by observing that insurance is incomplete in coverage. Is there an alternative institutional arrangement that seems to offer superior economizing? There may well be such an arrangement, but Arrow has not demonstrated it and, therefore, his allegation of inefficiency may well be wrong and certainly is premature.

Turning now to the possibility of reducing risk through the device of pooling, we find that Arrow takes the following position:

> The central economic fact about the processes of invention and research is that they are devoted to the production of information. By the very definition of information, invention must be a risky process. . . . Since it is a risky process, there is bound to be some discrimination against investment in inventive and research

[14] Arrow employs the moral hazard argument in his paper, 'Uncertainty and the Welfare Economics of Medical Care', *American Economic Review*, LIII (1963) 941–73. Mark V. Pauly criticized this use of the moral hazard argument and Arrow replied to the criticism in *American Economic Review*, LVIII (1968) 531–8. My criticism of Arrow's argument is much the same as Pauly's. Two parts of Arrow's reply to Pauly should be noted. First, Arrow concedes 'that the optimality of complete insurance is no longer valid when the method of insurance influences the demand for the services provided by the insurance policy'. So far so good. However, secondly, Arrow states that 'If the amount of insurance payment is in any way dependent on a decision of the insured as well as on a state of nature, then optimality will not be achieved either by the competitive system or by an attempt by the government to simulate a perfectly competitive system.' The supporting argument given by Arrow in defense of this second statement leaves much to be desired since it assumes that contracts between the insurer and insured that ration the insurance service are somehow outside the competitive system, that the decision to consume more of the service is somehow a 'bad' even though the price of the insurance covers the full cost of the service, and, implicitly, that adherence to contractual agreements is not an important feature of the competitive system.

K

activities. . . . The only way, within the private enterprise system, to minimize this [moral factor] problem is the conduct of research by large corporations with many projects going on, each small in scale compared with the net revenue of the corporation. Then the corporation acts as its own insurance company. But clearly this is only an imperfect solution.[15]

The centralization of research does provide a more diversified portfolio of investment projects that allows owners to reduce the variance of the outcome of their inventive efforts. To some extent firms do centralize research efforts. But a real social cost is borne if this procedure is pushed too far. The more centralized is the production or financing of invention, the smaller is the degree to which the advantages of specialization can be enjoyed and the less keen is the stimulus offered by competition. These costs must be taken into account in identifying the efficient institutional arrangement, and I suppose that these costs do play a major role in limiting the voluntary centralization of research by industry. The efficient arrangement generally will be one that falls between complete centralization and complete specialization.

It may be that government production or financing of invention is a superior arrangement, in which case extensive use of market arrangements can be criticized. Government *can* take a risk-neutral attitude (although I doubt that this is a desirable attitude in the nuclear age). But I do not know what attitude actually will be taken toward risk by government. Government is a group of people, each of whom in the absence of compensation to do otherwise, presumably is risk-averse. The psychological propensity to be risk-averse, if it is present, is found in employees of government as well as in employees of private enterprise, and a government probably is averse to political risks.

I suspect that the government will be less risk-averse in some of its activity. The attempt to place a man on the moon by 1970 probably never will be subjected to careful market measures of risk and rate of return, but if it were, it is unlikely that it would appear worthwhile even if it is successful in the technological sense. In some cases, a technological success carries great weight in achieving political success and here government will be less risk-averse.

[15] Arrow, op. cit., p. 227 above.

In other governmental activities, however, the government is likely to behave toward risk in a much more risk-averse fashion than is private enterprise. For example, inventing and innovating a superior postal service, although it has some risk associated with it, seems to be technologically possible and economically promising. But the adverse political developments that could follow from the laying off of many postal employees leads the government to hold back. It is very averse to the risk of being voted out of office.

Arrow's analysis of risk merely states that the market copes with risk differently than it would if risk could be shifted or reduced costlessly, or than it would if people were neither risk-averse nor susceptible to moral hazard. But a relevant notion of efficiency must refer to scarcity and people as they are, not as they could be.

In his discussion of the inappropriability of new knowledge, Arrow recognizes that if information is to be produced privately, its producers must be able to realize revenues from the use or sale of information. For this to be possible, information must be appropriable, and Arrow is not optimistic about the ease with which the value of information can be captured by its discoverer. Some part of Arrow's pessimism, I believe, is attributable to his tendency to see special and unique problems in establishing property rights to information when the problems are neither special nor unique.

Appropriability is largely a matter of legal arrangements and the enforcement of these arrangements by private or public means. The degree to which knowledge is privately appropriable can be increased by raising the penalties for patent violations and by increasing resources for policing patent violations.

It is true that all 'theft' of information cannot be eliminated at reasonable cost. But knowledge is not unique in this respect, since the same can be said of any valuable asset. The equilibrium price that is paid to producers of automobiles will in part reflect the fact that there is a positive probability that the purchaser will have his automobile stolen. The problem of theft is as pervasive as the problem of moral hazard, and although there may be differences in the cost of reducing the theft of different types of assets there is no difference in principle. It may be argued, as Arrow does, that the ease of theft of knowledge is heightened by the fact that knowledge once used becomes easily known by others. But the theft of an automobile also is made easier when it is removed from the home garage.

One characteristic of knowledge that increases the cost of enforcing private rights is the possibility of stealing information without thereby depriving its owner of the 'ability' to use the information, although, of course, the profitability to the owner of using the information may be reduced if the thief uses it. Compared with more tangible assets the detection of the theft of knowledge may need to rely to a greater extent on discovering its subsequent use by others. But if Arrow is correct in asserting that '[t]he very use of information in any productive way is bound to reveal it, at least in part,'[16] then detecting its subsequent use by nonowners may be relatively easy. In any case, the reduction in theft of knowledge can be accomplished, without increasing the probability of detection, by raising the penalties to the thief if he is apprehended. A harsher schedule of penalties always can be used to enhance the appropriability of knowledge.[17]

The truth of the matter is that I, at least, have no more than casual notions about the cost, per dollar value of knowledge, of establishing property rights in information. Given the appropriate legal apparatus and schedule of penalties it may be no more difficult to police property rights in many kinds of knowledge than it is to prevent the theft of automobiles and cash. And even if some kinds of information are more difficult to protect, I am not sure which institutions yield the better solution to the problem or what public policy deduction should be made.

We now turn to what Arrow identifies as the problems of indivisibility (or, in more current terminology, the problem of public goods):

> The cost of transmitting a given body of information is frequently very low. If it were zero, then optimal allocation would obviously call for unlimited distribution of the information without cost. In fact, a given piece of information is by definition an indivisible commodity, and the classical problems of allocation in the presence of indivisibilities appear here. . . .[18]

[16] Ibid., p. 225 above. Arrow states this to support his notion that theft of knowledge is easy.

[17] For a definitive analysis of the role of penalties in crime prevention (and of other aspects of the economics of crime), see Gary S. Becker, 'Crime and Punishment: An Economic Approach', *Journal of Political Economy*, LXXVI (1968) 196–217.

[18] Arrow, op. cit., p. 225 above.

As we have seen, information is a commodity with peculiar attributes, particularly embarrassing for the achievement of optimal allocation. . . . [A]ny information obtained . . . should, from the welfare point of view, be available free of charge (apart from the cost of transmitting information). This insures optimal utilization of the information but of course provides no incentive for investment in research. In an ideal socialist economy, the reward for invention would be completely separated from any charge to the users of information. In a free enterprise economy, inventive activity is supported by using the invention to create property rights; precisely to the extent that it is successful, there is an underutilization of the information.[19]

The partitioning of economic activity into the act of producing knowledge and the act of disseminating already produced knowledge is bound to cause confusion when the attempt is made to judge efficiency. It is hardly useful to say that there is 'underutilization' of information if the method recommended to avoid 'underutilization' discourages the research required to produce the information. These two activities simply cannot be judged independently. Since one of the main functions of paying a positive price is to encourage others to invest the resources needed to sustain a continuing flow of production, the efficiency with which the existing stock of goods or information is used cannot be judged without examining the effects of production.

If, somehow, we knew how much and what types of information it would be desirable to produce, then we could administer production independently of the distribution of any given stock of information. But we do not know these things. Arrow's assertion that '[i]n an ideal socialist economy, the reward for invention would be completely separated from any charge to the users of information' begs this whole problem. How would such a system produce information on the desired directions of investment and on the quantities of resources that should be committed to invention? There are ways, of course. Surveys of scientists and managers could be taken and a weighting scheme could be applied to the opinions received; no doubt there are many other ways of making such decisions. But the practice of creating property rights in information and allowing its sale is not clearly inefficient in comparison with these real alternatives.

[19] Ibid., p. 227 above.

Arrow does acknowledge the adverse incentive effects that
would obtain in a private enterprise economy if information
were made freely available, but this does not deter him from
asserting that the capitalistic method is inefficient in its distribution of information. This ambiguity and looseness in
Arrow's analysis is attributable directly to his viewpoint and
approach. If he were to compare a real socialist system with a
real capitalistic system the advantages and disadvantages of
each would stand out, and it would be possible to make some
overall judgment as to which of the two is better. But Arrow
compares the workings of a capitalistic system with a Pareto
norm that lends itself to static analysis of allocation but, nonetheless, that is poorly designed for analyzing dynamic problems
of production. He finds the capitalistic system defective. The
socialist ideal, however, resolves static allocation problems
rather neatly. But this is only because all the dynamic problems
of production are ignored. The comparison of a real capitalistic
system with an ideal socialist system that ignores important
problems is not a promising way to shed light on how to design
institutional arrangements for the production and distribution of
knowledge.

Indivisibilities in the use of knowledge become important
only when the costs of contracting are relatively large. This point
generally has been ignored. If everyone is allowed the right to
use already available knowledge because one person's use of
existing knowledge does not reduce its availability to others,
there will tend to be underinvestment in the production of
knowledge because the discoverer of knowledge will not enjoy
property rights in the knowledge. But this underinvestment
works to the disadvantage of others who would have the output
of any additional investment made available to them at no cost.
If the cost of contracting were zero, these prospective 'freeloaders' would be willing to pay researchers to increase the
investment being made. Research activity would be purchased
just as any other good.

The relevance of contracting cost is most clearly seen by
supposing that there are two prospective freeloaders and one
inventor. If the freeloaders are allowed to use successful
research without paying the inventor, he will reduce his
research efforts. But then the two freeloaders will find it in their
interest to buy additional research effort from the researcher.

The only implication of indivisibilities in the use of information is that it will pay for the freeloaders to join forces in buying this additional research, for by doing so they can share the required payment. If the cost of arriving at such an agreement is negligible, the resources devoted to experimentation will be the same as if the freeloaders were *required* to pay a fee to the inventor for the use of his successful experiments.

The objective of bargaining between those who produce knowledge and those who use it, whether the researcher has rights to the knowledge he produces or whether this knowledge is freely made available to all, is the production of knowledge at efficient rates. For if knowledge is produced at efficient rates, the social value of the research effort will be maximized. The bargaining between the interested parties will determine how this value is shared. If the cost of contracting, broadly interpreted, is zero, it will be in everyone's interest to reach an agreement that maximizes the value of the research effort because all will have a larger pie to share.

If the cost of contracting is positive, the kind of property rights system that is established may change the allocation of resources in the production of knowledge. If freeloading is allowed, that is, if users of knowledge are given the right to knowledge without paying for it, some prospective users will be inclined to stay out of any cooperative agreement between users. There will be an incentive to users jointly to pay researchers to increase the resources being committed to research, but if some users can remain outside this cooperative effort, they stand to benefit from research paid for by other users. This may lead to an underinvestment (underpurchase?) in research.

It might seem that the tendency for a user to remain outside any cooperative purchasing effort is independent of contracting costs. But this is not so. Broadly interpreted, such costs will include not only the cost of striking a bargain but also the cost of enforcing any bargain that is made. The property rights system that makes produced information freely available to all increases the cost of enforcing agreements. Let the user's purchasing organization attempt to acquire members. What does it have to offer prospective members? It cannot guarantee that those who join will have exclusive rights to the research output purchased, for the law says that anyone can use knowledge. The cost of enforcing a contract that promises exclusivity in the use of whatever knowledge is purchased is raised inordinately by this public policy, and that is why there will be a strong inclination to remain outside the buyer's cooperative effort.

If the legal system is changed so that producers of research have property rights in their research output, they will be able to transfer legal title to purchasers who can then exclude nonpurchasers from the use of the research. The incentive to remain a nonpurchaser is diminished with private appropriation of knowledge precisely because the cost of enforcing exclusive contracts is reduced.

The last assertion in the above quotation from Arrow's paper, 'In a free enterprise economy, inventive activity is supported by using the invention to create property rights; precisely to the extent that it is successful, there is an underutilization of the information', does not constitute an argument against the creation of property rights. The indivisibility problem may very well be handled best by a private property system that reduces the cost of contracting and raises the cost of freeloading while, at the same time, it provides incentives and guidance for investment in producing information.

III

The problem discussed in this section is qualitatively different from those discussed above. Here our attention is directed to the structure of the industry in which the knowledge is used.[20] Arrow discusses the relevance of industry structure in that section of his paper subtitled 'Competition, Monopoly, and the Incentive to Innovate'. The objectives and conclusions are stated by Arrow as follows:

> I will examine here the incentives to invent for monopolistic and competitive markets, that is, I will compare the potential profits from an invention with the costs. The difficulty of appropriating the information will be ignored; the remaining problem is that of indivisibility in use, an inherent property of information. A

[20] I am indebted to Professor Aaron Director for sharing with me his revealing insights into the problem discussed in this section, and, in particular, for suggesting that the results of Arrow's analysis are affected significantly by the difference in scale between the competitive industry and monopoly industry that is implicit in his approach. I would also like to thank Professor George J. Stigler, for his critical review of an earlier draft.

competitive situation here will mean one in which the industry produces under competitive conditions, while the inventor can set an arbitrary royalty for the use of his invention. In the monopolistic situation, it will be assumed that only the monopoly itself can invent. Thus a monopoly is understood here to mean barriers to entry; a situation of temporary monopoly, due perhaps to a previous innovation, which does not prevent the entrance of new firms with innovations of their own, is to be regarded as more nearly competitive than monopolistic for the purpose of this analysis. It will be argued that the incentive to invent is less under monopolistic than under competitive conditions but even in the latter case it will be less than is socially desirable.[21]

Arrow arrives at these conclusions under the two varieties of circumstances that are implied by the way in which the problem is set up:

> We will assume constant costs both before and after the invention, the unit costs being c before the invention and $c' < c$ afterward. The competitive price before invention will therefore be c. Let the corresponding demand be x_c. If r is the level of unit royalties, the competitive price after the invention will be $c' + r$, but this cannot of course be higher than c, since firms are always free to produce with the old methods.[22]

The basic point at issue can be brought forward best by discussing the circumstance in which $c' + r$ is less than c if the royalty is set at its profit-maximizing level.

Arrow's argument can be put into geometric form with the aid of Fig. 14.1. Let c and c', respectively, be the per unit cost of production before and after the invention. The inventor selling to a competitive industry sets the per unit royalty, r, so as to maximize the size of the rectangle $c'puv$; that is, the inventor sets the royalty so that the quantity demand is where marginal revenue, MR, is equal to c'. This results in a price for the competitive industry's product equal to p. Following Arrow's terminology, let $P' = c'puv$. An inventor selling to the competitive industry illustrated in Fig. 14.1 would be willing to invest in inventing so long as the cost of the invention to him is less than P'.

Arrow, in posing the alternative situation in which the industry is a monopoly owned by the inventor, reasons that before

[21] Arrow, op. cit., p. 230 above.
[22] Ibid., pp. 230–1 above.

the invention the inventor, acting as would any monopolist, has set price at w to hold the quantity demanded to that rate of output for which $c = \mathrm{MR}$. His profit, P, equals rectangle *cwxy*. After his invention, his cost per unit will be lowered from c to c'. Maximizing profits with his new cost he will set price at p. This yields a new profit rectangle equal to P'. The basic conclusion reached by Arrow, that 'the incentive to invest is

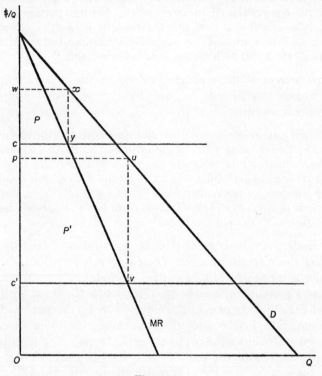

Figure 14.1

less under monopolistic than under competitive conditions', is now clear. The inventor selling to a competitive industry would be willing to invent if his cost is less than P' but the inventor who is a monopolist in the product market would be willing to invent only if the cost of inventing is less than $P' - P$, for this precisely measures to him the increase in profits attributable to the invention. Since $P' - P$ always is less than P', Arrow concludes that the incentive to invent is less under monopoly.

Arrow's conclusion, however, does not lend itself to a clear interpretation since he has allowed two extraneous issues to influence his analysis: (1) Arrow's inventor not only produces an invention but, in addition, he possesses the monopoly power to discriminate in the royalty charges he sets for the two industries. (2) Arrow neglects to take account of the normal monopoly incentives in the monopoly purchasing the invention; monopoly models generally deduce that a monopolist will use less of all inputs, including an invention, because he produces less output; the demonstration of any *special* effect of monopoly on the incentive to invention requires that adjustments be made for this normally restrictive monopoly behavior. When proper account is taken of these two matters we find that Arrow's conclusions are false.

Let us suppose that competitive inventions or regulations restrict the inventor to charging all users of the invention identical unit royalties, and let $p - c'$ in Fig. 14.1 measure that royalty. In this case, both the competitive industry and the monopolist accept $p - c'$ as the price of an input. The competitive industry would then pay a total royalty equal to P' to the inventor while the monopoly would pay half this amount since the monopoly's output would increase only to the intersection of pu with MR. The monopoly does offer to pay less total royalty because it produces at a smaller output rate than does the competitive industry. This comes as no surprise. One of the better-known deductions in economics is that a nondiscriminating monopolist will sell fewer units of output and use fewer units of input than would be used in the same industry if it were competitively organized.

To remove from the analysis the normal restrictive effect of monopoly on output, let us define MR in Fig. 14.1 to be the demand curve facing the competitive industry. For any given unit cost, both the monopoly and the competitive industry will produce the same output rate. At a royalty per unit equal to $p - c'$ both industries will produce where pu intersects MR and both will pay the same total royalty to the inventor.

By eliminating the inventor's monopoly power to charge different royalties and simultaneously by adjusting the demand curve facing the competitive industry to eliminate the normal restrictive effect of monopoly on input use, we arrive at the conclusion that a competitive industry will offer no greater incentive to invention than a monopoly. There is no special adverse effect of monopoly on the incentive to invention.

Let us now consider the case where rivalry between inventors, or where regulation, fails to equalize the royalties. What will be the incentive to invention offered by the two industries after adjusting their sizes to remove the normal restrictive effects of a prior monopoly? We shall see that in this case the incentive to invention is just the reverse of what Arrow concluded; for industries that would operate at the same levels of output in the absence of the invention, the development of a monopoly invention with price-discriminating power will receive greater rewards from a buying industry that is a monopoly.

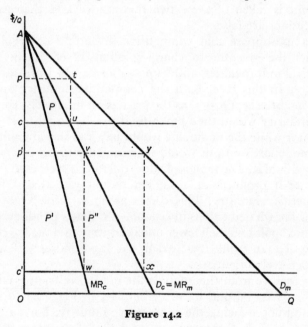

Figure 14.2

In Fig. 14.2 let D_m and MR_m be the demand and marginal revenue facing the monopolist and let D_c and MR_c characterize the industry demand facing the competitive industry. Assume that $MR_m = D_c$ so that for any given constant unit cost both industries will produce the same output rates. At cost $= c$ the competitive industry produces output cu, since demand must equal marginal cost under competition, while for monopoly the output rate cu will be selected because marginal cost must equal marginal revenue. Hence, the size of the two industries will be the same for any given constant unit cost. The effect of monopoly on the size of output has been removed.

At cost c, the monopoly receives profit $P = cptu$, whereas with the cost-reducing invention the monopoly profit is $P'' = c'p'yx$. The incentive to monopoly invention given by the monopoly industry is $P'' - P$. The best that the inventor can do if he sells his monopoly invention to an *equal-sized* competitive industry is to ask a per unit royalty equal to $p' - c'$ for this will cause the competitive industry to produce an output rate $p'v$ that maximizes the inventor's total royalty $c'p'vw$. We wish to ascertain whether the incentive to invention offered by the competitive industry, $c'p'vw = P'$, is larger or smaller than $P'' - P$. Fig. 14.2 indicates that the incentive to invention offered by the competitive industry is smaller since $P'' - P'$ clearly is greater than P. However, to make sure that this is no geometrical illusion, the reader will find an algebraic proof for the linear case in the Appendix. The Appendix also presents a counterexample to Arrow's conclusion for a case where both industries start at the same output rate and confront the same demand curve.

The traditional belief that monopoly restricts output may suggest that some measure of antitrust is desirable. If Arrow's analysis is taken to suggest, as I think it must, that there are special adverse effects of monopoly on the incentive to invention, a framer of public policy would deduce that antitrust should be pursued more diligently than is dictated by considerations of output restrictions only. But he would be wrong. If it is thought desirable to encourage invention by granting monopoly power through the patent or through secrecy, the above analysis suggests that antitrust should be pursued less diligently than is dictated by considerations of output restrictions only, for, at least in the linear model of two industries of equal output size, the more monopolistic will give the greatest encouragement to invention.

IV

The problem of efficiency and the possibilities of achieving efficiency through reform were associated historically with the grant of monopoly and tariff privileges by governments. In their historical settings, criticisms of inefficiency took on the characteristic of the comparative institution and not the nirvana approach. Critics of governmental policies who asked for reform were seeking to substitute an institutional arrangement that was both real and fairly well understood. They were confident of the beneficial results and of the practicality of allowing market enterprise to allocate resources. And, although the operation of political forces had not been subjected to the same careful study, the critics did know what they expected if govermentally created protection from those market forces were removed.

A process of refining the analytical concept of competition then set in, culminating in the currently accepted necessary conditions for perfect competition. These conditions, of course, can be only approximated by real institutions. On top of these are placed additional conditions on the nature of production, commodities, and preferences that are necessary if the equivalence of perfect competition and Pareto efficiency is to be established.

While the application of these conceptual refinements is an aid to solving some economic problems, especially in positive economics, their application to normative problems has led to serious errors. If an economy has no serious indivisibilities, if information is complete, etc., then the modern analysis can describe the characteristics of an efficient long-run equilibrium; this description is the main result of modern welfare analysis. But modern analysis has yet to describe efficiency in a world where indivisibilities are present and knowledge is costly to produce. To say that private enterprise is inefficient because indivisibilities and imperfect knowledge are part of life, or because people are susceptible to the human weaknesses subsumed in the term 'moral hazards', or because marketing commodity-options is not costless, or because persons are risk-averse, is to say little more than that the competitive equilibrium would be different if these were not the facts of life. But, if they are the facts of life, if, that is, they cannot be erased from life at zero cost, then truly efficient institutions will yield different long-run equilibrium conditions than those now used to describe the ideal norm.

It is one thing to suggest that wealth will increase with the removal of legal monopoly. It is quite another to suggest that indivisibilities and moral hazards should be handled through nonmarket arrangements. The first suggestion is based on two credible assumptions, that the monopoly can be eliminated and that the practical institutional arrangement for accomplishing this, market competition, operates in fairly predictable ways. The second assertion cannot claim to have eliminated indivisibilities, risk-averse psychology, moral hazard, or costly negotiations, nor can it yet claim to predict the behavior of the governmental institutions that are suggested as replacements for the market.

I have stated elsewhere what I believe to be the basic problem facing public and private policy: the design of institutional arrangements that provide incentives to encourage experimentation (including the development of new products, new knowledge, new reputations, and new ways of organizing activities) without overly insulating these experiments from the ultimate test of survival. In the context of the problems discussed in Arrow's paper, these institutional arrangements must strive to balance three objectives. A wide variety of experimentation should be encouraged, investment should be channeled into promising varieties of experimentation and away from unpromising varieties, and the new knowledge that is acquired should be employed extensively. No known institutional arrangement can simultaneously maximize the degree to which each of these objectives is achieved. A difficult-to-achieve balance is sought between the returns that can be earned by additional experimentation, by giving directional guidance to investment in experimentation, and by reducing the cost of producing goods through the use of existing knowledge. The concepts of perfect competition and Pareto optimality simply are unable at present to give much help in achieving this balance.

APPENDIX

All notation is consistent with Fig. 14.2 of the text. In this part of the Appendix we allow the inventor to produce a monopoly invention that he markets to a monopoly and a competitive industry. The industries are defined so that at any given marginal cost the rates of output will be the same.

Let

$$P = A - Bq \tag{1}$$

be monopoly demand, then total revenue is

$$\text{TR} = Aq - Bq^2 \tag{2}$$

and marginal revenue is

$$\text{MR}_m = A - 2Bq. \tag{3}$$

At unit cost c, the monopoly maximizes profits where

$$c = \text{MR}_m = A - 2Bq \tag{4}$$

which allows us to calculate monopoly output as

$$q = \frac{A - c}{2B}. \tag{5}$$

Monopoly profit at c cost is

$$P = \text{TR} - cq = \frac{(A - c)^2}{4B} \tag{6}$$

and the incentive to invention with monopoly is

$$P'' - P = \frac{(A - c')^2 - (A - c)^2}{4B} \tag{7}$$

where c' is the new lower unit cost.

Under competition, the inventor calculates the marginal revenue associated with the industry demand curve

$$D_c = \text{MR}_m = A - 2Bq \tag{8}$$

so that

$$\text{MR}_c = A - 4Bq. \tag{9}$$

The inventor then selects that per unit royalty such that the resulting output rate is where $c' = \text{MR}_c$. That is, where

$$c' = A - 4Bq. \tag{10}$$

The competitive industry's output rate will then be

$$q = \frac{A - c'}{4B} \tag{11}$$

and the incentive to invention is

$$P' = (A - c')q - 2Bq^2 = \frac{(A - c')^2}{8B}. \tag{12}$$

Comparing $P'' - P$, from (7), to P', we find that P' must always be less in the case under consideration since

$$(P'' - P) - P' = (A - c') - 2(A - c)$$

and

$$(A - c') > 2(A - c) \text{ if } p' < c.$$

The Arrow proposition is incorrect even if less acceptable but more lenient restrictions are considered. Again, let us assume that the inventor has a monopoly, but let both the competitive industry and the monopoly face the same demand curve. However, assume that the initial per unit cost, k, in the competitive industry is sufficiently above the monopoly's initial cost, c, to yield the same preinvention output rates. Then, let the cost in each industry be reduced by the same amount as a result of the invention. In this way, we pose a situation in which initial output levels are the same but one in which the invention moves both industries along identical demand curves. An arithmetic counterexample of Arrow's proposition follows.

Let the demand curve facing both industries be

$$p = 100 - q. \tag{1}$$

Marginal revenue then is

$$\text{MR} = 100 - 2q. \tag{2}$$

Let $c = \$90$ and $c' = 10$; and in each instance equate marginal revenue to marginal cost to derive the monopoly profit-maximizing q's:

$$90 = 100 - 2q; q = 5 \tag{3}$$

$$10 = 100 - 2q; q = 45. \tag{3'}$$

Profit P at $q = 5$ and P'' at $q = 45$ are

$$p = 100 - 5 = \$95 \tag{4}$$

$$p' = 100 - 45 = \$55 \tag{4'}$$

$$P = (\$95 - 90) \, 5 = \$25 \tag{5}$$

$$P'' = (\$55 - 10) \, 45 = \$2025. \tag{5'}$$

The amount that the monopolist would be willing to pay for this cost-reducing invention is $P'' - P = \$2000$.

We now wish to compare this with the rate of return to invention for a competitively organized industry of the same initial scale as the monopoly. To accomplish this while using the same market demand curve, $p = 100 - q$, let us set the competitive industry's preinvention per unit and marginal cost, k, at a high enough level to generate an output rate equal to the initial monopoly output rate of $q = 5$. Since the competitive industry will produce that output rate where $p = mc$, k must be \$95. Now let the invention reduce this cost by the same absolute magnitude as $c - c' = \$80$. For the competitive industry, then, the postinvention marginal cost, k', will be \$95 − \$80 = \$15.

The inventor now will pick a per unit royalty such that the competitive industry will produce where $k' = MR$ for this will result in the largest possible total royalty payment. Using equation (2), we find this output rate to be

$$15 = 100 - 2q; \qquad q = 42 \cdot 50. \tag{6}$$

The inventor's royalty per unit will be the difference between price and $k' = 15$. From equation (1), we find that $p = \$57 \cdot 50$ (at $q = 42 \cdot 50$), so that the inventor's total royalty in the competitive case, P', will be

$$P' = (57 \cdot 50 - \$15) \, 42 \cdot 50 = \$1806 \cdot 25 \tag{7}$$

and we find that this is \$193·75 *less* than the inventor could have earned if he sold the invention to a monopoly of the same initial size.[23]

---

[23] If this problem is repeated for the same percentage reductions in cost for the monopoly and the competitive industry, we would find that the incentives to invention would be equally great.

Notes on Contributors

ARROW, KENNETH JOSEPH, B.S., *City College of New York* (1940); M.A., *Columbia* (1941), Ph.D. (1951). Assistant Professor of Economics at the University of Chicago 1948–9; Assistant Professor of Economics and Statistics at Stanford University 1949–50; Associate Professor 1950–3; Professor 1953–68; Professor of Economics at Harvard University since 1968. A leading economic theorist, Arrow has made pioneering contributions in the border territory of economics and political science, as well as substantive contributions in the economic theory of technological change. His book *Social Choice and Individual Values* should be compulsory reading for all concerned with the economic theory of public policy, and many of his articles in leading journals are required reading within the economics graduate schools.

BURROWS, HOWARD PAUL, B.Sc.(Econ.), *London School of Economics* (1962); D.Phil., *York* (1967). Lecturer in Economics at the University of York since 1965. Burrows has specialised in public finance and has contributed several articles in the leading professional journals. He is also the author of a book concerned with the economics of social policy. He is especially interested in the application of econometric techniques in public sector analysis.

COMANOR, WILLIAM S., A.B., *Haverford College* (1959); Ph.D., *Harvard* (1964). Special Economic Assistant in the Antitrust Division of the U.S. Department of Justice 1965–6; Assistant Professor of Economics at Harvard University 1966–8; Associate Professor of Economics at Stanford University since 1968. Comanor has specialized in the economics of industrial organization where he has contributed articles to the leading economic journals. He is also interested in econometrics and in urban economics.

CREW, MICHAEL ANTHONY, B.Com., *Birmingham* (1963); Ph.D., *Bradford* (1972). Lecturer in Economics at the University of Bradford 1967–9; Visiting Assistant Professor of Economics at Carnegie-Mellon University 1968–9; Lecturer in Economics at the University of Kent 1969–70; Lecturer in Economics at the London Graduate School of Business Studies 1970–1; Lecturer in Economics at the University of Southampton since 1971. Crew has specialized in public sector economics and in the economics of industrial organisation. He has contributed a number of articles in these fields to the leading economic journals.

DEMSETZ, HAROLD, B.S., *Illinois* (1953); M.A., M.B.A., *Northwestern* (1950), Ph.D. (1959). Assistant Professor at the University of Michigan 1958–60; Assistant Professor at the University of California at Los Angeles 1960–3; Associate Professor at the University of Chicago 1963–7; Professor of Economics at the University of Chicago since 1967. Demsetz is an economic theorist who has specialized in the economics of industrial organization. He has made pathbreaking contributions in the theory of property rights and in the analysis of transaction costs and their relevance for the economic theory of public policy. An imaginative and stimulating economist with a gift for reopening discussions which are widely accepted to be closed.

HEAD, JOHN GRAEM, B.Ec., *Adelaide* (1954); B.Phil., *Oxford* (1957). Lecturer in Economics at the Australian National University 1957–64; Senior Lecturer in Economics at the Australian National University 1964–8; Professor of Economics at Dalhousie University since 1968. Head has specialized in public finance and has published many articles in the leading journals. He is especially wellknown for his contributions in the economic theory of public goods.

KAFOGLIS, MILTON ZACH., B.S., *Kentucky* (1949), M.A. (1951); Ph.D., *Ohio State* (1958). Professor of Economics at the University of Florida since 1958. Kafoglis is the author of several books and of many articles dealing with the application of welfare economics to public policy problems, especially in the fields of industrial organization and public finance.

LEIBENSTEIN, HARVEY, B.A., *Northwestern* (1945), M.A. (1946); Ph.D., *Princeton* (1951). Professor of Economics at the University of California at Berkeley 1951–67; Andelot Professor of Economics at Harvard University since 1967. An economic theorist with specialist interests in economic growth and development and in the economics of population. His contribution of the X-efficiency concept to economics has opened up a wide field of analysis not only in welfare economics but also in the economics of industrial organization and the theory of the firm.

ROWLEY, CHARLES KERSHAW, B.A., *Nottingham* (1960), Ph.D. (1964). Lecturer in Economics at the University of Nottingham 1962–5; Lecturer in Economics at the University of Kent 1965–8; Senior Research Fellow at the University of York 1968–9; Senior Lecturer in Economics at the University of Kent 1969–70; Senior Lecturer in Social and Economic Statistics at the University of York 1970–1. Reader 1972;

David Dale Professor of Economics at the University of Newcastle upon Tyne since 1972. Rowley has specialized in the economics of industrial organization and public sector economics. He is the author of three books and a number of articles.

SAMUELSON, PAUL ANTHONY, B.A., *Chicago* (1935); M.A., *Harvard* (1936), Ph.D. (1941). Assistant Professor at M.I.T. 1940–4; Associate Professor 1944–7; Professor of Economics at M.I.T. since 1947. Author of a best-selling textbook and one of the world's most distinguished and prolific economic theorists, Samuelson has recently been honoured by the award of the Nobel Prize for his contributions to economics.

TELSER, LESTER G., A.B., *Roosevelt* (1951); M.A., *Chicago* (1953), Ph.D. (1956). Assistant Professor at Iowa State University 1955–6; Served with A.U.S. 1956–8; Associate Professor in the Graduate School of Business at the University of Chicago 1958–65; Professor of Economics at the University of Chicago since 1965. Telser has specialized in the economics of industrial organization and has contributed many important articles, both of an analytic and an applied econometric nature.

WILLIAMSON, OLIVER EATON, S.B., *Massachusetts Institute of Technology* (1955); M.B.A., *Stanford* (1960); Ph.D., *Carnegie Institute of Technology* (1963). Assistant Professor at University of California at Berkeley 1963–5; Consultant to the Rand Corporation 1964–6; Associate Professor at the University of Pennsylvania 1965–8; Professor of Economics at the University of Pennsylvania since 1968. Williamson is probably the leading specialist in industrial organization, with many important contributions in the theory of the firm (his book *The Economics of Discretionary Behavior*, 1964, is a classic), in the theory of peak-load pricing and in the economics of anti-trust. He is the author of several books and a wide range of articles in the leading economic journals.

WISEMAN, JACK, B.Sc.(Econ.), *London School of Economics* (1949). Lecturer in Economics at the London School of Economics 1949–61; Reader in Economics 1962–4; Professor of Applied Economics and Director of the Institute of Social and Economic Research at the University of York since 1964. Wiseman has specialized in public finance and in the economics of human resources, but he has made important contributions also in the economics of industrial organization. Best known for his pioneering contributions (with A. T. Peacock) in analyzing the growth of public expenditure, Wiseman is the author of several books and many articles in the leading economic journals.

Index